Identifying, Assessing, and Treating Conduct Disorder at School

Developmental Psychopathology at School

Series Editors:

Shane R. Jimerson, *University of California, Santa Barbara, CA, USA*
Stephen E. Brock, *California State University, Sacramento, CA, USA*

A continuation Order Plan is available for this series. A continuation order will bring delivery of each new volume immediately upon publication. Volumes are billed only upon actual shipment. For further information please contact the publisher.

Tammy L. Hughes   Laura M. Crothers
Shane R. Jimerson

Identifying, Assessing, and Treating Conduct Disorder at School

 Springer

Tammy L. Hughes
Duquesne University,
Pittsburgh, PA,
USA
hughest@duq.edu

Laura M. Crothers
Duquesne University,
Pittsburgh, PA,
USA
CrothersL@duq.edu

Shane R. Jimerson
University of California,
Santa Barbara, CA,
USA
jimerson@education.ucsb.edu

Library of Congress Control Number: 2007937161

ISBN: 978-0-387-74393-6   e-ISBN: 978-0-387-74395-0

Printed on acid-free paper.

9 8 7 6 5 4 3 2 1

springer.com

Dedicated to
This book is dedicated to those children, families, and educational professionals who
confront and overcome the challenges associated with conduct disorder. We hope
that this book contributes valuable information that will facilitate their success.
And also to our children and families who inspire us and remind us
of the importance of our efforts;

Mason Hughes Miller, Jeffrey A. Miller
John Lipinski, III, Conrad B. and Linda H. Metz, Nancy M., Katherine A.,
and Mitchell D. Cazenas
Gavin O'Brien Jimerson, Taite Justine Jimerson, Kathryn O'Brien

Acknowledgments

As with any project of this magnitude, we feel it is important to acknowledge the individuals who contributed to our efforts. First, Dr. Hughes would like to acknowledge Dr. Michael Tansy, who works tirelessly to train and prepare professionals to differentiate emotional disturbance from social maladjustment. Dr. Hughes and Dr. Crothers would both like to express their gratitude to the support of their colleagues at Duquesne University. Additionally, Dr. Crothers would like to acknowledge Ph.D. candidates Sarah O'Neill and Ron Bell for their excellent work in contributing to this book, and the Educational and School Psychology faculty at Indiana University of Pennsylvania for providing an excellent foundation for her career in school psychology. Finally, Dr. Jimerson would like to acknowledge his colleagues at the University of California at Santa Barbara, Dr. Michael Furlong and Dr. Gale Morrison, for their superb scholarship and bringing science-to-practice through their contributions to numerous initiatives aimed at enhancing the outcomes of youths and families facing social, emotional, behavioral, and mental health challenges. He would also like to express his sincere gratitude to Susan Gionfriddo, Martin Conoley, Scott DuPree, and many other professionals in the Santa Barbara Juvenile Justice division of the Santa Barbara County Probation Department, as their commitment to providing support services for youths is commendable and has resulted in numerous collaborative projects to advance understanding and promote positive outcomes for the youths and their families. Finally, Dr. Jimerson would like to acknowledge Dr. Byron Egeland and Dr. Alan Sroufe of the Institute of Child Development at the University of Minnesota for their important contributions to his understanding of developmental psychopathology.

Table of Contents

1
Introduction

Conduct disorder (CD) is the diagnostic classification applied to children who display a pervasive and persistent pattern of problem behaviors characterized by aggression, destruction, deceitfulness, and serious violations of rules (American Psychiatric Association, 2000). The estimated lifetime prevalence of CD in the United States is 9.5% (12% among males and 7% among females) (Nock, Kazdin, Hiripi, & Kessler, 2006). The U.S. Department of Health and Human Services (1999) reports that CD affects 1% to 4% of schoolchildren. In the United States, CD symptoms are the primary presenting problems for psychiatric referral among children and adolescents (Kazdin, 1995). It is estimated that between 30% and 50% of all child psychiatry referrals involve CD (Kazdin, 1997). Moreover, children diagnosed with CD have higher levels of distress and impairment in almost all domains of adjustment, relative to children with other mental health disorders (Lambert, Wahler, Andrade, & Bickman, 2001). Early-onset conduct problems in childhood are a major risk factor for the development of delinquency, violence, antisocial behavior, impoverished social ties, and drug or substance abuse in later years (Bassarath, 2001; Patterson, DeGarmo, & Knutson, 2000). Thus, it is clear that school professionals need to be prepared to identify and provide support services for children with CD.

Why School Professionals Should Read This Book

The importance of understanding CD results in part from the fact that it constitutes one of the most frequent bases for referral of children and adolescents for psychological and psychiatric problems, criminal behaviors, and social maladjustment by the time they become adults (Kazdin, 1995). Beyond the prevalence of CD there is a common perception of increasing violence among children and adolescents. Further, how and where to serve children and adolescents with CD are difficult and controversial questions. Some may need to be served in alternative or special education setting and others in general education settings. To appropriately address the needs of all children and to address public perceptions, school psychologists and other educational professionals need to be prepared to identify, assess, and treat children with CD in the school setting. In this section, we review some of the key issues regarding the importance of addressing the needs of children with CD.

Significant School Adjustment Difficulties

Conduct disorder is associated with behaviors that interfere with school success (Walker, Ramsey, & Gresham, 2004). In the classroom, children with CD show poor adjustment, as academic and social skill deficits are associated with poor peer relationships and low academic achievement. Children with CD may behave aggressively at school (e.g., fighting, bullying, intimidating, physically assaulting), requiring discipline referrals and at times resulting in suspension or expulsion from school (Schubiner et al., 2000). In addition to being out of school because of school discipline, these children also are truant more frequently and are more likely to fail to graduate from high school. Further, many children with CD may meet special education eligibility criteria.

Section 504 of the Rehabilitation Act of 1973

Section 504 delineates the provision of special services to ensure that "disabled students receive a free and appropriate public education (FAPE)." Under Section 504, a qualified student is defined as any person who has a mental or physical impairment that substantially limits a major life activity (e.g., learning). Thus, depending on the severity of symptoms, children with CD may or may not qualify under Section 504 (see Appendix 1.1 for further details). Thus, children thought to have CD should be evaluated to determine whether they qualify for services.

Individuals with Disabilities Education Improvement Act (IDEIA, 2004)

Under the new IDEIA, if a special-education student has a disciplinary plan, and receives a disciplinary referral, the referral team must investigate and determine if the student's actions were a direct result of his or her disability. For the child with CD who also meets special-education eligibility criteria, school districts must ensure that disciplinary procedures do not interfere with the provision of a free and appropriate public education. The IDEIA directs the individualized education program (IEP) team to focus on addressing behavioral problems of children with disabilities to enhance their success in the classroom. For instance, in IDEIA, it is specifically required that (1) the IEP team explore the need for strategies and support systems to address any behavior that may impede the learning of the child with the disability or the learning of his or her peers; and (2) the school districts address the in-service and pre-service personnel needs (including those of professionals and paraprofessionals who provide special education, general education, related services, or early intervention services) as they relate to developing and implementing positive intervention strategies. Thus, it is imperative that both general-education and special-education professionals are prepared to provide educational services to children with CD.

Inclusion of Children with CD in General Education Classrooms

Children with disabilities are increasingly placed in general-education settings (Sailor, Gerry, & Wilson, 1990). Given that support services may be offered in both the general- or special-educational settings regardless of eligibility status, it is typical that educational professionals in both contexts will be responsible for facilitating these children's education. Hence, all educational professionals (in both special and general education) need to have up-to-date information on CD.

Importance of Early Identification and Intervention

Early identification and intervention are important influences upon the outcome for children with CD. Recognizing early signs of CD and identifying risk factors is an important step in preventing a child's progression to CD (Holmes, Slaughter, & Kashani, 2001). If early problem behaviors are not addressed, antisocial behaviors are likely to persist when the child becomes an adult. Studies of young offenders have suggested that 50% to 70% of children and adolescents who are arrested for committing crimes have antisocial behaviors that persist into adulthood (Loeber, 1982; McCord, 1979).

Conduct Disorder Is Typically Identified During the School-Age Years

The median age of onset is 11.6 years (Nock et al., 2006); thus, educational professionals across the elementary, middle, and high school years must be knowledgeable and prepared to identify symptoms and to provide support services. Early childhood indicators include behaviors associated with oppositional defiant disorder (ODD), which is characterized by irritability, argumentativeness, and noncompliance. Holmes et al. (2001) emphasize that the first step in preventing the progression from juvenile delinquency to adult antisocial behavior is under-standing and recognizing risk factors and contributing influences in early and middle childhood.

Conduct Disorder Is Often Experienced Concurrently with Other Childhood Problems

Conduct disorder behaviors are also frequently found among children diagnosed with attention deficit/hyperactivity disorder (AD/HD) and other disruptive disor-ders, and among children with bipolar disorder. In addition, rates of depression and rates of suicidal thoughts, attempts, and completions are all higher in children diagnosed with CD (Pavuluri, Birmaher, & Naylor, 2005; Shaffer et al., 1996). The National Comorbidity Survey Replication study indicates that CD typically precedes mood and substance use disorders, but most often occurs after impulse control and anxiety disorders (Nock et al., 2006).

School-Based Professionals Have Daily Opportunities to Support Students

Because most children with CD attend school, there is an opportunity to establish support services to help address the needs of these children. Among those children who continue to attend school, educational professionals are in a unique position to help facilitate adaptive and prosocial behaviors (Waller, Waller, Schramm, & Bresson, 2006; Webster-Stratton, Reid, & Hammond, 2004).

Education and Learning Are Important for Future Success

Low achievement, truancy, and school dropout rates all interfere with children's engagement in education activities. For children with CD, facilitating and maintaining their engagement in the educational process helps to provide them with the skills and knowledge that will benefit them in the future (Walker et al., 2004). Also, educational successes promote subsequent adaptation and well-being.

Effective Interventions Are Essential to Offset Long-Term Societal Costs

Long-term economic costs associated with unresolved CD are estimated to exceed $1 million per individual over his or her lifetime (Muntz, Hutchings, & Edwards, 2004). Ultimately, the importance of implementing effective interventions to promote the prosocial adjustment and healthy adaptation of children with CD can extend across the life span (Brestan & Eyberg, 1998).

Conduct Disorder Defined

Conduct disorder is one of three disruptive behavior disorders defined in the *Diagnostic and Statistical Manual of Mental Disorders*, text revision, 4th edition (DSM-IV-TR; American Psychiatric Association, 2000); the others are ODD and AD/HD (Figure 1.1). Behaviors among children diagnosed with CD may vary. The following provides a brief summary of the criteria according to the DSM-IV-TR (see Chapter 5 for the full criteria). Conduct disorder is a repetitive and persistent pattern in which the rights of others or the societal norms or rules are violated as manifested by the presence of at least three of the following criteria in the past 12 months (with at least one criterion present in the past 6 months): (1) being aggressive to people and animals, being physically cruel to people

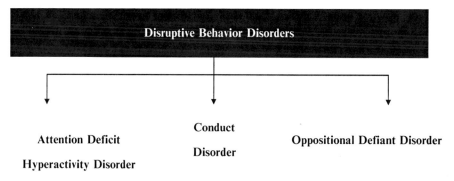

FIGURE 1.1. Disruptive behavior disorders include three different diagnostic categories.

or animals, stealing while confronting a victim (e.g., mugging, purse snatching, extortion, armed robbery), or forcing someone into sexual activity; (2) destruction of property; (3) deceitfulness or theft, such as breaking into someone's home, building, or car, lying to obtain goods or favors or to avoid obligations (i.e., "conning" others) or stealing items of nontrivial value without confronting a victim (e.g., shoplifting, but without breaking and entering; forgery); (4) serious violation of rules, such as staying out at night despite parental prohibitions, running away from home overnight, or being truant from school.

The DSM-IV-TR specifies "childhood-type" as at least one criterion characteristic of CD occurring prior to age 10 years, and "adolescent-onset type" as the absence of all criteria characteristic of CD prior to age 10 years. Conduct disorder differs from other childhood disorders in its characteristic antisocial behavior, the chronic nature of such behavior, as well as the severe impairment of functioning of those exhibiting such behaviors. Although it is possible for a child to be given a diagnosis of CD without a record of overt physical aggression, the symptoms commonly include these behaviors.

Oppositional defiant disorder is characterized by a persistent or consistent pattern of defiance, disobedience, and hostility toward various authority figures including parents, teachers, and other adults. Typical problem behaviors include persistent fighting and arguing, being touchy or easily annoyed, and deliberately annoying or being spiteful or vindictive to other people. Children with ODD may repeatedly lose their temper, argue with adults, deliberately refuse to comply with requests or rules of adults, blame others for their own mistakes, and frequently are angry and resentful. Oppositional defiant disorder can precede or co-occur with CD.

Attention deficit/hyperactivity disorder is characterized by inattention, hyperactivity, and impulsivity. At least six symptoms of inattention and hyperactivity-impulsivity must be present for 6 months. Some, but not all, symptoms, must occur by the age of 6, and must be disruptive and inappropriate to the child's developmental level. Additionally, disruptive symptoms must occur in at least two settings, where there is clear evidence of impairment in social, school, or work functioning. Attention deficit/hyperactivity disorder and CD often are found to co-occur.

Conduct Disorder and Educational Support Services

Meeting the DSM-IV-TR (American Psychiatric Association, 2000) criteria for CD (or any DSM diagnostic category, for that matter) does not necessarily qualify a child for a special-education placement or related services. Depending on the severity of the child's CD, he or she may be considered eligible for services or related assistance under Section 504 of the Rehabilitation Act of 1973 or IDEIA (2004). This section discusses educational regulations that govern the provision of special services to ensure that the children with CD receive a free and appropriate public education (FAPE).

If a child with CD is judged to be eligible (see Appendix 1.1), then Section 504 of the Rehabilitation Act of 1973 emphasizes that the individual is entitled to a FAPE. This may include either regular or special-education–related assistance and services (Davila, Williams, & MacDonald, 1991). An IEP is one way to provide FAPE, although it is not required under 504. If special-education services are not appropriate for the child with CD (and the student is judged to be a "handicapped person" as described by 504), then appropriate support services should be provided in the general-education setting. Moreover, general-education classroom teachers are explicitly identified as being important in the identification of required instructional adaptations and interventions.

The accommodations for children eligible under 504 need to be individualized to be effective; thus, there is no single plan that will fit the needs of each child. The Center for Child Welfare and Education (2004) at the University of Northern Illinois offers an example of a 504 accommodation for a high school student with CD who cannot walk in the hallways without being bumped by other students during the change in classes. When bumped, the student is confrontational with other students. A plan may be developed that allows the student with CD to go to his next class five minutes before the bell rings, thus precluding the opportunity to confront others when bumped.

The Americans with Disabilities Act of 1990 (ADA) also applies to children with CD, as the ADA prohibits discrimination against persons with disabilities at work, at school, and in public accommodations, and also applies to institutions that do not receive federal funds. Because the ADA has been interpreted as incorporating many of the Section 504 requirements, it has been suggested that by meeting 504 requirements, school districts fulfill their ADA obligations (Soleil, 2000). Furthermore, meeting IDEIA requirements also fulfills 504 requirements.

If a child with CD is found to qualify for special-education services according to IDEIA (2004), then the child would receive specially designed instruction, at no cost to the parents, to meet the unique needs of the child with a disability.

Under the protection of special education, the child with CD has the right to (1) procedural safeguards to ensure that parents are provided a written notice regarding identification, evaluation, or placement, or any change in placement of their child in special education; (2) a comprehensive evaluation by a multi-disciplinary team focused on serving the child in the least restrictive environ-ment; and (3) an impartial due-process hearing for parents who disagree with the identification, evaluation, or placement of their child. Some children diag-nosed with CD may qualify for special education under the eligibility category of emotional disturbance, while others may not qualify as they may not reach the diagnostic threshold (e.g., behaviors do not interfere with their learning or the learning of others) or their behavior difficulties are better described as social maladjustment (SM) (also see Appendix 1.1 for further discussion). Guidelines regarding how to determine special-education eligibility are dis-cussed in Chapter 6.

Purpose and Plan of This Book

This book offers school professionals information they need to be better prepared to identify and address the needs of children with CD. Chapter 2 provides a review of the multiple influences and complex etiology of CD. Chapter 3 describes the prevalence and related epidemiological information for CD. Chapter 4 provides information about early warning signs and programming opportunities to prevent CD. Chapter 5 details the assessments available to determine if CD is present. Chapter 6 details the consideration of CD symptoms for psychoeducational assessments and special-education eligibility. Chapter 7 summarizes the research examining the effectiveness of interventions for children with CD, and discusses implementation considerations for the school setting.

Appendix 1.1. Question and Answers Regarding Section 504 Coverage of Children with Conduct Disorder

QUESTION: What is conduct disorder?

ANSWER: Conduct disorder (CD) is the diagnostic classification applied to children who display a pervasive and persistent pattern of problem behaviors characterized by aggression, destruction, deceitfulness, and serious violations of rules (American Psychiatric Association, 2000). To meet diagnostic criteria, three or more of the criteria must be present in the past 12 months, with at least one criterion present in the past 6 months. There are two subtypes, a childhood-onset type, which requires onset of at least one criterion characteristic of CD prior to age 10 years, and an adolescent-onset type, which is the absence of all criteria characteristic of Conduct Disorder prior to age 10 years.

QUESTION: Are all children with CD *automatically* protected under Section 504?

ANSWER: No. Some children with CD may have a disability within the meaning of Section 504; others may not. Children must meet the Section 504 definition of disability to be protected under the regulation. Under Section 504, a "person with disabilities" is defined as any person who has a physical or mental impairment that substantially limits a major life activity (e.g., learning). Thus, depending on the severity of their condition, children with CD may or may not fit within that definition.

QUESTION: Must children thought to have CD be evaluated by school districts?

ANSWER: Yes. If parents believe that their child has a disability, whether it be CD or any other impairment, and the school district has reason to believe that the child may need special education or related services, the school district must evaluate the child. If the school district does not believe the child needs special education or related services, and thus does not evaluate the child, the school district must notify the parents of their due-process rights.

QUESTION: Must school districts have a different evaluation process for Section 504 and the IDEIA?

ANSWER: No. School districts may use the same process for evaluating the needs of students under Section 504 that they use for implementing IDEIA.

QUESTION: Can school districts have a different evaluation process for Section 504?

ANSWER: Yes. School districts may have a separate process for evaluating the needs of students under Section 504. However, they must follow the requirements for evaluation specified in the Section 504 regulation.

QUESTION: Is a child with CD who has a disability within the meaning of Section 504 but not under the IDEIA entitled to receive special education services?

ANSWER: Yes and no. If a child with CD is found to have a disability within the meaning of Section 504, he or she may receive any special-education services the placement team decides are necessary; however, he or she is entitled to either regular or special education services that provide an education comparable to that provided to students without disabilities.

QUESTION: Can a school district refuse to provide special-education services to a child with CD because he or she does not meet the eligibility criteria under the IDEIA?

ANSWER: Yes and no. School districts are only required to provide special-education services to anyone who is identified. They can, however, provide services to nonidentified youngsters if they wish to do so. Alternately, they may provide regular education accommodations to ensure that the child's education is comparable to that provided to children without disabilities.

QUESTION: Can a child with CD who is protected under Section 504 receive related assistance and services in the regular educational setting?

ANSWER: Yes. If it is determined that a child with CD has a disability within the meaning of Section 504 and needs only adjustments in the regular classroom, rather than special education, those adjustments are required by Section 504.

QUESTION: Can parents request a due-process hearing if a school district refuses to evaluate their child for CD?

ANSWER: Yes. In fact, parents may request a due process hearing to challenge any actions regarding the identification, evaluation, or educational placement of their child with a disability, whom they believe needs special education or related services.

QUESTION: Must a school district have a separate hearing procedure for Section 504 and the IDEIA?

ANSWER: No. School districts may use the same procedures for resolving disputes under both Section 504 and the IDEIA. In fact, many local school districts and some state education agencies are conserving time and resources by using the same due-process procedures. However, education agencies should ensure that hearing officers are knowledgeable about the requirements of Section 504.

QUESTION: Can school districts use separate due-process procedures for Section 504?

ANSWER: Yes. School districts may have a separate system of procedural safeguards in place to resolve Section 504 disputes. However, these procedures must follow the requirements of the Section 504 regulation.

QUESTION: What should parents do if the state hearing process does not include Section 504?

ANSWER: Under Section 504, school districts are required to provide procedural safeguards and inform parents of these procedures. Thus, school districts are responsible for providing a Section 504 hearing even if the state process does not include it.

Note: The above is a modification of the 1993 Memorandum from the United States Department of Education entitled, Clarification of School Districts' Responsibilities to Evaluate Children with Attention Deficit Disorders (ADD). The original document focused exclusively on ADD; however, the information is also applicable to conduct disorder (CD).

2
Causes

While it is clear that some mental health disorders have an organic basis, the underlying causes, and exactly how they are manifested is typically much more controversial. This chapter discusses the complex and multifaceted interaction of genetic, neurological, and environmental factors implicated in the development of conduct disorder (CD). As is the case with many forms of psychopathology, the specific causal factors linked to the development of CD have not yet been identified. However, research completed within the last two decades has yielded several correlates of the development of this disorder. Because numerous different causal factors in the development of CD have been suggested and linked through research to this form of psychopathology, it appears evident that one single primary cause does not exist. Instead, an interplay of organic factors, including neuroanatomical features/processes and genetics, and environmental conditions influence the manifestation of CD. The contributing factors that have been linked to the development of CD are considered below.

Underlying Neurological Causes

This section reviews the regions of the brain associated with CD, including anatomical features, hormones, and neurotransmitters of the human neurological systems (Figure 2.1).

Neuroanatomy

Numerous neurobehavioral models suggest that aggressive behavior may be a result of a functional failure of the regions of the brain responsible for emotional regulation, including the amygdala and prefrontal areas (Blair, 2001; Sterzer, Stadler, Krebs, Kleinschmidt, & Poustka, 2005). Individuals who exhibit a proclivity toward aggression and those with known brain lesions in the amygdala have marked neurobehavioral similarities (Angrilli et al., 1996; Patrick, Bradley, & Lang, 1993; Sterzer et al., 2005). In brain imaging studies, the amygdala in those exhibiting normal behavior and emotion processing activates in response

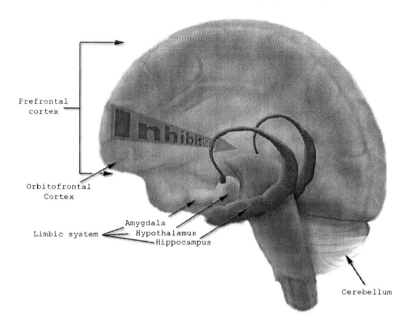

Prefrontal cortex

Orbitofrontal Cortex

Limbic system
Amygdala
Hypothalamus
Hippocampus

Cerebellum

FIGURE 2.1. The brain regions implicated in aggressive behavior.

to fear or threat while viewing unpleasant pictures (Büchel, Morris, Dolan, & Friston, 1998; LaBar, Gatenby, Gore, LeDoux, & Phelps, 1998; Lane et al., 1997; Morris, Frith, Perrett, Rowland, & Young, 1996; Sterzer et al., 2005; Whalen et al., 1998). There is evidence that those with CD have lower level amygdala responses when viewing unpleasant pictures (Davidson, Putnam, & Larson, 2000). For example, Sterzer and colleagues (2005), in response to the belief that aggression and antisocial behavior stem from a deficiency in responding to emotional cues in the social environment, used functional magnetic resonance imaging (fMRI) in 13 adolescent boys between the ages of 9 to 15 years diagnosed with severe CD and 14 healthy age-matched control subjects to measure brain activation while passively viewing pictures with neutral or strong negative affective valence. Functional magnetic resonance imaging involves the use of MRI to measure the hemodynamic response related to neural activity in the brain. In explanation, oxygen is delivered to neurons through the hemoglobin in capillary blood cells. When neuronal activity is increased, a corresponding demand for oxygen results, manifesting in a local response of a greater blood flow to the regions of heightened neural activity (University of Oxford, 2007). After controlling for anxiety and depressive symptoms, differential neural activity in adolescents with CD was found in comparison with the control group in the left amygdala. Interestingly, the CD group also demonstrated a lower level of responsiveness in the left amygdala to aggressive behavior, which reduces their sensitivity to environmental cues regulating emotion (Davidson et al., 2000).

Similarly, lesions in the prefrontal areas of the brain, specifically in the orbit-ofrontal cortex (OFC) and the anterior cingulated cortex (ACC), also appear to contribute to emotion processing and social functioning (Anderson, Bechara, Damasio, Tranel, & Damasio, 1999; Bechara, Damasio, Damasio, & Anderson, 1994; Blair & Cipolotti, 2000; Damasio, 1994; Hornak et al., 2003; Sterzer et al., 2005). The OFC appears to assign emotional significance to complicated stimuli as well as trigger social emotions, the dorsal portion of the ACC plays a part in higher cognitive functions such as response conflict and error monitoring, while the ventral and anterior ACC regulates emotional behavior (Bush, Luu, & Posner, 2000; Damasio, 2003). In their research, Sterzer and colleagues (2005) found differential neural activity in the right dorsal ACC in adolescents with CD in comparison with the control group. These investigators indicate that the activity difference in the ACC was attributed to an abnormal deactivation in adolescents with CD during the viewing of negative (but not neutral) pictures, perhaps reflecting an impaired ability to constrain emotional behavior outbursts and resulting in susceptibility toward impulsive aggression.

Other research further explicates the role of the frontal lobe in the onset of CD, in that executive cognitive functioning (ECF) appears to mediate the relationship between language competence and antisocial behavior in adolescent girls with CD. Investigators discovered that adolescent girls with CD demonstrated inferior language skills and lower ECF in comparison to controls. Even after age and socioeconomic status had been controlled for, ECF still mediated the relationship between language competence and antisocial behavior (Giancola & Mezzich, 2000).

Event-Related Potential and Arousal

The brain waves or electrical activity in the brains of adolescents with CD also seem to be somewhat different than non–behavior-disordered youngsters, with slower brain waves, greater amplitude, and shorter latency periods being observed among those demonstrating antisocial behavior (Bauer & Hesselbrock, 2001; Mpofu, 2002). Other studies have suggested that children with CD may have comorbid temporal lobe seizures that render them vulnerable to aggressive behaviors, with electroencephalographic potential (ERP) measures, which assess electric potentials on the scalp, a record of electrical activity of the brain being predictive of later criminal or psychopathic behavior (Gabrielli & Mednick, 1983; Mpofu, 2002; Raine & Venables, 1987). It is unknown, however, whether the ERP measures are a cause or consequence of violent behavior. Additionally, the inconsistent reliability of ERP readings limits the generalizability of such findings (Mpofu, 2002; Volavka, 1990).

Other physiological correlates of CD in children and adolescents have been identified, with lower resting heart rates and skin conductance resting level responses (EDR, a measure of the level of general tension or activation) found in children who exhibit antisocial behavior, both of which have been found to be predictive of criminal or antisocial behavior in adulthood (Raine, Venables, & Williams, 1990). Interestingly, EDR levels have been correlated with anatomical differences in central nervous system (CNS) structures, such as the prefrontal cortex, pons, amygdala, and temporal lobe, believed to be important factors in impulse control and aggression (Gray, 1987; Mpofu, 2002; Quay, 1993). Another related finding is the weak mobilization of endocrinological stress responses in children and adolescents with CD (Buitelaar, Montgomery, & van Zwieten-Boot, 2003; Van Goozen, Matthys, Cohen-Kettenis, Buitelaar, & van Engeland, 2000; Van Goozen et al., 1998). Similarly, in a study of the autonomic responsiveness of boys with CD with and without attention-deficit/hyperactivity disorder (AD/HD) in comparison to controls, the CD and the CD–AD/HD group reported lower levels of emotional response to aversive stimuli and lower autonomic responses with corresponding physiological deficits in autonomic responsivity. These findings suggest a deficit in the associative information processing systems that normally produce adaptive cognitive-emotional reactions (Herpertz et al., 2005). In summary, the underarousal of the autonomic and endocrinological systems appears to be associated with CD symptomatology.

Neurohormones

Additional evidence for neurological differences between children and adolescents diagnosed with CD and those who are not afflicted is provided by studies investigating cortisol concentrations, a neurohormone, in aggressively behaving populations. Neurohormones are chemical substances produced by the neurosecretory cells in the nervous system that can change the structure or function or direct the activity of an organ or organs. Oosterlaan, Geurts, Knol, and Sergeant (2005) measured basal salivary cortisol (the amount of cortisol, a lipophilic steroid stress hormone, in saliva is reflective of the amount of this substance in blood) in a sample of children with CD, with teacher-reported conduct disorder symptoms being predictive of 38% of the variance in cortisol concentrations, and with severe antisocial symptoms being associated with low cortisol levels. Researchers of this study conclude that their results support biologically-based models of antisocial behavior that involve reduced autonomic activity. Since cortisol is secreted in response to stressful or threatening situations, low levels may indicate how children will respond to potentially stressful situations. Individuals with lower cortisol levels may be less afraid of retribution by others, including punishment or reactive aggression, and are thus less inhibited in perpetrating aggressive acts (McBurnett, Lahey, Rathouz, & Loeber, 2000). In another investigation, examiners found decreased morning plasma cortisol levels in adolescent girls with CD in comparison to controls, with this diagnosis predicting 10% of the variance in cortisol levels. Interestingly, decreased cortisol levels appear to be most strongly associated with antisocial girls who do not have other psychiatric disorders (Pajer, Garnder, Rubin, Perel, & Neal, 2001).

Neurotransmitters

Neurotransmitters are chemicals produced by the nerve cells in the brain that send messages to other nerve cells through a tiny gap, a synapse, which separates the neurons in the brain. Neurotransmitters have been found to have an effect on such CNS activities as depression, control of appetite, addiction, sleep, memory, learning, temperature regulation, mood, and psychotic behavior, among others (Borne, 1998). Serotonin is a neurotransmitter that is found not only in the CNS, but also in blood vessels and the intestinal wall. Researchers have suggested that mental health concerns such as eating disorders, anxiety, obsessive-compulsive disorder, and depression may be due to serotonergic dysfunction, since increasing the amount of serotonin available in the brain appears to ameliorate symptoms associated with such illnesses (Emslie, Portteus, Kumar, & Hume, 2004).

There have been a few studies in which decreased levels of brain serotonin have been found in the cerebrospinal fluid of aggressive children and adolescents, but further research is warranted (Coccaro, Kavoussi, Cooper, & Hauger, 1997). However, in adolescents with CD and comorbid depression, treatment with imipramine or fluoxetine, antidepressants prolonging serotonin conductivity, thereby making serotonin more available in the brain, resulted in a reduction of CD symptoms in 85% and 87% of those studied, respectively, thereby supporting the existence of a link between serotonin augmentation and diminished aggression in children and adolescents (Mpofu & Conyers, 2003; Puig-Antich, 1982; Riggs, Mikulich, Coffman, & Crowley, 1997). Further, there is some limited evidence for norepinephrine involvement in aggressive behavior in children, with modulation or augmentation in norepinephrine levels achieved via neuroleptics, such as haloperidol and pimozide, yielding a reduction in CD and AD/HD symptoms (Campbell, Gonzalez, & Silva, 1992; Kolko, Bukstein, & Barron, 1999; Mpofu & Conyers, 2003). Other neurochemical factors have been associated with CD in children and adolescents. Specifically, behavioral activation and inhibition functions of the hypothalamic-pituitary-adrenal (HPA) axis, which comprises both direct influences and feedback interactions among the hypothalamus, the pituitary gland, and the adrenal or suprarenal gland, have been suspected of playing a part in the development of antisocial behavior (Mpofu, 2002).

In summary, there appear to be several neurological features and conditions that are predictive of a vulnerability to the development of CD symptomatology. First, left amygdala activation levels appear to be lower in children and adolescents with CD than in average youngsters in response to fear or threat. Second, researchers have found differential neural activity in the prefrontal areas of the brain in adolescents with CD in comparison with control groups, specifically in the right dorsal anterior cingulated cortex (Sterzer et al., 2005). Further, evidence of frontal cortex dysfunction and executive functioning deficits has been found among adolescents with CD symptomatology (Giancola & Mezzich, 2000). Third, slower brain waves, greater wave amplitude, shorter latency periods, temporal lobe seizures, and lower resting heart and electrodermal resting levels have been associated with CD in children and adolescents (Bauer & Hesselbrock, 2001; Gabrielli & Mednick, 1983; Mpofu, 2002; Raine & Venables, 1987; Volavka, 1990). Additionally, lower cortisol levels have been found in both boys and girls diagnosed with CD (Oosterlaan et al., 2005; Pajer et al., 2001). Finally, there are neurochemical factors that have been associated with CD, including low or poorly modulated levels of the neurotransmitters serotonin and norepinephrine and the behavioral activation and inhibition functions of the HPA axis (Mpofu, 2002). Clearly, there are numerous neurological factors that have been identified in children and adolescents with CD.

Underlying Genetic Causes

Although CD does not seem to result directly from genetic factors, current research suggests a strong genetic influence on the development of many disruptive behavior disorders (DBDs), including CD. Analyzing the potential genetic component of an area of psychopathology such as CD is referred to as the "heritability" of this disorder (Connor, 2002). Heritability estimates of 100% indicate that the disorder is entirely genetic. Estimates below 100% suggest that not all of the given disorder can be accounted for by genetic influences. A high comorbidity between independently diagnosed DBDs such as CD and oppositional defiant disorder (ODD) has been documented, which supports the assertion that a common genetic predisposition may result in multiple DBD diagnoses. For example, Eaves and colleagues (2000) found a high genetic correlation across sexes in vulnerability to CD and ODD, suggesting predisposition for these DBDs may be a common underlying condition. This line of research suggests genetic makeup and familial proclivity may be significant risk factors for developing CD. This section discusses the specific role of genetics and CD. Later sections explore the environmental factors and CD, and review the interactive effects of neurological factors, genetics, and the environment.

It is difficult in psychological research to discount the effects of the environment when studying the unique contribution of genes to the development of psychopathology. However, twin studies have been an effective research design for examining the influence of genetics on CD (Connor, 2002). Slutske et al. (1997) conducted a retrospective study of twin pairs, finding that genetics had a substantial role in the development of CD, with estimates of heritability at 71%, within the 95% confidence interval, a statistically significant result. No significant differences in genetic influences for CD were found between males and females. The findings of Slutske et al. (1997) have been further supported by research that utilized a female–female twin design and found a modest but significant degree of heritability for CD in this all-female sample (Goldstein, Prescott, & Kendler, 2001).

However, studies using a variety of twin types have limitations that must be acknowledged when interpreting the role of genetic and environmental factors (Slutske et al., 1997). For example, ensuring the uniform application of constructs under investigation is challenging since dissimilar twins were under examination. That is, it is nearly impossible to be certain that the shared environment was equivalent for monozygotic and dizygotic twin groups or for male–female, male–male, and female–female twin groups. Separating enmeshed and interactive factors such as environment and genetics increases the complexity and challenges of interpreting results from this type of study. Furthermore, complete confidence in such interpretations may not be possible without comparative data, such as data obtained from studying twins reared apart with fully separate environments (Gelhorn et al., 2006). Despite these cautions, the study conducted by Slutske et al. (1997) provides strong support for the general role of genetic factors in the development of CD.

Genome Screens

Research conducted by Dick and colleagues (2004) provides further support for the contribution of genetic factors in the development of CD. Previously conducted research had typically consisted of interviewed samples of adult or adolescent twins to examine the link between CD and genetic risk factors (Slutske et al., 1997). Although use of this methodology had provided support for the influence of genetics on CD, research identifying specific genes associated with the development of this psychopathology was lacking. Dick and colleagues sought to address this dearth of research by focusing on identifying the actual genes involved in CD development. Specifically, researchers conducted a genome-wide linkage analysis (genome scan) to identify the genes contributing to CD.

Genome screens, which provide an overview of which genes are likely related to certain behavior, were conducted on a sample of adults involved in the Collaborative Studies On Genetics of Alcoholism (COGA), sponsored by the National Institute on Alcohol Abuse and Alcoholism, whose retrospective reports indicated they experienced CD or CD symptoms during childhood. This sample was used because previously conducted twin studies have suggested that there may be some overlap in the genetic factors that contribute to both childhood CD and alcohol dependence (Dick et al., 2004). In fact, CD may be a risk factor that is partially responsible for mediating differential rates of alcohol dependence between ethnic groups (Luczak, Wall, Cook, Shea, & Carr, 2004). Genome linkage analysis, a method for identifying genomic regions related to disease phenotypes, yielded several regions on chromosomes 19 and 2 that may contain genes that present a risk for CD (Dick et al., 2004). The same region on chromosome 2 has also been linked to alcohol dependence, suggesting a shared genetic vulnerability for both disorders. Overall, the results of the study discussed offer emerging evidence for the influence of genetic makeup on childhood-onset CD; however, because Dick and colleagues (2004) are pioneers within this area of behavioral genetics, future research is necessary to replicate the findings.

Temperament

Just as neurological structures, processes, or neurochemistry may render someone at risk for developing CD, the phenotype of underlying genetic code, temperament, is another contributing factor to the manifestation of antisocial behavior. Center and Kemp (2003) used the empirically supported biosocial theory of personality developed by Hans Eysenck to assess the influence of temperament and personality on CD. The researchers summarize Eysenck's theory, asserting that personality results from "interaction between biologically based temperament source traits and socialization experiences" and note that of the three tiers of the personality/temperament structure—extroversion (E), neuroticism (N), and psychoticism (P)—high P levels are linked directly to CD (Center & Kemp, 2003). Perhaps more interesting is the ability to predict later antisocial behavior in very young children using information about temperament; toddlers' difficult temperaments rated by their mothers at age 3 have strong links to the manifestation of conduct disorder by age 17 (Bagley & Mallick, 2000).

Researchers of the Pittsburgh Youth Study, Pardini, Obradovic, and Loeber (2006), note that boys who exhibit interpersonal callousness (IC) are at risk for persistent delinquency in later adolescence. Further evidence for this finding was provided by Dadds, Fraser, and Frost (2005), who explain that callous-unemotional traits (CU) provide unique predictive value for early-onset CD. Similar results were obtained by researchers studying these constructs in boys and adolescent males in Sweden, with high levels of callous-unemotional (CU) traits (lack of empathy, remorselessness, and shallow affect) in boys and adolescent males with CD, associated with more pervasive, varied, and aggressive disruptive behavioral problems, in comparison with boys with CD and adolescent males low in CU tendencies. Interestingly, higher levels of conduct problems in children and adolescents with CU traits were not explained by AD/HD or ODD, and such youngsters were more likely to be diagnosed with dysthymia in comparison to those with low CU tendencies (Enebrink, Andershed, & Långström, 2005). While girls diagnosed with CD are more likely to exhibit an adolescent-onset of severe antisocial behavior, they tend to resemble boys in personality traits such as poor impulse control, and a CU interpersonal style (Silverthorn, Frick, & Reynolds, 2001).

The propensity for risk-taking is another temperamental trait that appears to be common in adolescents diagnosed with CD. Crowley, Raymond, Mikulich-Gilbertson, Thompson, and Lejuez (2006) found that in a sample of adolescents diagnosed with CD and substance use disorder, in comparison to controls, CD patients took more risks, suggesting an initial risk-taking proclivity. However, patients' slower responses on an experimental task argued against the stereotype of thoughtless, impulsive behavior. These findings suggest that although children and adolescents with CD may be less risk averse than those who are not diagnosed with CD, their propensity toward potential peril or jeopardy is not thoughtless, but may be calculated (Crowley et al., 2006). Frick, Lilienfeld, Ellis, Loney, and Silverthorn (1999) and Frick and colleagues (2003) echo this finding, indicating that children with both CD and CU traits seem to demonstrate a preference for novel, exciting, and dangerous activities. Conduct-disordered youth are also less reactive to threatening and emotionally distressing stimuli (Blair, 1999; Frick et al., 2003; Loney, Frick, Ellis, & McCoy, 1998), and are less sensitive to cues of punishment (Morris, 2007) particularly when primed for a reward-oriented response set (Barry et al., 2000; Fisher & Blair, 1998; Frick et al., 2003; O'Brien & Frick, 1996). The previously described characteristics define a temperamental style that has been referred to as low fearfulness (Rothbart & Bates, 1998) and high daring (Lahey & Waldman, 2003), among others, and may be associated with lower levels of conscience development as compared to nonafflicted peers (Frick, 2004).

Thus, there appear to be numerous genetic influences that are associated with CD. In studies of twin pairs, genetics has been found to play a modest to substantial role in the manifestation of CD (Goldstein et al., 2001; Slutske et al., 1997). Genome linkage analysis yielded several regions on chromosomes 19 and 2 that may contain genes that present a risk for CD. Using Eysenck's theory of personality, high levels of the psychoticism (P) tier of the temperament structure are linked to CD (Center & Kemp, 2003). Difficult temperament levels at age 3 are predictive of the development of CD in adolescence (Bagley & Mallick, 2000), and a callous-unemotional personality style (lack of empathy, remorselessness, and shallow affect) is associated with delinquency and conduct-disordered behavior in both males and females (Dadds et al., 2005; Enebrink et al., 2005; Pardini et al., 2006; Silverthorn et al., 2001). Finally, the propensity for risk-taking, low reactions to threatening and emotional stimuli, reduced sensitivity to cues of punishment, and low levels of conscience and moral development are temperamental traits that appear to be common in adolescents diagnosed with CD (Barry et al., 2000; Blair, 1999; Crowley et al., 2006; Fisher & Blair, 1998; Frick, 2004; Frick et al., 1999, 2003; Loney et al., 1998; O'Brien & Frick, 1996).

Underlying Environmental Causes

Many of the studies discussed in this section have a common thread regarding the role of environmental risk factors; they are an influential component of the development of CD even when these factors fail to reach statistical significance in research studies and are frequently enmeshed with the genetic risk of heritability. A primary environmental factor linked to CD and other DBDs is parenting (Barton, 2003). Although parenting may not intuitively present as a risk falling within the environmental arena, parenting styles and behaviors are responsible for creating various types of home environments in which children develop.

Parental Factors

In an examination of the relationship between maternal antisocial behavior (ASB) and child conduct problems, with a mediator of negative parenting, researchers found that maternal ASB was directly related to their poor parenting, which in turn was predictive of child CD behaviors and difficulties in social competence. Negative parenting partially mediated the relationship between maternal ASB and child CD, although the pattern of relations differed by sex; in boys, maternal ASB was directly related to conduct problems, independent of parenting, whereas in girls, maternal ASB was strongly related to their poor parenting, but not to girls' conduct problems (Rhule, McMahon, & Spieker, 2004). A poor attachment between a mother and infant during the first 12 to 18 months of life is also predictive of aggression in the youngster in later childhood (Kann & Hanna, 2000). Burke, Loeber, and Birmaher (2002) summarize research suggesting a link between child–parent attachment and antisocial behavior, reporting connections between disorganized attachment (Lyons-Ruth, Alpern, & Repacholi, 1993), insecure-avoidant attachment (Pierrehumbert, Milijkovitch, Plancherel, Halfon, & Ansermet, 2000), or coercive insecure attachment (DeVito & Hopkins, 2001), while other studies have found no predictive relationship to the severity or diagnosis of disruptive behavior disorders (Speltz, DeKleyen, Calderon, Greenberg, & Fisher, 1999). Thus, further research is necessary to clarify whether parent–child attachment styles may be predictive of CD.

Further, young maternal age at first birth is associated with CD in children, although controlling for pre- and postnatal history of maternal problem behavior reduced the association of young maternal age at first birth with CD in boys (Wakschlag et al., 2000). Additionally, maternal depression occurring after the birth of a child is associated with childhood ASB, with intraindividual change analyses suggesting that children exposed to their mother's depression between the ages of 5 and 7 demonstrate a subsequent increase in CD behavior by age 7 (Kim-Cohen, Moffitt, Taylor, Pawlby, & Caspi, 2005).

Brennan, Hall, and Bor (2003) and Thompson, Hollis, and Richards (2003) examined familial and social risks for CD such as maternal report of a negative attitude toward an infant, maternal harsh discipline style (authoritarian parenting), maternal permissiveness, poor educational background, exposure to consistent poverty, frequent family transitions (such as moving from home to home) in relation to biological risk factors such as birth complications, maternal illness during pregnancy, and parental temperament problems. In the Thompson et al. (2003) study, researchers found that maternal approval of authoritarian child-rearing attitudes is predictive of the development of CD problems in children. In the Brennan et al. (2003) investigation, the interaction of familial and social risk factors was then examined in relationship to aggressive behavior. Results indicated that children who have experienced both types of risk factors are at increased likelihood of developing problems with aggressive behavior, such as often seen in children diagnosed with CD.

School Factors

Along with risks stemming from parenting and parental behavior, there are school-related factors influencing the onset of CD, including attending classes in which there is little focus on academic work, low teacher expectations for students, and the unavailability of teachers to address problems that students encounter (Delligatti, Akin-Little, & Little, 2003). Another aspect of schooling that may affect children's behavior is their social connections with other youngsters. Peer relationships, specifically peer rejection instead of positive, meaningful relationships, may contribute to the development of CD. Repeated peer rejection is associated with aggressive behavior on the part of the victim, as well as the forming of relationships with individuals who share a proclivity for aggression and disruptive behavior, thus reinforcing this maladaptive way of responding as well as maintaining it (Barton, 2003).

Community Factors

In addition to the family- and school-based environmental risks discussed above, factors stemming from the community and society cannot be overlooked. Such risks identified by Barton (2003) include low socioeconomic status (SES) and community disorganization. Lahey and colleagues (2000) report that high crime rates in the area where one is raised, as well as the availability of drugs, are additional factors that must be considered, as is the role of low SES on parenting, a previously identified environmental risk. Burke et al. (2002) indicate that multiple researchers have also identified specific social and economic risk factors, including neighborhood violence (Guerra, Huesmann, Tolan, Van Acker, & Eron, 1995), unemployment (Fergusson, Horwood, & Lynskey, 1993), living in low-income community housing (Wikström & Loeber, 2000), the presence of neighborhood adults involved in crime (Herrenkohl et al., 2000) and exposure to racial prejudice (Hawkins et al., 1998).

Child Abuse

Physical and sexual abuse appear to be predictive of the onset of CD, with Dodge, Pettit, Bates, and Valente (1995) finding that abused children are likely to demonstrate the following social processing deficits: hostile attribution biases, encoding inaccuracies, and positive evaluation of aggressive behavior, which mediate conduct problems. Trickett and Putnam (1998) also note that conduct problems are very likely in those children who have been sexually abused. The characteristics of the abuse, such as the severity, duration, frequency, the relationship between perpetrator and victim, and the severity of violence of the abuse appear to have an effect upon the demonstration of CD in the victims of the abuse, but additional research is necessary in order to fully understand the role that such abuse plays in the development of later CD behavior.

In addition, Hilarski (2004) examined the relationship between history of victimization and CD in children. Researchers hypothesized that early exposure to victimization, a traumatic experience, was associated with the development of CD or the demonstration of antisocial behaviors. This hypothesis was grounded in the theory that early exposure to victimization is associated with later acting-out behavior, such as aggressive acts and assault. Severe externalizing behaviors may prevent individuals from receiving therapeutic counseling or other services to meet needs resulting from their past experience with trauma. Indeed, results indicated that early exposure to victimization (e.g., before age 11) was a significant factor in predicting the individual's demonstration of CD behavior later in the same year as well as at age 18. Clearly, these results suggest the need for more appropriate assessment to ensure children's external behaviors do not mask internal psychopathology and the resulting need for effective treatment.

In summary, there are several environmental risk factors that have been associated with the development of CD in children and adolescents. First, there are parental, familial, and social risk factors that may render children vulnerable to developing antisocial behaviors. For example, maternal antisocial behaviors, young maternal age at first birth, maternal depression, authoritarian parenting, negative parenting, maternal permissiveness, poor educational background, exposure to consistent poverty, and frequent family transitions, as well as biological risk factors such as birth complications, maternal illness during pregnancy, and parental temperament problems have been found to be related to the onset of CD (Brennan et al., 2003; Kim-Cohen et al., 2005; Rhule et al., 2004; Thompson et al., 2003; Wakschlag et al., 2000). Second, poor attachment between a mother and infant during the first 12 to 18 months of life has been found to be a predictor of aggression and antisocial behavior in children in some studies (DeVito & Hopkins, 2001; Kann & Hanna, 2000; Lyons-Ruth et al., 1993; Pierrehumbert et al., 2000), while other investigations have yielded no predictive relationship between attachment and the severity or diagnosis of disruptive behavior disorders (Speltz et al., 1999). Third, school factors, such as attending classes in which there is little focus upon academic work, low teacher expectations for students, and the unavailability of teachers to address problems that students encounter, as well as peer rejection and negative peer relationships, are associated with the development of CD (Barton, 2003; Delligatti et al., 2003). Fourth, community factors, such as low SES, community disorganization, high crime rates and neighborhood violence, living in low-income community housing, the presence of neighborhood adults involved in crime, the availability of drugs, high unemployment rates, and exposure to prejudice (Barton, 2003; Burke et al., 2002; Fergusson et al., 1993; Guerra et al., 1995; Hawkins et al., 1998; Herrenkohl et al., 2000; Lahey et al., 2000; Wikström & Loeber, 2000) may be risk factors that heighten an individual's likelihood of developing antisocial behaviors. Finally, child physical and sexual abuse and early exposure to victimization seem to predispose children to exhibit aggressive, conduct-disordered behavior (Dodge et al., 1995; Hilarksi, 2004; Trickett & Putnam, 1998).

The Interaction of Neurological, Genetic, and Environmental Factors

In addition to neurological factors, genetics, and the role of environmental factors in the development of CD, the interaction between genetic predisposition/heritability and adverse environmental risks has also been recognized (Cadoret, Yates, Troughton, Woodworth, & Stewart, 1995; Connor, 2002; Mason & Frick, 1994; Rutter, Silberg, O'Connor, & Simonoff, 1999). Kim-Cohen et al. (2005) contend that studies ignoring genetic transmission overestimate the social transmission effects on CD because both genetic and environmental processes appear to create risk for antisocial behavior in children. There is a growing body of evidence that the interaction effects of genes and the environment play a significant role in the development of CD, both from adoption studies and from investigations using measured genotype.

The link between genotype and environment provides an interesting perspective on the role of nature versus nurture in the development of CD. Pike, McGuire, Hetherington, Reiss, and Plomin (1996) found that genetic factors contributed to the association between familial negativity, an environmental risk factor, and adolescent antisocial behavior, which is typically displayed by adolescents with CD. The adolescents' psychological adjustment to negative environmental factors was primarily mediated by genetic factors, but nonshared familial factors, such as environmental processes, also contributed, albeit modestly. Adoption studies in which researchers have examined the role of genetic heritability from biological parents, coupled with the role of environmental factors established by non-biological adoptive parents, is yet another strategy for understanding the role of nature and nurture. This type of design has consistently resulted in the finding of a genetic predisposition toward antisocial behavior, aggression, and adult crime (Connor, 2002).

In addition to posing a risk factor for developing CD, individuals' genetic makeup can also contribute to how they experience their environment. This correlation between individuals' genetic makeup and their perception of their environment effectively links genetic risk factors and environmental ones (Pike et al., 1996). An example of this is research conducted by Foley, Eaves, and Wormley (2004), in which investigators found that low monoamine oxidase A (MAO-A) activity increased the risk for CD only in the presence of an adverse childhood environment, with neither a passive nor an evocative genotype-environment correlation accounting for this interaction. Monoamine oxidase A is an enzyme that catalyzes the oxidation of monoamines, which are derived from amino acids, the basic structural building units of proteins in the body. When this enzyme is either too low or high, neurotransmitters may become inactive, thus contributing to maladaptive behavioral changes.

Consistent findings in genetic studies investigating the etiology of CD have suggested genetics are an influential factor in its development; however, Gelhorn et al. (2006) investigated whether differences in genetic and environmental influence exist among CD symptoms, domains (e.g., aggressive vs. nonaggressive), and diagnoses of full-scale CD. Researchers examined the likelihood of inheriting a predisposition toward developing particular CD symptoms/domains to determine if differences existed in the degree of heritability, thus resulting in differences in the role of genetic factors. The general findings of this study suggest individual symptom heritability is highly variable. Between-symptom differences in genetic as well as environmental factor influence were reported. Genetic influence fell within the moderate-substantial range, while shared environmental factors demonstrated a modest-moderate influence on CD symptomatology. Results suggest that both aggressive and nonaggressive CD types demonstrate strong heritability. Overall, Gelhorn and colleagues have concluded that individual CD symptoms may differ in regard to degree of heritability, but CD domains and full diagnoses are influenced strongly by genetic factors.

In Slutske and colleagues' (1997) research, in addition to investigating the role of genetic makeup on the development of CD, the researchers also examined the role of shared family environment and the environment specific to each individual (e.g., environmental factors vs. genetic ones) as well as sex differences in CD etiology and whether nonclinical conduct problems share the same genetic and environmental risk factors as diagnosable CD. Shared environment contributed a modest effect on CD that failed to reach statistical significance. However, the researchers asserted that shared environment could have accounted for as much as 32% of the variation in CD diagnosis, despite not reaching statistical significance. No significant differences in environmental influences for CD were found between males and females. While researchers caution against overemphasizing the importance of the specific heritability value (e.g., the specific percentage of accountability assumed by genetics), they acknowledge the important role genes play in the development of CD. Overall, the study conducted by Slutske and colleagues provides strong support for the potential interaction of genetic and environmental factors in the development of this form of psychopathology. Other research has provided greater credence for the role of environment in the development of CD in children and adolescents. Burt, Krueger, and McGue (2001) studied twins from the Minnesota Twin Family Study, finding that although CD was influenced by both genetic and environmental factors, a single shared environmental factor comprised the largest contribution to the covariation among AD/HD, ODD, and CD.

Button, Scourfield, and Martin (2005) examined the interaction of family dysfunction, a previously explained environmental risk, with genes on the development of conduct problems in children and adolescents. The researchers were extending previous research that identified a link between family dysfunction and conduct problems by framing this association in a gene–environment interaction study design. Results from the study conducted by Button and colleagues yielded significant positive results in support of previous research findings. Conduct disorder was found to have a significant association with family dysfunction in addition to being under the influence of genetics. The heritability of the predisposition to exhibit conduct problems, as well as the influence of family environment on their development, was not found to differ across age or sex of the child/adolescent. In fact, the interaction between heritability and family dysfunction comprise a majority of the variance in participant's conduct problem scores. Despite the significance of this finding, the researchers caution against overinterpretation and failing to acknowledge the existence of other environmental factors that could be entangled with genetics while contributing to CD development. Although this study is not without limitations, it supports the hypothesis that genes and environment interact in their influence on CD development. Overall, it remains reasonable to conclude that the genetic makeup of certain individuals increases their vulnerability to environmental risks, resulting in the development of conduct problems.

Gelhorn et al. (2006) used the twin study method to investigate the etiology of aggressive and nonaggressive CD domains. Given the assumptions inherent in twin studies as discussed above, the researchers sought to understand the distinct and interactive effects of genetic and environmental risk factors on the CD domain, while recognizing the limitations in the study design. In addition, unlike the retrospective accounts utilized by Slutske et al. (1997), Gelhorn et al. (2006) directly interviewed adolescents in order to assess *Diagnostic and Statistical*

Manual of Mental Disorders, 4th edition (DSM-IV) CD criteria. Results suggest that CD domains are influenced by unique genetic and nonshared environmental factors, though shared environmental factors cannot be completely disregarded. Researchers reported a majority of the covariation in domains stems from genetic factors, with a specific estimate of 61% versus 39% for nonshared environmental factors.

Similarly, in a study designed to examine the interaction of genes and family dysfunction in contributing to conduct problems in children and adolescents, parents of monozygotic and dizygotic twin pairs (ages 4 to 18), drawn from the CaStANET birth cohort twin register, were interviewed regarding zygosity, conduct problems, and family environment. Using structural equation modeling, the researchers tested for main and interactive effects of genes and family dysfunction, which the investigators modeled as an environmental moderator variable, finding highly statistically significant main and gene–environment interactions. Consequently, the examiners concluded that a risk genotype rendering an individual vulnerable to family dysfunction accounts for most of the variance in antisocial symptomatology in childhood and adolescence (Button et al., 2005).

Connections between genetic and environmental risk factors can be drawn from research conducted by Jaffee, Belsky, Harrington, Caspi, and Moffitt (2006). This study was based on the presupposition that mothers with histories of adolescent-onset CD are at an increased likelihood to expose their children to a variety of environmental risk factors associated with the development of CD, thus perpetuating an intergenerational continuity of antisocial behavior. Although the proposed mediational hypothesis regarding the link between parent psychopathology (CD) and child temperament could not be tested with confidence, the researchers suggest the following: children of parents diagnosed with CD are at elevated risk for developing internalizing and externalizing problems, such as CD, because of their temperamental reactivity and exposure to adversity, which are genetic and environmental risk factors, respectively. Jaffee and colleagues assert there is a need for future research to examine "biological vulnerabilities" for disruptive behavior disorders such as CD that are passed from parents to children. Moreover, parents who have a history of early-onset CD and engage in assortative mating, in which they choose partners with a history of antisocial behavior, are likely to experience numerous negative long-term effects in their adult lives.

In summary, the interaction between genetics and the environment appears to contribute to the etiology of CD. The correlation between one's genetic makeup and one's perception of his or her environment effectively links genetic and environmental risk factors (Foley et al., 2004; Pike et al., 2006). Heredity and genetics, along with environmental conditions or characteristics such as family dysfunction, family negativity, and exposure to adversity, are predictive of adolescent antisocial behavior (Burt et al., 2001; Button et al., 2005; Gelhorn et al., 2006; Jaffee et al., 2006; Pike et al., 1996; Slutske et al., 1997). Overall, it is reasonable to conclude that the dynamic interplay of genetic makeup of certain individuals and their vulnerability to environmental risks, results in the development of conduct problems (Button et al., 2005).

Understanding the Confluence of Risk Factors

While the multiple risk factors and correlates of CD described above are notable, an important question that remains is the interplay of these factors. The dynamic and reciprocal influence of multiple factors impacts on the development of both healthy and maladaptive outcomes (Sroufe & Rutter, 1984). There are three conceptual models that have been offered to further understand the confluence of the numerous risk factors: additive, interactive, and transactional.

Additive Models

Rutter, Cox, Tupling, Berger, and Yule (1975) found that the number of distal factors present (rather than any single risk factor) provided the strongest prediction of later antisocial behavior, and the authors thus propose a cumulative risk model. Studies by Dodge and colleagues (1995) illustrate the value of simultaneously considering multiple factors. For instance, one study assessed 20 different biological, contextual, and life experience risk factors during preschool, and revealed significant but weak associations with conduct problems 5 years later. However, the cumulative risk, considering all factors, accounted for about half of the variance in conduct problems (Deater-Deckard, Dodge, Bates, & Petit, 1996). Another study that included four diverse risk factors during early elementary school (difficult biological temperament, low SES at birth, early experience of physical abuse, and peer rejection), found low risk of problems in grades 6 or 7 for students with none of these risk factors, moderate risk for students with one of the risk factors, and high risk for students with all four risk factors (Dodge, 1996).

Interactive Models

Interactive models propose that certain risk factors operate only in the presence or absence of other risk factors. Such diathesis-stress models have been supported and further enhance the understanding of the development of CD. For instance, research reveals that the risk associated with family and neighborhood poverty may be moderated by parental supervision (Pettit, Laird, Bates, & Dodge, 1997). Garmezy and Rutter (1983) characterize protective factors as those characteristics that buffer a child from the deleterious effects of risk factors. Indeed, the interaction of risk and protective factors is an important consideration in understanding the development of CD in children.

Transactional-Ecological Developmental Models

Whereas both the additive and interactive models are empirically supported and may predict antisocial outcomes, these models offer a paucity of information regarding the process or development of CD over time. Understanding the developmental psychopathology of CD is further advanced by considering a transactional-ecological developmental model (Collins & Sroufe, 1999;

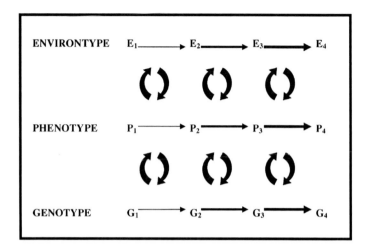

FIGURE 2.2. The transactional developmental model, in which genotype and environtype change the phenotype as each is reciprocally changed by the phenotype over time. Subscripts represent times 1, 2, 3, and 4. [Adapted from Sameroff (2000), with kind permission of Springer Science and Business Media.]

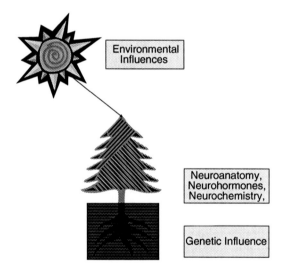

FIGURE 2.3. Interaction between genetics and the environment in the development of conduct disorder.

Sameroff, 1995; Sameroff & Chandler, 1975). At its simplest, the transactional model stipulates that the contact between individuals and their environment becomes a mutual transaction through which each is altered by the other, which then impacts subsequent interactions in an ongoing and continuous fashion. However, this model builds in complexity as it also takes into account the social and cognitive states of the individual while simultaneously acknowledging behavior as highly contextual (Bronfenbrenner, 1986; Sameroff, 1995). Thus, current adaptation is influenced by the individual's past and current circumstances, ecological contexts, and previous developmental history. Contemporary scholarship reveals the dynamic interplay among the phenotype (i.e., the child), the environtype (i.e., the source of external experience), and the genotype (i.e., the source of biological organization; Kashani, Jones, Bumby, & Thomas, 1999; Sameroff, 1995; 2000; Tolan, 2001; Figure 2.2). Development is a transactional process between individuals and their environments, whereby these components mutually influence each other (Cicchetti & Toth, 1995). The transactional-ecological developmental model aims to promote the understanding of developmental outcomes through exploration of developmental trajectories.

Conclusion

This chapter illustrates the complexity of identifying the causes of CD. A review of the literature reveals that there is not one single developmental trajectory that leads to CD, but rather an evolution through periods of quiescence and more dynamic increases over time (Patterson & Yoerger, 2002). Children and adolescents engaged in antisocial and aggressive behaviors represent a heterogeneous group (Jimerson, Morrison, Pletcher, & Furlong, 2006). The current consensus regarding the etiology of CD is reflected in a transactional-ecological developmental model that incorporates the dynamic and reciprocal influences of biological, individual, and contextual factors over time (Figure 2.3). Further research is needed to clarify the complex interplay among multiple factors that contribute to the development of CD.

3
Incidence and Associated Conditions

This chapter explores the lifetime incidence of conduct disorder (CD), as well as rates of CD in both general- and special-education school populations. Additionally, CD's association with other conditions is examined, with special attention being given to issues associated with dual diagnoses and concurrent and future maladjustment.

Incidence

The lifetime incidence of CD in the general population has been established in numerous studies, with evidence of variable rates of the disorder both in the United States and internationally. Despite the differential rates reported, however, it appears clear that CD is a common disorder of childhood and adolescence. Lifetime incidence rates of the disorder vary considerably. One investigation estimated the lifetime incidence of CD in the U.S. population to be 1.1% (Compton, Conway, Stinson, Colliver, & Grant, 2005); however, other epidemiological studies have placed the incidence rates at 9.5% (12.0% for males and 7.1% for females) (Nock, Kazdin, Hiripi, & Kessler, 2006). Among international studies, lifetime incidence rates have also been found to vary significantly, from 21% in Turkey, (Doğan, Önder, Doğan, & Akyüz, 2004) to 5.4% in Great Britain (Vostanis, Meltzer, Goodman, & Ford, 2003). Maughan, Rowe, Messer, Goodman, and Meltzer (2004) provide a synthesis of six international studies from the U.S., Canada, and New Zealand, which represents the variation in the prevalence of CD (Table 3.1).

Three recent studies (two in the U.S. and one in Scotland) of the incidence of CD in children in regular education yield modest to moderate estimates of the disorder. In a nonreferred, population-based sample of 4-year-old children in the U.S., the incidence of CD and moderate-to-severe CD was 6.6% and 2.2%, respectively (Kim-Cohen et al., 2005). In another sample of over 3000 children of ages 3 to 18 in the U.S., teacher reports of CD symptomatology ranged from 1% to 2% (Nolan, Gadow, & Sprafkin, 2001). Further, in a sample of almost 2000 Scottish 15-year-olds participating in a school-based survey of health and lifestyles, 14.0% of males and 2.9% of females met the criteria for CD (West, Sweeting, Der, Barton, & Lucas, 2003).

TABLE 3.1. Prevalence of conduct disorder in recent epidemiological studies.

Authors	DSM/ICD	Interview	Informant[1]	Gender	n	6	7	8	9	10	11	12	13	14	15	16	17	18
Simonoff et al., 1997	DSM-III-R	CAPA	P,C,**J**	Boys	1275				4.5			4.7			9.0			
Loeber et al., 1998	DSM-III-R	DISC-P	P,C,**J**	Girls	1478				2.1			2.3			4.8			
				Boys	1517		5.6				5.4		8.3					
Breton et al., 1999	DSM-III-R	DISC-2.25 Dominio	P,C,**T**	Boys	2400		1.7			3.0			3.2					
				Girls			2.1											
Lahey et al., 2000	DSM-III-R	DISC-2.3	P,C,**J**	Boys	1274					3.4			7.9			13.2		
				Girls						0.6			1.4					
Romano et al., 2004	DSM-III-R	DISCC-2.25	P,C,**J**	Boys	1201					1.4			4.5		6.3	3.6		
				Girls											2.9			
Moffitt et al., 2001[‡]	DSM-IV	Mixed	P,C,T,**J**	Boys	843/934						10		13		14			14
				Girls							3		5		8			3

CAPA, Child and Adolescent Psychiatric Assessment; DISC, Diagnostic Interview Schedule for Children.
[1]Informant: P, parent, C, child, T, teacher, J, joint, boldface type indicates informant cited.
[¶]Additional data kindly provided on request.
[‡]n's vary by age/wave.
[§]Two-stage sample.
From Maughan, Rowe, Messer, Goodman, & Meltzer, 2004, with permission.

In special-education populations the rates of CD appear to be considerably greater than that found in general-education students. For example, among students receiving special education services at school in Quebec, Canada, approximately 33% met the criteria for CD (Déry, Toupin, Pauzé, & Verlaan, 2004).

Finally, as might be expected, among children who commit law violations, the rates of CD are quite high; in a sample of delinquent adolescents in Brazil, the CD rate was found to be 77% (Andrade, Silva, & Assumpçáo, 2004). Further, in a German prison population, 21.7% of inmates were found to meet the criteria to be diagnosed with CD (Rösler et al., 2004).

Developmental Level

The median age of onset of CD is 11.7 years of age (Nock et al., 2006), with one of the earliest symptoms of CD, animal cruelty, exhibited at a mean age of 6.75 years (Frick et al., 1993). Preschool-age children who have older siblings exhibiting antisocial behavior are at an increased risk of developing CD (Brotman, Gouley, O'Neal, & Klein, 2004). Loeber, Burke, Lahey, Winters, and Zera (2000) report that some research is suggestive of the incidence of CD tending to increase from middle childhood to adolescence, while other studies have concluded that no age differences exist in the incidence of CD (Cohen et al., 1993; Lewinsohn, Hops, Roberts, Seeley, & Andrews, 1993).

Nonaggressive CD behaviors, including serious theft, breaking-and-entering, and fraud; covert conduct problems; and serious aggression, such as robbery, rape, and attempted/completed homicide all appear to increase during adolescence, while physical fighting appears to decrease (Loeber et al., 2000). Moffitt and Caspi (2001) offer a comparison between childhood risk factors of males and females exhibiting childhood-onset and adolescent-onset antisocial behavior, utilizing data from the Dunedin, New Zealand, longitudinal study. The results reveal that outcomes associated with early onset are much more deleterious relative to those children who initiate behavior problems during adolescence.

Gender

Researchers have noted that boys are more likely to be diagnosed with CD in the *Diagnostic and Statistical Manual of Mental Disorders*, text revision, 4th edition (DSM-IV-TR), as well as to exhibit a higher frequency of CD symptoms than girls. The odds for CD in boys appear to be three to four times greater than for girls, at various ages (Lahey, Miller, Gordon, & Riley, 1999; Lahey et al., 2000; Loeber et al., 2000; Lumley, McNeil, Herschell, & Bahl, 2002). Interestingly, however, sex differences in disruptive behavior do not emerge until approximately age 6, at which time more boys begin to demonstrate overt forms of antisocial conduct (Loeber et al., 2000).

Ethnicity

Ethnic differences in rates of CD have been found in some research. In a study of prisoners in the United Kingdom, fewer black and South Asian, as compared to white prisoners, reported a history of CD (Coid et al., 2002). Researchers also examined the incidence of CD among Hispanics, who were subdivided into Island Puerto Ricans (IPR) and Mainland Hispanics (MH), African Americans (AA), and Mainland Non-Hispanic, Non-African Americans (MW). Results suggested that IPRs had a lower rate of CD than MHs, AAs, and MWs (Bird et al., 2001).

Socioeconomic Status

Conduct disorder appears to be more common in neighborhoods that suffer from high crime and social disorganization (Loeber et al., 2000). Children from low-income households have been found to have a rate of CD of 4.6% (Keenen, Shaw, Walsh, Delliquadri, & Giovannelli, 1997), and the disadvantages of poverty, including exposure to delinquency, unemployment, substance abuse, and neighbors who engage in criminal activity, are associated with the development of CD (Loeber et al., 2000).

Discussion

Numerous studies in the U.S. and internationally are suggestive of CD being a common diagnosis in childhood and adolescence. Incidence rates for the disorder in childhood and adolescence range from 1% to 6% in nonreferred samples (Kim-Cohen et al., 2005; Nolan et al., 2001), with 2.9% in females and 14.0% in males (West et al., 2003). Further, in special-education samples and samples of adjudicated children and adolescents, rates have been reported as 33% (Déry et al., 2004) and from 77% to 100% (Andrade et al., 2004; Myers & Scott, 1998). The median age of onset of CD is 11.7 years (Nock et al., 2006), with one of the earliest symptoms of CD, animal cruelty, exhibited at a mean age of 6.75 years (Frick et al., 1993). The odds for CD in boys appear to be three to four times greater than for girls at various ages (Lahey et al., 1999, 2000; Loeber et al., 2000; Lumley et al., 2002). Ethnic differences in rates of CD have been found in some research, with Caucasians, African Americans, and Mainland Hispanics being diagnosed with CD more often than Island Puerto Ricans, and white prisoners having self-reported higher rates of CD than African European or South Asian inmates (Bird et al., 2001; Coid et al., 2002). The risks of poverty and associated environmental conditions, such as crime, unemployment, and social disorganization, also appear to be associated with the incidence of CD (Keenen et al., 1997; Loeber et al., 2000).

Associated Conditions

There is significant evidence suggesting that CD is comorbid with other DSM-IV-TR disorders, which is the simultaneous occurrence of two or more conditions

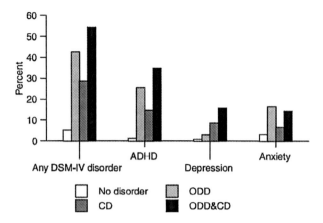

FIGURE 3.1. Rates of comorbid disorder in pure ODD, pure CD, and comorbid CD and ODD. (From Maughan, Rowe, Messer, Goodman, & Meltzer, 2004, with permission.)

(Caron & Rutter, 1991). Findings from one study support CD as a complex illness with a presentation of symptoms from both Axis I and Axis II in the DSM-IV-TR, as well as differences in symptom presentation between male and female children and adolescents (Burket & Myers, 1995). Studies in the U.S. and in other countries, such as Australia and Colombia, have suggested that CD is often diagnosed in conjunction with Axis I diagnoses of oppositional defiant disorder (ODD; 32%; Biederman et al., 1996), attention-deficit/hyperactivity disorder (AD/HD; 25% to 50%; Anonymous, 2000; Palacio et al., 2004), anxiety, obsessive compulsive disorder (OCD), depression (Drabick, Gadow, & Sprafkin, 2006), bipolar disorder (BD; 37–69%; Kovacs & Pollock, 1995; Schneider, Atkinson, & El-Mallakh, 1996) or the broad BD phenotype called severe mood dysregulation (SMD; 25.9%; Brotman et al., 2006), pervasive developmental disorder (PDD; Emerson, 2003), and Tourette syndrome; and Axis II diagnoses, such as aggressive personality disorders and borderline personality disorder (Burket & Myers, 1995; Kawa et al., 2005; Masi et al., 2006; Sanders, Arduca, Karamitsios, Boots, & Vance, 2005; Yang, Zhang, & She, 2005). Maughan, Rowe, Messer, Goodman, and Meltzer (2004) provide further discussion of comorbidity among children with CD symptoms (Figure 3.1).

Externalizing Disorders

Researchers have suggested that children are often diagnosed with ODD prior to being diagnosed as CD, with antisocial behavior in childhood being predictive of a CD diagnosis in adolescence (Mannuzza, Klein, Abikoff, & Moulton, 2004). However, in one study, ODD children who were not also concurrently diagnosed with CD at a baseline assessment in childhood were not found to be at increased risk for CD at the 4-year follow-up in mid-adolescence (Biederman et al., 1996). Thus, while comorbidity of ODD and CD is common, some children meet the criteria for only one classification.

Attention deficit/hyperactivity disorder, which is often diagnosed prior to the onset of CD (Tillman et al., 2003), is seen as a salient risk factor for the development of CD in boys (Côté, Tremblay, Nagin, Zoccolillo, & Vitaro, 2002; Mannuzza et al., 2004). Comorbid CD and AD/HD is associated with increased AD/HD symptom severity, earlier onset of antisocial behavior, social dysfunction, higher aggression, anxiety, and greater substance-abuse problems (Kuhne, Schachar, & Tannock, 1997; Thompson, Riggs, Mikulich, & Crowley, 1996). However, Lahey et al. (1999) and Loeber et al. (2000) have proposed a model in which only children with comorbid ODD and AD/HD will develop CD in childhood, with a group of these children also later developing antisocial personality disorder (ASPD).

Further, there is ample evidence, both in the United States and internationally, that other externalizing behaviors, such as substance abuse with both drugs and alcohol, are strongly correlated with CD (Kelly, Cornelius, & Lynch, 2002). One U.S. study found that 63% of girls and 82% of boys who were diagnosed with substance-abuse disorder, in which they excessively used alcohol, also demonstrated antisocial symptoms (Molina, Bukstein, & Lynch, 2002). Researchers in Taiwan found that CD was strongly associated with the use of methamphetamines in adolescence (Yen & Chong, 2006; Yen, Yang, & Chong, 2006), and in the United States, researchers have suggested a comorbidity of CD and drug abuse ranging from 24% to 82% (Couwenbergh et al., 2006; Latimer, Stone, Voight, Winters, & August, 2002). In other studies, males who exhibited comorbid CD and substance dependence (SD) demonstrated greater severity in their CD symptoms (Whitmore et al., 1997). Finally, in a sample of adults being treated for chemical dependency, 39% also met the criteria for CD (Schubiner et al., 2000).

Internalizing Disorders

The results of research on the relationship between anxiety disorders and CD have been mixed. Early epidemiological studies of prepubertal children with anxiety disorders without CD are suggestive of a reduced risk for CD development in adolescence. Conversely, in other studies, researchers have indicated that there is a higher probability than by chance of the comorbidity of CD and anxiety disorders in childhood and adolescence. Hence, anxiety in childhood appears to act as a protective factor against developing CD in adolescence, while CD in childhood or adolescence is predictive of the development of an anxiety disorder (Loeber et al., 2000).

Additionally, depression often occurs concomitantly with CD, although research has both supported (Drabick et al., 2006) and negated (Loeber et al., 2000) the presence of depression as a precursor to the development of antisocial behavior (Loeber et al., 2000). Interestingly, the findings of one study suggest that there are few differences between children and adolescents with "pure" CD and antisocial symptomatology comorbid with other disorders. However, comorbidity accentuated depressive and emotional symptoms (such as CD with depression and anxiety), such that children and adolescents were more globally and severely impaired as compared to "pure" CD youngsters even after controlling for other disorders and symptom severity (Ezpeleta, Domènech, & Angold, 2006; Newcorn et al., 2004).

Furthermore, the DSM-IV-TR has identified CD as a risk for somatoform disorders, although Loeber et al. (2000) has reported that there is limited information about this relationship, and updated information is needed. In studies of ASPD and family-genetic studies of adults, a link of somatization and CD has been established (Lewis & Bucholz, 1991). However, only a few studies have been conducted that address the relationship between somatoform disorders and CD. One of which, conducted by Achenbach, Howell, McConaughy, and Stanger (1995), found that in girls a high somatization score in adolescence was predictive of high delinquency scores, while the same was not true for boys.

There has also been research conducted on the relationship of BD and CD. Some researchers have recommended that since CD and BD are often distinct yet co-occurring diagnoses in children, neither should be seen as a secondary disorder to the other (Biederman et al., 2003). Children with comorbid CD and BD appear to be at an increased risk for SD, with one study revealing that 64% of parents of such youngsters reported substance abuse in their children (Kovacs & Pollock, 1995). Other studies have provided contradictory evidence of the comorbidity of CD with other disorders, such as BD, explaining that the link between disruptive behavior disorders (DBDs) and BD is tenuous (Jaideep, Reddy, & Srinath, 2006).

Discussion

Studies in the United States and in other countries, such as Australia and Colombia, have suggested that CD is often diagnosed in conjunction with Axis I diagnoses of ODD (Biederman et al., 1996), AD/HD (Palacio et al., 2004), anxiety, OCD, depression (Drabick et al., 2006), BD (Schneider et al., 1996), SMD (Brotman et al., 2006), and Tourette syndrome; and Axis II diagnoses, such as aggressive personality disorders and borderline personality disorder (Burket & Myers, 1995; Kawa et al., 2005; Masi et al., 2006; Sanders et al., 2005; Yang et al., 2005). Research has suggested that children are often diagnosed with externalizing behavior disorders such as ODD, AD/HD, and SD prior to or in addition to being diagnosed as having CD (Biederman et al., 1996; Côté et al., 2002; Couwenbergh et al., 2006; Kelly et al., 2002; Kuhne et al., 1997; Lahey et al., 1999; Latimer et al., 2002; Loeber et al., 2000; Mannuzza et al., 2004; Molina et al., 2002; Schubiner et al., 2000; Thompson et al., 1996; Tillman et al., 2003; Whitmore et al., 1997; Yen & Chong, 2006; Yen et al., 2006). Finally, there is frequently comorbidity between CD and internalizing disorders, such as anxiety, depression, somatoform disorder, and BD (Achenbach et al., 1995; Biederman et al., 1996; Drabick et al., 2006; Ezpeleta et al., 2006; Jaideep et al., 2006; Kovacs & Pollock, 1995; Lewis & Bucholz, 1991; Loeber et al., 2000; Newcorn et al., 2004), although whether any of these are predictive of CD the research has yet to firmly establish.

The Difficulty with Dual Diagnosis

The comorbidity of CD with ODD, AD/HD, and BD may make it difficult for clinicians to distinguish these disorders from one another (Rowland, Lesesne, & Abramowitz, 2002). For example, disruptive behavior of more than 2000 ten- to twelve-year-olds in the general Dutch population was assessed through the Achenbach Child Behavior Checklist (CBCL) and Youth Self-Report (YSR). Through latent class analysis, researchers found three classes of preadolescents: (1) those characterized by high scores on AD/HD, CD, and ODD items; (2) a group typified by high probabilities of AD/HD and ODD symptoms; and (3) group that scored low on all items. The researchers concluded that because they could not isolate the symptoms from various DBDs from one another, it is questionable whether diagnostic distinctions in general population studies are useful (Sondeijker et al., 2005). However, other studies provide contradictory information.

In another investigation, researchers used several structured diagnostic assessments to determine whether CD adolescents could be distinguished from controls, and found that adolescents' self-report (including the CBCL) significantly discriminated CD adolescents from nonafflicted controls, suggesting the utility of such methods in reaching differential diagnoses (Crowley, Mikulich, Ehlers, Whitmore, & Macdonald, 2001). In yet another investigation of the comorbidity of major depression and conduct disorder, four variables distinguished between the two mental illnesses: anxiety, witness to family violence, illegal behavior, and impulsive behavior. Anxiety proved to be the strongest discriminating variable between CD and depression, with anxiety being associated with depression alone (Meller & Borchardt, 1996). Greene et al. (2002), Kuhne et al. (1997), and Loeber et al. (2000) report that the majority of empirical evidence supports a distinction between ODD, AD/HD, and CD, as well as BD (Kim & Miklowitz, 2002), although there is symptom overlap.

Moreover, some studies have suggested difficulty in discriminating between several disorders because of symptom overlap, and speculate regarding the utility of diagnostic distinctions (Rowland et al., 2002; Sondeijker et al., 2005). Other research, however, provides evidence supporting the distinction between CD and disorders such as depression, ODD, AD/HD, and BD (Crowley et al., 2001; Greene et al., 2002; Kuhne et al., 1997; Loeber et al., 2000; Meller & Borchardt, 1996). The controversy with respect to comorbidity continues to fuel debates regarding the value and meaning of the classification criteria delineated in the DSM-IV-TR, with some scholars proposing alternative procedures for assessment and case formulation among children (Achenbach, 1998).

Concurrent and Future Maladjustment

Conduct disorder in childhood is associated with a number of other concurrent developmental problems, including being bullied (Johnson et al., 2002), having a learning disability, the likelihood of repeating a grade in school, being suspended or expelled from school, demonstrating an earlier age at onset of alcohol dependence, and undergoing a greater number of treatments for drug abuse (Schubiner et al., 2000). There are factors that mediate the symptom presentation of CD and other associated conditions, such as socializing with a deviant peer group. Researchers reveal that high levels of CD symptomatology moderate the deviant peer pathway to substance use in children with AD/HD (Marshal & Molina, 2006).

Research conducted in the United Kingdom and Japan has suggested that having an intellectual disability or a significantly lower verbal IQ in comparison to performance IQ is associated with CD (Emerson, 2003; Harada et al., 2002). Not surprisingly, children with CD tend to exhibit poor social competence, and may also have low self-esteem (Renouf, Kovacs, & Mukerji, 1997).

Other researchers have suggested that children with comorbid CD, such as a dual diagnosis of CD and depression, are at extreme risk for school failure, peer rejection, violent behavior, drug and alcohol abuse, suicide, and serious criminality (Kelly et al., 2002; Rapp & Wodarski, 1997). Unfortunately, the presence of CD in depressed adolescents may shroud their affective symptoms from mental health personnel, potentially resulting in an underdiagnosis of depression, and consequently less effective treatment (Herkov & Myers, 1996). Personality traits associated with CD include high neuroticism or psychoticism, which may also make an accurate diagnosis more challenging to mental health practitioners (Center & Kemp, 2003; Khan, Jacobson, Gardner, Prescott, & Kendler, 2005).

As for future maladjustment, CD in childhood is predictive of having serial employment in adulthood (Schubiner et al., 2000), adult psychiatric illness (when comorbid with other disorders) (Kelly et al., 2002; Rapp, 1997), and has been found to be a strong risk factor for later substance abuse in schizophrenic adult males and those with major affective disorders (Mueser et al., 1999; Swartz et al., 2006).

Conduct disorder exhibited during childhood and adolescence is a necessary precondition to be diagnosed with ASPD, a DSM-IV-TR Axis II diagnosis, which cannot be diagnosed prior to the age of 18 (American Psychiatric Association, 2000). Researchers have found that the onset of deviant conduct at or before age 10, a greater diversity of deviant behavior, and more extensive pretreatment drug use is predictive of progression to ASPD (Myers, Stewart, & Brown, 1998). In a study of a nationally representative sample of 1422 adults with ASPD, researchers examined the different symptom presentations in those who had been diagnosed with CD in childhood as compared to those who had been diagnosed with CD in adolescence. Childhood-onset CD individuals were more likely than the adolescent-onset CD sample to admit to CD criteria involving aggression against persons, animals, and property prior to the age of 15, and to report more childhood criteria and lifetime violent behavior. Further, childhood-onset CD respondents demonstrated significantly increased odds of lifetime social phobia, generalized anxiety disorder, drug dependence, and paranoid, schizoid, and avoidant personality disorders, while curiously evidencing a decreased risk for lifetime tobacco dependence. Researchers conclude that childhood-onset CD is associated with a more polysymptomatic and violent form of ASPD and an increased risk for various Axis I and Axis II disorders (Goldstein, Grant, Ruan, Smith, & Saha, 2006).

Conclusion

Conduct disorder is associated with concurrent developmental maladjustment in childhood and adolescence, and is predictive of future behavioral impairment in adulthood. Children with CD often suffer from other developmental problems, including being bullied (Johnson et al., 2002), having poor social competence and low self-esteem (Renouf et al., 1997), being intellectually disabled or having a lower verbal IQ than performance IQ (Emerson, 2003; Harada et al., 2002), having a learning disability, an increased likelihood of repeating a grade in school, being suspended or expelled from school, demonstrating an earlier age at onset of alcohol dependence, undergoing a greater number of treatments for drug abuse (Schubiner et al., 2000), and associating with a deviant peer group, which heightens the symptom severity in children with comorbid AD/HD (Marshal & Molina, 2006). Research also reveals that children with comorbid CD are at extreme risk for school failure, peer rejection, violent behavior, drug and alcohol abuse, suicide, serious criminality, and adult psychiatric illness (Kelly et al., 2002; Rapp & Wodarski, 1997). In adulthood, CD is associated with serial employment and substance abuse in schizophrenic males (Mueser et al., 1999; Swartz et al., 2006). Conduct disorder exhibited during childhood or adolescence is a necessary precondition to be diagnosed with ASPD, with deviant conduct at or before age 10, a greater diversity of deviant behavior, and more extensive pretreatment drug use predicting a likely progression to ASPD (Myers et al., 1998). Individuals with ASPD who demonstrated CD in childhood also evidence significantly increased odds of lifetime social phobia, generalized anxiety disorder, drug dependence, and paranoid, schizoid, and avoidant personality disorders, while curiously evidencing a decreased risk for lifetime tobacco dependence (Goldstein et al., 2006). Clearly, CD is associated with numerous negative childhood and adult conditions.

4
Case Finding, Screening, and Referral

Considering the findings described in Chapters 1 and 3, it is apparent that school professionals need to be aware of the symptoms of conduct disorder (CD). Specifically, all school professionals need to be informed about the risks and symptoms of CD, its typical developmental course, as well as how to engage in screening procedures, and make appropriate referrals for psychoeducational evaluation. This chapter reviews how to use empirical evidence to inform practice in the applied school setting. For instance, the age and development of the child can impact symptom presentation of CD. In addition, developmental considerations should inform school district policies regarding culpability and ultimately the provision of support services in schools. How to gather and understand relevant information is reviewed along with a list of screening techniques. The formal process of diagnosis, psychoeducational evaluation, and treatment are discussed in detail in Chapters 5, 6, and 7.

Critical Information from School Personnel

In the school context, teachers are often the first to notice behavioral warning signs and risks associated with CD. Along with parents, teachers have the opportunity to observe patterns in a child's behavior that may be more significant than isolated incidents (Loeber et al., 1993). Teachers can also provide the context for discrete behaviors observed by others. For example, while observing that a child has hit someone is important, knowing the history associated with how and why hitting occurs may affect interpretation of this behavior. Thus, teacher input is critical for understanding behavioral events.

Understanding How to Use Risk Factors is Critical

Chapter 2 detailed the risk factors associated with the development of CD, emphasizing that there is no risk factor that singularly accounts for the manifestation of the disorder. Rather, there is general agreement in the literature that there is a complex web of different but interrelated dynamic, interacting individual, and contextual factors that combine to result in CD and other aggressive phenotypes (Hughes, 2001; Rutter, Giller & Hagell, 1998).

Understanding how to interpret a risk factor is important because some of the symptoms of CD (e.g., aggression) are low-base-rate behaviors (i.e., they do not occur often). When a symptom is rare, occurring only or mostly at the extreme ranges of a population distribution, the magnitude of the entire distribution will decrease or underestimate the magnitude of the effect of that symptom on the individual (Rutter et al., 1998). The impact of a risk factor (e.g., being male) upon a low-base-rate behavior (e.g., aggression) within correlational research is likely to inaccurately represent the strength of the effect of that risk. In this case, the strength of the effect of a risk factor is meaningful only when considered at the individual level. Thus, idiographic (individual data), rather than nomothetic (group data), comparisons are needed for understanding the importance of a risk factor. Second, as discussed in Chapter 2, there can be indirect influences, such as coercive parenting practices, on causal pathways of developing CD (Rutter et al., 1998). Consider for example the individual who possesses a risk factor to act aggressively. Possession of a risk factor alone does not necessarily result in the commission of an aggressive act; rather, it is the dynamic transactions of risk factors and situational factors over time. That is, risk factors constitute a predisposition for aggressive behaviors, rather than deterministic factors, that are facilitated by situational factors such as the opportunity or psychological press to act in an aggressive manner (Hughes, 2001).

Bohman (1996), in his Swedish adoption study, compared groups of children with and without a biological risk with those reared with and without the environmental risk of adult criminality. His results showed that the risk of adult criminality is 3% for unexplained factors, 6% for environmental risk alone, 12% for genetic influence alone, and 40% for both genetic and environmental risk factors. These results are consistent with previous findings reported by Cadoret et al. (1995) and Crowe (1974). Thus, regarding intervention, it is important to consider how disposition (possessing a risk factor) results in the process of engaging in an aggressive act in a particular place and a particular time (Farrington, 1995).

As noted in Chapter 2, there is some evidence of the importance of considering the balance of risks and promotive factors in understanding the importance of a risk factor. For instance, a higher number of risks predict higher rates of CD in children (Farrington, 1997). Factors aggregate to produce increased vulnerability in these children. An excellent example of this was the Cambridge Study in Delinquent Development (Farrington, 1997), in which 411 boys in working-class London were followed from ages 8 to 40. Vulnerability scores were calculated based on five risk factors: low family income at age 8, large family size by age 10 (four or more biological siblings), low nonverbal IQ at ages 8 to 10, and poor parenting (harsh or inconsistent discipline and parent conflict) at age 8. For those with no risk factors, convictions for violence were increased by only 3% compared to controls. However, having four or five factors present increased one's risk for demonstrating violent behavior by 31%. Thus, the interaction between individual and environmental risk factors determines the overall variance in the outcome of these children. Similarly, high rates of protective factors (explaining desistance from delinquency) can offset or moderate risks that might otherwise result in CD (Lewis, 2002).

Sameroff (2000) emphasizes that promotive factors (the positive end of the risk dimension explaining nondelinquency) are important to consider. For example, one study summed promotive factors and examined their relationship to adolescent outcomes, revealing that families with many promotive factors did substantially better than families in contexts with few promotive factors (Sameroff, Seifer, & Bartko, 1997). Sameroff (2000) stated, "The more risk factors, the worse the outcomes; the more promotive factors, the better the outcomes" (p. 35). Thus, considering the array of influences on child development, many variables (e.g., the biology, the individual characteristics, the parents, the family, the neighborhood, and the culture) seem to be dimensional, facilitating development at one end and inhibiting it at the other end.

The single most robust risk factor in developing antisocial behavior is being male. Most children with CD are male; in fact, one's risk of CD is 18.55 times greater for males relative to females (Rutter et al., 1998). However, static risks (e.g., one's sex) are not subject to alteration. Alternatively, dynamic risks (e.g., exposure to coercive parenting styles) are subject to modification and are often targets for interventions (discussed at length in Chapter 7).

School Personnel Must Consider All Psychosocial Risk Factors

In Bassarath's (2001) biopsychosocial review, the risk factors for CD are categorized into strongly, moderately, and mildly predictive (Tables 4.1 to 4.3). Individual, family, or environmental risk factors have been demonstrated in numerous research studies to increase a child's risk of future conduct problems (Barton, 2003; Brennan et al., 2003; Burke et al., 2002; Delligatti et al., 2003; DeVito & Hopkins, 2001; Dodge et al., 1995; Fergusson et al., 1993; Guerra et al., 1995; Hawkins et al., 1998; Herrenkohl et al., 2000; Hilarksi, 2004; Kann

TABLE 4.1. Strongly predictive risk factors of conduct disorder.

- Prior antisocial behavior: stealing, property destruction, early sexual intercourse, drug trafficking, etc.
- Antisocial peers: children with CD are frequently rejected by prosocial peers, tend to have problematic families, and attach to mutual friends of delinquents or other children with criminal histories (Vitaro, Tremblay, & Bukowski, 2001)
- Social ties: usually low in popularity, involved in few social activities, rejected by peers and likely to be bullied; they can also be socially aggressive and disruptive in class
- Substance abuse: early cigarette smoking, alcohol and/or other substance abuse, particularly before age 12
- Male gender: statistics have consistently shown boys to be at higher risk than girls by a ratio of 5:1
- Antisocial parents and siblings: having a convicted mother, father, or sibling significantly predicts boys' convictions; it is unclear if this is due to genetics or learned behavior

Adapted from Bassarath (2001).

TABLE 4.2. Moderately predictive risk factors of conduct disorder.

- Early aggression: careful history of the developmental course of various oppositional, aggressive, and conduct behaviors may suggest a life-course persistent trajectory, and its implied need for intensive treatment and resources
- Low family socioeconomic status: good parenting, stable family environment, and good early health and development can mitigate the effects of impoverishment and unemployment; thus, the perceived association of poverty with crime may be justified only if there are biological and psychosocial vulnerabilities operating together
- Psychological characteristics: high activity level, risk taking, impulsiveness, and short attention span; attention deficit/hyperactivity disorder, oppositional defiant disorder, and recently diagnosed depression and anxiety have all consistently been linked to CD
- Parent–child relations: includes mixed, inconsistent and punitive discipline practices, low parent involvement, poor supervision, low emotional warmth, and negative attitude toward the child; numerous studies have shown that these parenting practices are consistently linked with later delinquency, substance abuse, and violence (Capaldi & Patterson, 1996)
- School attitude/performance: includes low interest in education, dropping out, low school achievement, and truancy; Poor academic achievement in elementary school and particularly in high school has been related to later conduct difficulties (Maguin & Loeber, 1996)
- Medical/physical conditions: includes pertinent findings in developmental history, medical conditions, and physical development; prenatal and delivery complications have been fairly predictive of later violent offending in particular (Connor, 2002); zinc deficiency has also been linked to CD
- Intelligence quotient (IQ): most studies have found that IQ scores of children with CD are on average lower than those of nondelinquent children, even when other variables such as socio-economic status, ethnicity, academic achievement, and motivation are statistically controlled; another consistent finding is that Performance IQ is greater than Verbal IQ (Connor, 2002), which strongly suggests specific language difficulties and possibly neuropsychological dysfunction in conduct disordered children and adolescents

Adapted from Bassarath (2001).

TABLE 4.3. Mildly predictive risk factors of conduct disorder.

- Other family characteristics: high family stress, large family size, and marital discord
- Broken home: includes both family breakdown (e.g., divorce) and separation from parents for other reasons (e.g., parent or child incarceration)
- Abusive parents: includes all abuse categories such as emotional, physical, sexual abuse as well as maltreatment and neglect

Adapted from Bassarath (2001).

& Hanna, 2000; Kim-Cohen et al., 2005; Lahey et al., 2000; Lyons-Ruth et al., 1993; Pierrehumbert et al., 2000; Rhule, McMahon, & Spieker, 2004; Speltz et al., 1999; Thompson et al., 2003; Trickett & Putnam, 1998; Wakschlag et al., 2000; Wikström & Loeber, 2000). Risk factors are optimal targets for intervention and should be addressed without delay. The best treatment outcomes occur when children are early in the development of CD and before the age of 8 (Frick, 1998a; Kazdin 1996; McMahon & Wells, 1998; Shaw, Dishion, Supplee, Gardner, & Arnds, 2006). School psychologists should routinely train school personnel regarding the importance of identifying children at risk.

Warning Signs

Although risk factors indicate an increased probability that CD may develop, warning signs are the hallmark symptoms of this disorder. In CD, the primary red flag or warning sign is cruelty to animals. Parental retrospective reports on the emergence of CD symptoms in their children indicate 6.5 years as the median age of onset for hurting animals—earlier than bullying, cruelty to people, vandalism, or fire setting (Frick et al., 1993). The diagnostic value of this symptom is also supported in a report by Spitzer, Davies, and Barkley (1990), which was based on national field trials for developing DSM-III–R (American Psychiatric Association, 1987), wherein cruelty to animals first appears in the criteria for diagnosis.

Cruelty to animals is predictive of subsequent violent acts and ongoing anti-social behaviors. Arluke, Levin, Luke, & Ascione (1999) reviewed the files of the Massachusetts Society for the Prevention of Cruelty to Animals and located the records of 153 individuals (146 males and seven females) ranging from 7 to 11 years of age who had been prosecuted for intentional physical cruelty (not neglect) to animals. In addition, 153 individuals with no record of cruelty-to-animal complaints (matched for age, gender, socioeconomic status, and neighborhood) were selected for comparison. The State of Massachusetts criminal records for adult arrests were reviewed for each individual in both groups. All violent, property, drug, or public order offenses were collected. Results showed that individuals prosecuted for animal abuse were more likely to have an adult arrest in each of the four crime categories than the comparison group. The differences between percentages for abusers and nonabusers were highly significant ($p < .0001$) for all four types of offenses. Arluke and colleagues concluded that animal abusers are not only dangerous to their animal victims, but in the longer term may also jeopardize human welfare.

The Context of Development

When risks and warning signs are noted by school personnel, the next step is to conduct a screening for CD. However, there are several issues related to child cognitive, moral, and social development that are critical to consider for accurate interpretation of screening results. In addition, how conduct problems develop over the life span needs to be examined. Ultimately, developmental levels can inform issues of placement and treatment.

Understanding typical development and the wide range of age-appropriate behaviors is critical for all professionals working with children. The multiple influences on development—sociological, environmental, and physiological—need to be considered in assessing the etiology and developmental trajectory of CD. In this way, the influence and impact of proximal and distal risk factors on one another across time can be examined (Dodge, 2000). In addition, symptoms preceding the development of CD can be considered for their contribution to the developmental course of the disorder (Angold, Costello, & Erkanli, 1999).

Examining the course of the child's CD symptoms allows for comparison of the typicality of a specific antisocial behavior. Moffitt (1993) argues that there is a subgroup of children with adolescent time-limited conduct problems who present with less severe symptoms that will desist when adult (psychological, financial, and educational) independence is reached. This is supported by the findings that the majority of children with CD do not develop lifelong patterns of antisocial behavior, and as a general therapeutic rule, children with less severe symptoms tend to subsequently engage in prosocial and adaptive behaviors more frequently than more disturbed children (Connor, 2002). Moffitt's research underscores the need to identify child or adolescent onset of CD symptoms listed in the DSM criteria.

Developmental Course of the Disorder

Longitudinal research focusing on the development of delinquent behaviors in males has provided valuable information that informs understanding developmental trajectories of disruptive behavior problems and ultimately the diagnosis of CD. Specifically, delinquent behaviors have been shown to influence the onset of symptoms and CD diagnosis (Burke, Loeber, Mutchak, & Lahey, 2002). Loeber and his colleagues have spent over 20 years researching the development of problem behaviors that lead to delinquency. They suggest that the development of disruptive and delinquent behavior occurs in an orderly and progressive fashion, with less serious problem behaviors preceding more serious problem behaviors (Kelly, Loeber, Keenan, & DeLamarte, 1997). Loeber and colleagues (1993) provided empirical evidence for three developmental pathways to delinquency in males extending from childhood to adolescence. The three pathways are referred to as authority conflict, overt aggression, and covert aggression. Several studies have replicated the three-pathway model (e.g., Loeber, Keenan, & Zhang, 1997; Tolan & Gorman-Smith, 1998).

Authority Conflict

In the three-pathway model the authority-conflict pathway is the first and earliest occurring entry pathway. The authority-conflict pathway represents conflict with, and avoidance of, authority figures. Three stages to this pathway are described in a sequential manner starting with stubborn behavior, then defiance (refusal, disobedience), and then authority avoidance, such as truancy (Loeber et al., 1993). As described by Loeber and colleagues, this pathway can only be entered (with stubborn behavior) prior to the age of 12 years, and behaviors typically increase in severity. After the age of 12, children tend to exhibit behavior consistent with the highest stage of this pathway (authority avoidance).

Overt Aggression

The overt pathway is the second pathway of delinquency. As opposed to positive problem solving, this pathway is marked by aggression. The three stages that comprise this pathway are minor aggression (annoying, bullying); physical fighting (gang fights); and violence (rape, assault) (Loeber et al., 1993).

Covert Aggression

The third and final pathway to delinquency is the covert pathway. This pathway is characterized by lying, vandalism, and theft, versus respect for property and honesty, and can only be entered prior to the age of 15 years as described by Loeber et al. (1993). Again, this pathway is considered in terms of stages starting with minor covert behavior (lying, shoplifting), then property damage (vandalism, fire setting), and finally serious property damage (burglary, theft).

Persisters Versus Desisters

These researchers have shown that those boys who entered a pathway at the earliest stage (authority) with behaviors before the age of 12 were more likely to be persisters. Children who persist show behavioral indicators on assessments from one year to another. In contrast experimenters (inconsistent behavior recorded from one assessment to another) were more likely to enter at any pathway (Loeber et al., 1997). Loeber and colleagues (1993) also investigated whether it is possible for a boy to enter multiple pathways, and found that as the boys grew older they would in fact progress through two or three pathways. This appears to indicate a rise in total number and type of problem behaviors over time. In addition, boys with advanced overt behavior were more likely to advance in the covert pathway as well. Conversely, boys with advanced covert behavior were not as likely to also advance in the overt pathway. Finally, entry into the authority conflict pathway was noted as a forerunner to later escalation in covert or overt actions.

Similarly, Stahl and Clarizio (1999) suggest that there is also a typical developmental sequence of disruptive behavior disorders. They suggest that one disorder tends to predispose individuals to develop additional disorders. Specifically, oppositional defiant disorder (ODD) typically precedes the occurrence of CD, which in turn precedes antisocial personality disorder (ASPD) in adulthood (Loeber et al., 2000). The median age of onset for CD is 11.7 years; early onset is reported between the ages of 4.5 and 5 years of age (Nock et al., 2006). Further, Stahl and Clarizio assert that in most cases, one disorder is primary, and associated, comorbid disorders are a complication of this primary diagnosis. For example, attention deficit/hyperactivity disorder (AD/HD) commonly exists alongside of ODD and CD diagnoses; however, researchers hypothesize that this disorder does not impact the developmental course of CD without a preexisting diagnosis of ODD before the age of 7 years (Loeber et al., 2000).

Childhood Rates of Conduct Disorder

In fact, there is general agreement that the prevalence of CD increases over the course of development steadily from early childhood to middle childhood and adolescence (Brotman, Gouley, O'Neal, & Klein, 2004; Burke et al., 2002; Kim-Cohen et al., 2005; Loeber, Burke, Lahey, Winters, & Zera, 2000); however, there are studies that have concluded that there are no age differences (Cohen et al., 1993; Lewinsohn, Hops, Robert, Seeley, & Andrews, 1993), and age differences do not hold for females. Maughan, Rowe, Messer, Goodman, & Meltzer (2004) reported prevalence rates for girls remained low and fixed across early and middle childhood, and then increase steadily in adolescence. However, as discussed, this issue is complicated by early rather than late symptom onset, the type of symptom, and the age and sex of the child. For example, boys with CD who showed covert aggressive behaviors (i.e., serious theft, breaking and entering, and fraud) and overt conduct problems (i.e., serious aggression, robbery, rape, and attempted/completed homicide) all showed increasing rates during adolescence; however, the symptom of physical fighting appears to decrease (Loeber et al., 2000). Children with CD who were younger than 10 were 8.7 times more likely to demonstrate at least one aggressive behavior, in comparison to individuals receiving adolescent-onset CD diagnosis (Lahey et al., 1998).

While researchers continue to examine the complex web that results in and is associated with CD, for school personnel it is important to recognize symptoms, know that they may occur early in development, and understand that the prognosis various for different groups and that the course of development may be altered. Further, for school personnel to be responsive to these complexities, it is critical to be able to understand and negotiate school policies.

Screenings

Developmental screening processes are undertaken to assess all children to determine which youngsters might require further assessment to determine possible need or eligibility for specially designed instruction, thereby providing early detection of a problem. Screenings are not for determining diagnosis; rather, they are for those who are not yet symptomatic. Many developmental screening instruments can be administered by a variety of school personnel in a short amount of time, although training school personnel must be a priority to provide accurate information.

Screenings are an efficient way to begin to clarify information regarding risk factors, warning signs, and developmental lags. Developmental lags are delays in an individual's development as compared to the maturational timeline and typical sequence that most children experience. Such a lag may or may not reach the threshold of a diagnosis, but can result in a need for intervention. Here, the purpose of intervention is to help the child return to the typical developmental sequence or to continue along the developmental course, albeit at a rate slower than others.

School systems often use screenings for Child Find activities and during designated mental health days. In fact, the Individuals with Disabilities Education Improvement Act (IDEIA, 2004) requires states to provide early identification and provision of services to infants and toddlers with (1) developmental delays; (2) established conditions that are associated with developmental delays; and (3) at the state's option, children at risk for developmental delays. States that do not serve the at-risk population are encouraged to monitor these children for changes that would warrant a referral. Table 4.4 list the developmental screeners that can be used by school personnel. For instance, the Systematic Screening for Behavior Disorders (SSBD; Walker & Severson, 1992) provides a multigating, mass screening process to identify students who may develop behavior disorders by giving general classroom teachers uniform behavioral standards, to help reduce the idiosyncratic nature of teacher referrals. A brief summary of the SSBD is provided in Table 4.5.

Although developmental screenings are appropriate for both preschool and school-age children, school personnel should always rule out learning problems when considering behavioral disorders such as CD. In addition, the developmental issues discussed above including those related to culpability should be explored for all children, especially for those younger than age 12.

Behavior Observations

Observing behaviors directly has many advantages. Duration, frequency, and intensity can be documented along with a basic functional analysis of what happened just before and after an event. During observations, it is helpful to compare the child to a peer for analysis purposes. At a minimum, a comparison peer should be matched to the targeted youngster by sex and classroom location. Other variables to consider for matching are peer status and similar rates of acquisition and retention of academic material. Although perhaps intuitively inconsistent, it is not

TABLE 4.4. Screening tools for behavioral problems.

The Brief Infant-Toddler Social and Emotional Assessment	Briggs-Gowan, Carter, Irwin, Wachtel, & Cicchetti (2004)
Parents' Evaluation of Developmental Status	Glascoe (2006)
Pediatric Symptom Checklist	Jellinek & Murphy (n.d.)
Preschool and Kindergarten Behavior Scales, 2nd edition	Merrell (2003)
Systematic Screening for Behavior Disorders (SSBD)	Walker & Severson (1992)

TABLE 4.5. Three phases of the Systematic Screening for Behavior Disorders (SSBD).

1. Teacher nominations of children whose characteristic behavior patterns most closely resemble profiles of behavior disorders occurring in the school setting and ranking of those students
2. Screening of teacher-nominated students, using a series of rating items to identify behavioral severity and define the specific content of their behavior problems
3. Systematic observation of students using a classroom code and a playground code

Adapted from Walker & Severson (1992). Available from Sopris West; http://store.cambiumlearning.com.

helpful to identify and compare the observed student with the most well-behaved high-performance student, as it only creates artificially disparate results.

Observations should occur across structured and unstructured settings and where academic tasks are varied (individual work, small and large group instruction). The child should be observed in environments known to be problematic and successful for them. It is critical that the student is not identified as the target for the observations. Professionals should initiate observation activities in advance, making sure to discuss how the teacher can quietly and discreetly identify the student to the observer (if unknown). Often teachers will write a description on a piece of paper early in the day and then hand it to the observer. For example, "Johnny has blond hair, is wearing a red flannel shirt, and is seated in the third row of the classroom."

The Hawthorne effect should not be underestimated; it states that, when being observed, people alter their behavior (Roethlisberger & Dickson, 1939). This principle applies to everyone in the classroom environment—the children as well as the teacher. After the observation, it is important to ask the teacher whether the class and the student's behavior were typical. This tactic not only improves the interpretation of the observation, but also provides information about the alterability of the child's behavior. Many teachers are frustrated that the child's poor behavior does not occur during the observation. However, this is not uncommon, particularly in the case of low-base-rate behaviors. Rather than conclude that the behavior is not the severe problem described by the teacher, this information provides evidence that the environment can be altered in a manner that affects the child's behavior. Explaining to students that an authority figure will walk through the classroom and observe their learning in random intervals is one of the easiest interventions to implement in the classroom.

When to Refer

If the information from screening procedures, teacher and parent input, observations and ineffective interventions leads to the question of whether a disorder is present, then professionals should refer the child for a formal evaluation. School psychologists are adequately trained to identify a variety of DSM behavior disorders that are disruptive, including CD. In addition, school psychologists can translate those diagnoses for multidisciplinary teams to determine special education eligibility decisions.

Conclusion

It is an important role of the school psychologist to alert school personnel to risk factors and warning signs of CD. Further, school psychologists should be instrumental in leading screening activities for children in schools so that specific behaviors can be evaluated in terms of their deviation from the expected developmental path.

5
Diagnostic Assessment

Assessment of conduct disorder (CD) is a critical element of the treatment process, since a thorough analysis of a child or adolescent's psychosocial strengths and needs guides intervention planning (Frick, 1998b). Although many of the symptoms associated with CD may seem obvious, in a study of clinicians' diagnosis of antisocial behavior based on case vignettes it was found that the consistency of diagnosis was affected by context, and varied by profession, with social workers seeming particularly reluctant to use a CD diagnosis (Kirk & Hsieh, 2004). To accurately diagnose antisocial behavior, when assessing CD, it is important to use measurement techniques that consider the age and the cognitive level of the child being tested. Since CD frequently involves multiple causes and a heterogeneous group of behaviors that range in type and severity, the choices of treatment strategies may be narrowed using the information gleaned in the measurement of antisocial symptoms (American Psychiatric Association, 2000).

Developmental considerations are particularly important. For example, CD is not an appropriate diagnosis in very young, preschool-age children, due to their inadequate level of social understanding and the allowances that are made for them as a result. As detailed in Chapter 4, preschool children may not yet have the cognitive abilities to understand the ramifications of their behaviors, which is why CD is not an appropriate diagnosis for them (American Psychiatric Association, 2000).

In addition, there is evidence suggesting that childhood-onset CD is more strongly related to individual and familial factors, whereas adolescent onset is more related to environmental disadvantages associated with ethnic minority status and exposure to deviant peers (McCabe, Hough, Wood, & Yeh, 2001). Such findings should not be considered the rule, but rather a guide that may assist the approach to assessment. Furthermore, it is essential for all professionals to keep in mind that "although almost all adults with antisocial aggressive behavior exhibited these patterns as children, many antisocial children (conduct disordered) do not become antisocial adults" (Frick, 1998a). With these caveats in mind, this chapter identifies the diagnostic criteria for CD, discusses the different assessment strategies that may be used with children and adolescents, and reviews assessment methods and instruments, including best-estimate procedures, broad-band behavioral rating scales, narrow-band behavioral rating scales, observations, interviews, laboratory and performance-based measures, personality inventories, and pictorial assessments.

Diagnostic Criteria

As briefly discussed in Chapter 1, CD is a childhood diagnostic category found in the *Diagnostic and Statistical Manual of Mental Disorders*, text revision, 4th edition (DSM-IV-TR) (American Psychiatric Association, 2000). The diagnostic criteria for CD are listed in Table 5.1. The essential features of CD are the repetitive and persistent pattern of behaviors that violate the basic rights of others or major age-appropriate societal norms or rules. The behaviors fall into four categories: (1) causing or threatening physical harm to others, (2) causing property loss or damage, (3) deceitfulness or theft, and (4) serious violations of rules. For a diagnosis, three or more characteristic behaviors must be present in the past 12 months, with at least one characteristic behavior in the previous 6 months. Moreover, the disturbance in behavior must cause clinically significant impairment in social, academic, or occupational functioning. The age of onset determines the type of CD, and the severity is gauged by the extent of harm to others. Behaviors characterizing mild severity include the following: lying, truancy, and staying out after dark without permission. Moderate severity may include vandalism and stealing without confronting the victim. Severe conduct problems include forced sex, physical cruelty, use of a weapon, and breaking and entering. As specified in the diagnostic criteria, for individuals over 18 years, a diagnosis of CD can only be given if the criteria for antisocial personality disorder (ASPD) are not met (individuals under 18 may not be diagnosed with ASPD).

Included in the diagnostic criteria for oppositional defiant disorder (ODD) are behaviors characteristic of CD. The diagnostic criteria for ODD are listed in Table 5.2. Negative and defiant behaviors characteristic of ODD are often manifested as persistent stubbornness, resistance to directions, and unwillingness to compromise or negotiate with adults or peers. Behaviors such as disobedience and opposition to authority figures are characteristic of both CD and ODD. However, the behaviors characteristic of ODD are generally less severe than those of individuals with CD and typically do not include aggression toward people or animals, destruction of property, or a pattern of theft or deceit. Oppositional defiant disorder criteria do not include the persistent pattern of the more serious behavior problems (e.g., violations of the basic rights of others). When an individual's pattern of behavior meets the criteria for both ODD and CD, the diagnosis of CD takes precedence.

Symptom Onset

The DSM-IV-TR specifies two subtypes of CD based on the age at onset: childhood-onset type and adolescent-onset type. These two subtypes also differ in the nature of the presenting conduct symptoms, developmental course and prognosis, and gender incidence, although both subtypes can occur in mild, moderate, and severe forms. When assessing age of onset, both the child and caregiver

TABLE 5.1. *Diagnostic and Statistical Manual of Mental Disorders*, text revision, 4th edition (DSM-IV-TR) diagnostic criteria for Conduct Disorder. (American Psychiatric Association, 2000, pp. 98–99).

A. A repetitive and persistent pattern of behavior in which the basic rights of others or major age-appropriate societal norms or rules are violated, as manifested by the presence of three (or more) of the following criteria in the past 12 months, with at least one criterion present in the past 6 months:

Aggression to people and animals

1. Often bullies, threatens, or intimidates others
2. Often initiates physical fights
3. Has used a weapon that can cause serious physical harm to others
4. Has been physically cruel to people
5. Has been physically cruel to animals
6. Has stolen while confronting a victim
7. Has forced someone into sexual activity

Destruction of property

8. Has deliberately engaged in fire setting with the intention of causing serious damage
9. Has deliberately destroyed others' property

Deceitfulness or theft

10. Has broken into someone else's house, building, or car
11. Often lies to obtain goods or favors to avoid obligations
12. Has stolen items of nontrivial value without confronting a victim

Serious violation of rules

13. Often stays out at night despite parental prohibitions, beginning before age 13 years
14. Has run away from home overnight at least twice while living in parental or parental surrogate home
15. Is often truant from school, beginning before age 13 years

B. The disturbance in behavior causes clinically significant impairment in social, academic, or occupational functioning.

C. If the individual is 18 years or older, criteria are not met for antisocial personality disorder.

Code type based on age at onset

Conduct disorder childhood-onset type: onset of at least one criterion characteristic of conduct disorder prior to age 10 years

Conduct disorder adolescent-onset type: absence of any criteria characteristic of conduct disorder prior to age 10 years

Conduct disorder, unspecified onset: age at onset is not known

Specify severity

Mild: few if any conduct problems in excess of those required to make the diagnosis and conduct problems cause only minor harm to others

Moderate: number of conduct problems and effect on others is intermediate between "mild" and "severe"

Severe: many conduct problems in excess of those required to make the diagnosis *or* conduct problems cause considerable harm to others

---

From the *Diagnostic and Statistical Manual of Mental Disorders*, 4th edition, text revision. Copyright 2000, American Psychiatric Association, with permission.

should supply information, although because many behaviors may be concealed, caregivers may underreport symptoms and overestimate age of onset (American Psychiatric Association, 2000). The childhood-onset type is defined when at least one criterion characteristic of CD is exhibited prior to age 10 years. Individuals with childhood-onset type (1) are usually male, (2) frequently display physical aggression toward others, (3) are likely to have disturbed peer relationships, (4) may have had ODD during early childhood, and (5) usually have symptoms that

TABLE 5.2. DSM-IV-TR diagnostic criteria for oppositional defiant disorder. (American Psychiatric Association, 2000, p. 102).

A. A pattern of negativistic, hostile, and defiant behavior lasting at least 6 months, during which four (or more) of the following are present:
1. Often loses temper
2. Often argues with adults
3. Often actively defies or refuses to comply with adults' requests or rules
4. Often deliberately annoys people
5. Often blames others for his or her mistakes or misbehavior
6. Is often touchy or easily annoyed by others
7. Is often angry and resentful
8. Is often spiteful or vindictive
Note: Consider a criterion as being met only if the behavior occurs more frequently than is typically observed in individuals of comparable age and developmental level.
B. The disturbance in behavior causes clinically significant impairment in social, academic, or occupational functioning.
C. The behaviors do not occur exclusively during the course of a psychotic or mood disorder.
D. Criteria are not met for conduct disorder, and, if the individual is age 18 years or older, criteria are not met for antisocial personality disorder.

From the *Diagnostic and Statistical Manual of Mental Disorders*, 4th edition, text revision. Copyright 2000, American Psychiatric Association, with permission.

meet the full criteria for CD prior to adolescence. Additionally, many children with this subtype have concurrent attention-deficit/hyperactivity disorder (AD/HD). Individuals with childhood-onset type are more likely to have persistent CD as well as to develop adult ASPD in comparison with those with adolescent-onset type (American Psychiatric Association, 2000).

Adolescent-onset type is defined by the absence of all criteria of CD prior to 10 years of age. In comparison with those with childhood-onset type, individuals with adolescent-onset type are less likely to demonstrate aggressive behaviors and are more likely to have normative relationships with peers, although often they demonstrate antisocial behaviors along with peers. Such adolescents are also less likely to have persistent CD or to develop adult ASPD. Further, the ratio of males to females with CD is lower for the adolescent-onset type than for the childhood-onset type. One additional subtype, unspecified onset, is used if the age at onset of CD is not known (American Psychiatric Association, 2000).

There are also severity specifiers (mild, moderate, and severe) listed in the DSM-IV-TR:

- Mild symptoms refer to few, if any, conduct problems in excess of those required for the diagnosis. Conduct problems in this category also cause relatively minor harm to others, such as lying, truancy, and staying out after dark without permission.
- Moderate symptoms describe the number of conduct problems and the effect on others as intermediate between mild and severe, for example, stealing without confronting a victim or vandalism.
- Severe symptoms represent many conduct problems in excess of those required to make the diagnosis. Additionally, the conduct problems cause considerable

harm to others, such as forced sex, physical cruelty, use of a weapon, stealing while confronting someone, and breaking and entering (American Psychiatric Association, 2000).

Developmental Course

The developmental course of the disorder suggests that the onset of CD may occur as early as the preschool years, although the first significant symptoms usually are demonstrated during middle childhood to middle adolescence. Oppositional defiant disorder commonly occurs prior to the childhood-onset type of CD, and onset of CD is rare after the age of 16 years. The course of CD is variable, and in most individuals, the disorder remits by adulthood; however, a moderate number then meet the criteria for ASPD. Many of those with adolescent-onset type CD and those with milder symptoms demonstrate adequate social and occupational adjustment in adulthood. Early-onset CD predicts more severe symptoms and worse prognosis along with increased risk for ASPD and substance-related disorders. Further, individuals with CD are at increased risk for later mood disorders, anxiety disorders, somatoform disorders, and substance-related disorders (American Psychiatric Association, 2000).

Associated Features and Differential Diagnosis

Although ODD, which shares some of the features of CD, such as disobedience and opposition to authority figures, often occurs alongside of CD, children with ODD do not evidence some of the more serious forms of antisocial behavior in which the basic rights of others or age-appropriate societal norms or rules are compromised. When a child or adolescent meets both the criteria for ODD and CD, only CD is diagnosed.

Additionally, although children with AD/HD may demonstrate disruptive, hyperactive, and impulsive behavior, such symptoms alone do not violate age-appropriate societal norms, and thus do not meet criteria for CD. Unlike the ODD/CD diagnoses, when criteria are met for AD/HD and CD, both diagnoses are given.

Children and adolescents with mood disorder often exhibit irritability and conduct problems. However, these symptoms can be differentiated from those seen in individuals with CD based on the episodic course and accompanying symptoms that are indicative of mood disorder. Nonetheless, if criteria for both are met, diagnoses of both CD and the mood disorder should be given.

The diagnosis of adjustment disorder (with disturbance of conduct or with mixed disturbance of emotions and conduct) also may be given if clinically significant antisocial behavior that does not meet the criteria for another specific disorder develops in clear association with psychosocial stressor onset. Additionally, isolated antisocial behavior that does not meet the threshold for CD or adjustment disorder may be diagnosed as child or adolescent antisocial behavior, since CD is diagnosed only if the conduct problems are representative of a repetitive and persistent pattern associated with deficits in social, academic, or occupational functioning (American Psychiatric Association, 2000).

Age-Specific Features

Symptoms of CD vary with age as children or adolescents mature, developing increased physical strength, cognitive abilities, and sexual maturity. Less severe behavior, such as lying, shoplifting, and physical fighting, tends to be demonstrated first, while other symptoms, such as burglary, emerge later. The most severe conduct problems, such as rape or theft while confronting a victim, typically are the last to emerge. It is important to note, however, that there are large differences among individuals, with some children demonstrating the more damaging behaviors at an early age, which is also representative of a worse prognosis (American Psychiatric Association, 2000).

Gender-Related Features

Conduct disorder, particularly childhood-onset type, tends to be more common in males. Gender differences may also be found in specific types of conduct problems; males with a diagnosis of CD are likely to fight, steal, vandalize, and demonstrate school discipline problems, whereas females with CD tend to exhibit lying, truancy, running away, substance use, and prostitution. Generally, while males engage in confrontational aggression, females demonstrate nonconfrontational behaviors (American Psychiatric Association, 2000).

Best-Estimate Procedures

The best-estimate diagnostic (BED) procedure has become recognized as an important technique in assessment of psychiatric illnesses, including CD. The scientific rationale for the use of BED is that employing all sources of information tends to reduce diagnostic error, particularly since unlike other illnesses, mental conditions typically cannot be validated through laboratory tests or physical examinations. Best-estimate diagnosis procedures tend to include not only self-report data from individuals, but also information from family members and medical records. In a study comparing psychiatric diagnoses based on interview information with those based on BED procedures, the inclusion of family history data in BED yielded higher rates of sensitivity and specificity than did interviews in diagnosing CD (Bucholz et al., 2006). Thus, the use of multiple informants and varied diagnostic procedures in identifying antisocial behavior is warranted.

Broad-Band Behavioral Rating Scales

Behavior rating scales are a time-efficient method of collecting reliable information (Frick, 1998a). Broad-band behavior rating scales provide an assessment of several domains of behavior, often yielding information about healthy and maladaptive functioning, and can be completed by parents, teachers, and children (self-report) to obtain comparable information. Table 5.3 lists popular broad-band measures. Using multiple informants may enable the evaluator to achieve an understanding of the severity of conduct disorder in relation to the normative group. One study has suggested that despite previous research to the contrary (Andrews, Garrison, Jackson, Addy, & McKeown, 1993; Bergeron, Valla, & Breton, 1992; McGee et al., 1990; Offord, Boyle, Fleming, Munroe-Blum, & Rae-Grant, 1989), there may be high agreement on CD behaviors between adolescents and their mothers using latent class analysis, which uses a probabilistic model and not a specified cutoff value (Romano et al., 2004). Frequently, rating scales not only provide an assessment of the child's emotional and behavioral functioning, but also help to identify contextual factors that may be contributing to antisocial behavior.

Behavior Assessment System for Children

The Behavior Assessment System for Children, 2nd edition (BASC-2; Reynolds & Kamphaus, 2004) is a multisource, multidimensional assessment system that provides separate report measures for the child or adolescent (self-report), and for his or her parent (126 items) and teacher (138 items). Each form of the BASC includes multiple scales that reflect symptoms of psychopathology, including aggression, anxiety, attention problems, depression, conduct problems, and hyperactivity. Composite T-scores are yielded on the dimensions of externalizing problems, internalizing problems, behavior symptoms, and adaptive skills, with a school problem composite also provided on the teacher form. The individual scales of the BASC were constructed through rational sorting of items and item-level covariance structural analysis. Thus, each item contributes to a single homogeneous scale.

The BASC self-report scale combines a true/false measure with frequency scales, while the parent and teacher scales include items with 4-point frequency scales ranging from 0 (never) to 3 (always). Test-retest reliability coefficients (2 to 8 weeks) for the BASC parent form range from .84 to .92, while the internal consistency coefficients vary from .67 to .90 for boys to .64 to .89 for girls, on this same measure. Additionally, the BASC teacher form correlates modestly with the Conners' rating scales and the Revised Behavior Problems Checklist (RBPC), providing evidence of convergent validity (Conners, 1997; Crystal, Ostrander, Chen, & August, 2001; Quay & Peterson, 1987).

TABLE 5.3. Broad-band assessments of conduct disorder.

Behavior Assessment Systems for Children (BASC-2)	Reynolds & Kamphaus (2004)
Child Behavior Checklist (CBCL)	Achenbach (2007)
Teacher Report Form (TRF)	
Global Family Environment Scale (GFES)	Moos et al. (1974)
	Moos & Moos (1987)

Child Behavior Checklist and Teacher Report Form

The Child Behavior Checklist (CBCL; Achenbach, 1991a, 1999; Achenbach & Rescorla, 2001) is a measure for parents or caregivers to complete that has eight empirically defined scales for a set of items related to child psychopathology (withdrawn, somatic complaints, anxious/depressed, social problems, thought problems, attention problems, delinquent behavior, and aggressive behavior), and has been demonstrated to have adequate reliability (internal consistency values of .78 to .97 for the full scales) and validity in normative populations (Achenbach, 1991a; Brotman et al., 2004). In a clinical sample, the aggressive behavior subscale strongly related to CD and ODD symptoms (Edelbrock & Costello, 1998; Hudziak, Copeland, Stanger, & Wadsworth, 2004), while in another study, the aggressive behavior subscale was found to be reflective of overt CD behavior, such as initiating physical fights, while the delinquent scale assessed covert CD behaviors, such as stealing without confrontation (Tackett, Krueger, Sawyer, & Graetz, 2003).

One potential limitation of this measure is that each specific scale is not necessarily reflective of specific disorders, which creates a disparity between clinical practice and population descriptions (Rubio-Stipec, Walker, Murphy, & Fizmaurice, 2002). Other weaknesses include moderate interparent agreement, with values ranging from .26 to .78, item overlap, and lack of symptom measurement (Lengua, Sadowski, Friedrich, & Fisher, 2001; McMahon & Forehand, 1988; Silva et al., 2005).

The Teacher Report Form (TRF; Achenbach, 1991b) is designed to complement the CBCL, and is comprised of behavioral and emotional items that focus on problems that are likely to be demonstrated at school. Teachers are asked to rate a child's behavior in comparison with that of his or her age peers. The internal consistency values for the TRF in large normative samples range from .72 to .95, although there are no special education or clinical normative samples provided from which to base scoring (Achenbach, 1991b; O'Neill & Liljequist, 2002; Silva et al., 2005).

Global Family Environment Scale

A commonly used family functioning rating scale is the Global Family Environment Scale (GFES; Moos, Insel, & Humphrey, 1974), in which there is a focus on gaining information about family structure, organization, communication, and affective expression, thereby measuring the adequacy of the environment in which the child is raised (Frick, 1998a; Rey, Walter, Plapp, & Denshire, 2000). The GFES is a reliable, single-score measure with a structure similar to that of Axis V of the DSM-IV and includes 90 items related to different family constructs (Rey et al., 2000). Parents are asked to respond to questions regarding ten domains of family organization, including cohesion, expressiveness, conflict, independence, achievement, intellectual-cultural orientation, active-recreational orientation, moral-religious emphasis, organization, and control. Families of children with CD have been found to score low on the control domain, which is suggestive of less structure, rule setting, and rule enforcement in these households (Kazdin & Kolko, 1986).

Ratings reflect the lowest quality of the family environment for a period lasting at least 1 year prior to the age of 12 years of the referred child (Rey et al., 2000). On the GFES, high scores suggest a family environment that is stable, secure, and nurturing for the child, with consistent care, affection, and discipline and reasonable expectations; moderately high scores are indicative of a slightly unsatisfactory family environment that is mainly stable and secure but contains some conflicts and inconsistencies about discipline or expectations; average scores reflect a moderately unsatisfactory environment including moderate parental discord (which may have resulted in separation or divorce), inadequate or moderate conflict about discipline and expectations, moderately unsatisfactory parental supervision or care, and possible frequent changes of residence and school; moderately low scores reflect a poor family environment, such as persistent parental discord, hostile separation with problems about custody, exposure to more than one stepparent, substantial parental inconsistency or inadequate care, some abuse (by parental figures or siblings) or neglect, poor supervision, and very frequent changes of residence or school; low scores are suggestive of a very poor environment, including several usually short-term parental figures, severe parental conflict, inconsistent or inappropriate care, evidence of substantial abuse or neglect, or grave lack of parental supervision; and extremely low scores are reflective of a very disturbed family environment, often resulting in the child being made a ward of the state, institutionalized, or placed in foster care more than once with evidence of severe abuse or neglect or extreme deprivation (Rey et al., 1997).

Narrow-Band Behavioral Rating Scales

Narrow-band behavior rating scales provide an assessment of specific domains of behavior, and are typically completed by parents, teachers, or children (self-report). Table 5.4 lists popular narrow-band measures.

Attention Deficit Disorder with Hyperactivity: Comprehensive Teacher's Rating Scale

The Comprehensive Teacher's Rating Scale, which uses the approximate acronym of ACTeRS (Ullmann, Sleator, & Sprague, 2000), is an instrument that provides an evaluation of AD/HD in school-age children (grades K–8), with an emphasis on the attentional component of the disorder. The measure is available in both parent and teacher forms, each of which assesses attention, hyperactivity, social skills, and oppositional behavior, while the parent form also has an early child behavior subscale. The internal consistency of the subscales on the teacher form range from .92 to .97, and the parent form ranges from .76 to .96 (Silvia et al., 2005; Ullman et al., 2000). This instrument may be assistive in providing information about early antisocial behavior, or conduct problems associated with AD/HD.

TABLE 5.4. Narrow band assessments of conduct disorder.

ADD-H: Comprehensive Teacher's Rating Scale (ACTeRS)	Ullmann et al. (2000)
Conflict Tactics Scale (CTS)	Straus & Gelles (1990)
Conners' Rating Scale (CRS)	Conners (1997)
Diagnostic System for Psychiatric Disorders in Childhood and Adolescence (DISYP)	Doepfner & Lehmkuhl (1998)
Differential Test of Conduct and Emotional Problems (DT/CEP)	Kelly & Vitali (1990)
Disruptive Behavior Disorders Rating Scale (DBDRS)	Pelham et al. (1992)
Early Assessment Risk List for Boys (EARL-20B)	Augimeri, Koegl, Webster, & Levene (2001)
Eyberg Child Behavior Inventory (ECBI)	Eyberg & Robinson (1983); Robinson, Eyberg, & Ross (1980)
Inventory of Callous Unemotional Traits (ICT)	Essau et al. (2006)
Questionnaire for Factors of Aggression	Hampel & Selg (1975)
Rating Scale for Disruptive Behavior Disorders (RS-DBD)	Silva et al. (2005)
Revised Problem Behavior Checklist (RBPC)	Quay & Peterson (1987)
Scale for Assessing Emotional Disturbance (SAED)	Epstein & Cullinan (1998)
Self-Report Early Delinquency Scale (SRED)	Moffitt & Silva (1988)
Youth Psychopathy Traits Inventory (YPI) Psychopathy Checklist: Youth Version (PCL:YV)	Dolan & Rennie (2006) Forth, Kosson, & Hare (2003)

Conflict Tactics Scale

Developed by Straus (1979), the Conflict Tactics Scale (CTS) is an 18-item self-report inventory that provides an assessment of the frequency (on a 0 to 6 scale) of a variety of functional (e.g., calmly discussing a problem), verbally aggressive (e.g., insults or swearing), and physically aggressive (e.g., hitting) conflict tactics, which are translated into three subscales: reasoning, verbal aggression, and physical violence (Straus & Gelles, 1990; Street, King, King, & Riggs, 2003). The reliability of the CTS has been found to be strong [Cronbach's α = .87 for men, .88 for women] (Straus, 1979), and a factor analysis of the CTS (Barling, O'Leary, Jouriles, Vivian, & MacEwen, 1987) demonstrated that the measure comprises physical and psychological aggression factors (Heyman & Schlee, 1997). This measure may be used to classify adolescents' aggressive behaviors into verbally, physically, and psychologically aggressive domains, thereby assisting with both diagnosis and intervention.

Conners' Rating Scales

The Conners' Rating Scales–Revised (CRS-R) is a measure used primarily to identify behaviors of AD/HD in children and adolescents (ages 3 to 17), and is available in both short and long forms for the parent and teacher rating scales. The long version of the teacher scale contains 59 items, while the long version of the parent scale contains 80 items, both of which are categorized into the subscales of oppositional, cognitive problems/inattention, hyperactivity, anxious/shy, perfectionism, social problems, Conners' global index (restless-impulsive, emotional lability), AD/HD index, and DSM-IV symptoms subscales (inattentive, hyperactive-impulsive). In contrast, the short forms contain 27 items in the parent version and 28 items in the teacher version, which are grouped into four subscales: oppositional, cognitive problems/inattention, hyperactivity, and the AD/HD index. The internal consistency coefficients in the long forms range from .73 to .96, while ranging from .86 to .95 in the short forms (Conners, 1997; Conners, Sitarenios, Parker, & Epstein, 1998a,b; Conners et al., 1997). Although the Conners scales are helpful in identifying some antisocial behavior comorbid to attentional problems, it is not an instrument that is representative of all disruptive behaviors in the DSM IV-TR (Silva et al., 2005).

Diagnostic System for Psychiatric Disorders in Childhood and Adolescence

The Diagnostic System for Psychiatric Disorders in Childhood and Adolescence (DISYP) uses the DSM and International Classification of Diseases (ICD) criteria to identify CD (Doepfner & Lehmkuhl, 1998). This German instrument is commonly used in Europe, and is based on a semistructured interview of parents, covering all DSM-IV items listed in the corresponding diagnostic categories and subsuming a severity score for each item ranging from 0 to 3 (Herpertz et al., 2005).

Differential Test of Conduct and Emotional Problems and Scale for Assessing Emotional Disturbance

In light of the more recent focus in schools on the diagnosis of emotional disturbance and its exclusion of social maladjustment (conduct-related behaviors), the Differential Test of Conduct and Emotional Problems (DT/CEP) (Kelly & Vitali, 1990) is designed to distinguish between conduct problems and emotional disturbance. It is a behavior rating scale that assesses teacher perceptions of a student in the school environment, and operationally defines the distinction between CD and emotional disturbance (ED) by indicating that students with conduct problems use their behavior for purposeful gain, while students with ED tend to be impulsive and self-destructive with little or no identifiable gain. The DT/CEP contains 63 true/false statements concerning each subject, with items forming two scales: the conduct problem (CP) scale and the emotional disturbance (ED) scale. An example of a CP item is "constantly fighting or beating up others," while an item from the ED scale is "often complains of nightmares and bad dreams" (West & Verhaagen, 1999). Results of the efficacy of the DT/CEP have been mixed. For example, using the DT/CEP, Costenbader and Buntaine (1999) identified 79% of placed ED students as non-ED and 15% of social maladjustment (SM) students as ED. Moreover, although behavior rating scales can be an effective measure of conduct disorder, they provide only a retrospective assessment of a child's behavior; therefore, it is recommended to complement this tool with direct behavior observation.

Information from the Scale for Assessing Emotional Disturbance (SAED) is very limited. The SAED correlates well with the Achenbach Child Behavior Checklist (CBCL; Achenbach, 1991) for identifying emotional disorders; however, it does not appear to accurately differentiate between ED and SM (Dumont

& Rauch, 2000; Olympia et al., 2004). In fact, these two scales designed specifically to differentiate ED and SM have received limited empirical support.

Disruptive Behavior Disorders Rating Scale

The Disruptive Behavior Disorders Rating Scale (DBDRS) is presented in both a parent and teacher version, both of which have 45 items, although the versions differ slightly (Pelham, Evans, Gnagy, & Greenslade, 1992). On the teacher form, educators indicate whether each DSM-IV symptom of AD/HD, ODD, and CD was present (1 = not at all, 2 = just a little, 3 = pretty much, 4 = very much). Symptoms that are rated either 3 or 4 are considered to be present (Chronis et al., 2003). Pelham et al. (1992) report strong internal consistency for the ODD, inattention, and impulsivity-overactivity factor scales on the teacher form, which are .96, .95, and .95, respectively (Silva et al., 2005).

Early Assessment Risk List for Boys

In another study, researchers investigated the predictive and incremental validity of the Early Assessment Risk List for Boys (EARL-20B) (Augimeri, Koegl, Webster, & Levene, 2001), a structured clinical checklist designed for the professional judgment of risk for aggressive and disruptive behaviors and risk/needs factor-based management of this risk. Seventy-six boys consecutively referred to child psychiatric outpatient clinics in mid-Sweden were evaluated according to the EARL-20B and with independent (not EARL-20B–based) clinical evaluations. The participants were then followed for 6 and 30 months, with EARL-20B–based assessments positively and moderately associated with aggressive (reactive and proactive aggression) and disruptive behavior (including conduct problems and DSM-IV–diagnosed CD) at both subsequent evaluations. Interestingly, clinical evaluations made without the EARL-20B were not as consistently associated with outcome. Incremental predictive validity over unstructured clinical evaluations and CD at baseline suggested promising clinical utility, thus supporting the checklist as potentially useful in supporting clinical decision making for referred boys at risk for continued antisocial behavior (Enebrink, Långström, & Gumpert, 2006).

Eyberg Child Behavior Inventory

A popular rating scale for assessing CD in children of ages 2 to 16 is the Eyberg Child Behavior Inventory (ECBI; Eyberg, 1980), a 36-item scale completed by parents to assess problem behaviors for children and adolescents between the ages of 2 and 16 (Teichner et al., 2000). Scores from the ECBI correlate well with independent behavioral observations and also differentiate between clinic-referred and normal controls. The total behavior problems score on the ECBI has strong internal consistency (.98) and test-retest reliability ($r = .86$) (Beauchaine, Webster-Stratton, & Reid, 2005). A caveat to this instrument, however, is that it has yet to be published, requiring any interested professionals to obtain copies of the various published research articles to effectively utilize this instrument.

Inventory of Callous-Unemotional Traits

Since callous-unemotional behavior has been identified in children and adolescents diagnosed with CD, researchers examined the structure, distribution, and correlates of a new measure of self-reported callous-unemotional (CU) traits in 1443 adolescents (774 boys, 669 girls) between the ages of 13 and 18 years, developed by Essau, Sasagawa, and Frick (2006). The Inventory of Callous-Unemotional Traits (ICT) was subjected to exploratory factor analysis and confirmatory factor analysis, with exploratory factor analysis producing three factors: callousness, uncaring, and unemotional behavior. Fit indices suggested that the three-factor model, with a single higher-order factor, represented a satisfactory solution for the data, and this factor structure appears to fit well for both boys and girls. Callous-unemotional traits correlated significantly with measures of CD and psychosocial impairment. The researchers also indicated that the traits showed predicted associations with sensation seeking and the Big Five personality dimensions, supporting the construct validity of the measure of CU traits. The Big Five personality dimensions refers to a model providing a unifying, hierarchical taxonomy for traits (Goldberg, 1993), enabling the investigation of broad and narrow personality influences in a widely-accepted framework (Hampson, Goldberg, Vogt, & Dubanoski, 2006; Marshall, Wortman, Vickers, Kusulas, & Hervig, 1994; Smith & Williams, 1992) of five bipolar dimensions: extraversion and introversion, agreeableness and hostility, conscientiousness and unconscientiousness, emotional stability and neuroticism, and intellectualism/openness and unintellectualism" (Hampson et al., 2006). Thus, use of the ICT may be helpful in predicting which children may be susceptible to engaging in antisocial behavior (Essau et al., 2006).

Questionnaire for Factors of Aggression

The Questionnaire for Factors of Aggression (QFA; Hampel & Selg, 1975) is an instrument that provides an analysis of different forms of aggressive behavior. In an investigation of 103 young-adult male imprisoned offenders in Germany, those with antisocial behavior were found to differ from nondelinquents only in their reports of aggression toward the self (Hinrichs, 2001).

Rating Scale for Disruptive Behavior Disorders

Silva and colleagues (2005) developed the Rating Scale for Disruptive Behavior Disorders (RS-DBD) based on the DSM-IV items used to establish diagnoses for disruptive behavior disorders (DBDs), including AD/HD, CD, and ODD. The scale, which is available in English and Spanish, consists of 41 items from the DSM-IV, with 18 items on the AD/HD scale, eight items on the ODD scale, and 15 items on the CD scale, all of which are rated on a four-point scale (0 = not at all, 1 = just a little, 2 = pretty much, and 3 = very much). Interestingly, the RS-DBD scales provide a basis for comparing severity within diagnostic categories (AD/HD, ODD, and CD). The internal consistency for both parent and teacher scales ranged from .78 to .96, which is satisfactory for individual decision making, and convergent validity was established by relating the RS-DBD to the relevant Conners scales. The authors also report that parents and teachers tend to report very similar information regarding CD on each of the forms.

Revised Problem Behavior Checklist

Another narrow-band rating scale is the Revised Problem Behavior Checklist (RBPC), which provides an assessment of behaviors in six scales: conduct disorder, socialized aggression, attention problems–immaturity, anxiety-withdrawal, motor excess, and psychotic behavior. Internal consistencies across scales range from .70 to .95 (Hogan, Quay, Vaughn, & Shapiro, 1989; Quay & Peterson, 1987; Silva et al., 2005).

Self-Report Early Delinquency Scale and Self-Reported Delinquency Questionnaire

The Self-Report Early Delinquency Scale (SRED) utilizes both parent and child forms to provide information about antisocial behavior (Moffitt & Silva, 1988), while the Self-Reported Delinquency Questionnaire (SRD) is a self-report form that may also be used to measure delinquency (Elliot, Huizinga, & Ageton, 1985). Items included on the SRD range from overt antisocial behavior, such as running away from home, fire-setting, and selling marijuana or other drugs, to covert forms of CD behavior, including avoiding paying for goods or services, wrongfully using credit cards, and defrauding someone (Burke et al., 2002; Elliot et al., 1985).

Youth Psychopathy Traits Inventory and Psychopathy Checklist: Youth Version

In another study, researchers examined the convergent and predictive validity of the Youth Psychopathy Traits Inventory (YPI) and the Psychopathy Checklist: Youth Version (PCL:YV) (Forth, Kosson, & Hare, 2003) in 115 male adolescents with DSM-IV–diagnosed CD. Investigators noted that both measures assess moderately overlapping constructs in the lifestyle/social deviance domain, but do not correlate on the affective domain. Although both instruments yielded predictive accuracy for subsequent institutional infractions and violence with the lifestyle/ antisocial element, the PCL:YV was more highly accurate in its predictive capabilities (Dolan & Rennie, 2006).

Behavioral Observations

Behavioral observations are another important assessment tool that can be utilized in assessing CD. Table 5.5 lists popular behavior observation measures. By using observational techniques, the evaluator is able to assess the child's or adolescent's behavior without having to filter it through an informant's

TABLE 5.5. Observational systems.

Dyadic Parent–Child Interaction Coding System (DPICS)	Eyberg & Robinson (1983)
Family Interaction Coding System (FICS)	Reid, Baldwin, Patterson, & Dishion (1988)
Snap! Diagnostic Behavior Scale (SDBS)	Swanson et al. (1982)

perception. In addition, the child's or adolescent's behavior can be observed within the environmental context, thereby providing further insight regarding the causation and the overall assessment of CD with regard to the observed child or adolescent (Frick, 1998b). Observation of the behavior-environment interaction can also aid in identifying aspects of the environment that can be modified in a treatment plan (Merrell, 1999).

Dyadic Parent–Child Interaction Coding System

The Dyadic Parent–Child Interaction Coding System–Revised (DPICS-R), developed by Robinson and Eyberg (1981), is an observational measure that provides an evaluation of the behaviors evidenced by children with CD and their parents in the home environment. The DPICS-R has 39 behavioral categories for parents, and eight behavioral categories for children. This well-researched instrument correlates acceptably with informant-report indices of CD behavior and is also sensitive to behavioral change (Webster-Stratton, Hollinsworth, & Kolpacoff, 1989). In using the DPICS-R, a total child deviance score can be derived, which is the sum of the frequencies of whining, yelling, crying, physical negativity, "smart" talk, aggression, and compliance (Beauchaine et al., 2005; Webster-Stratton & Hammond, 1997; Webster-Stratton, Reid, & Hammond, 2001). This instrument is further discussed later in the chapter (see Laboratory and Performance-Based Measures).

Family Interaction Coding System

Another example of an observation tool is the Family Interaction Coding System (FICS), in which a child's behaviors and responses of others to this behavior are assessed. There are, however, some limitations to this assessment tool. First, it can be very time-consuming and costly. Second, there is the concern that children may not display their "true" behaviors if they are aware that they are being observed (Frick, 1998a). Nonetheless, when the testing is conducted in a mental health or school psychology clinic, McMahon and Forehand (1988) claim that clinic-based observations are more efficient and cost-effective and less obtrusive than home-based observations (as cited in Merrell, 1999, p. 223).

Snap! Diagnostic Behavior Scale

Another observational method is the Snap! Diagnostic Behavior Scale (SDBS), which was developed by Swanson, Nolan, and Pelham (1982) and provides a quantification of the DSM-III criteria for attention deficit disorder with hyperactivity (American Psychiatric Association, 1980; Kim-Cohen et al., 2005; Pelham, Atkins, Murphy, & White, 1981). The SDBS assesses problems in the following areas: inattention, impulsivity, hyperactivity, and peer problems. Test-retest reliabilities for the SDBS over a 2-week interval were .69, .78, .92, and .66 for the inattention, impulsivity, hyperactivity, and peer problems subscales, respectively (Mantzicopoulos & Morrison, 1994; Pelham et al., 1981). This observational rating technique may be used to identify antisocial behavior that is comorbid with AD/HD.

Interviews

Additional assessment methods that can be used in diagnosing CD are structured or semistructured interviews, which provide an assessment of the age of onset of behavior problems as well as of the duration of symptoms. These interviews can also help shed light on the developmental progression and the degree of impairment with regard to the CD (Frick, 1998b). Again, as with the behavioral rating scales, structured or semistructured interviews provide a detailed description of the child's or adolescent's emotional and behavioral functioning. Table 5.6 lists popular structured or semistructured measures. Due to potential social perception deficits, oppositional defiance to the assessment process, and other characteristic behaviors of CD that may lead to inaccurate or misleading responses, the use of multiple informants, such as parents, teachers, self, and peers, is considered best practice in diagnosing CD (Delligatti et al., 2003; Lahey et al., 2000). Moreover, clinical interviews are constantly updated to adapt to the changes made in the DSM system (Frick, 1998b).

Child and Adolescent Psychiatric Assessment

The Child and Adolescent Psychiatric Assessment (CAPA; Angold et al., 1995) was designed to combine the advantages of clinical interviews with epidemiological interview methods. The CAPA employs operationalized symptom definitions in order to standardize the interviewer's assessment of symptom constructs and

TABLE 5.6. Interview forms.

Child and Adolescent Psychiatric Assessment (CAPA)	Angold et al. (1995)
Child Assessment Schedule (CAS)	Hodges et al. (1982); Hodges, Cool, & McKnew (1989)
Composite International Diagnostic Interview (CIDI)	World Health Organization (1993); Kessler et al. (2005); Kessler & Ustun (2004)
Developmental and Well-Being Assessment (DAWBA)	Goodman et al. (2000)
Diagnostic Interview of Children and Adolescents (DICA)	Reich (2000)
Diagnostic Interview Schedule for Children (DISC)	Shaffer et al. (1996)
Schedule for Affective Disorders and Schizophrenia (SADS)	Ambrosini (2000); Stahl & Clarizio (1999)

thresholds, thereby minimizing variance between interviewers in coding symptoms (Foley et al., 2004). In using the CAPA, the parent and child are questioned separately by different interviewers, and the time frame for determining the presence of most psychiatric symptoms is the past 3 months (Costello, Mustillo, Erkanli, Keeler, & Angold, 2003), because of a greater accuracy of reports based on recent rather than distal symptomatology. The psychometric properties of the CAPA are modest, with the 1- to 11-day test-retest reliability of CAPA (Child Form; CAPA-C) symptoms .60 for CD (Angold & Costello, 1995).

Child Assessment Schedule

The Child Assessment Schedule (CAS) is a structured clinical interview that was revised and used to assess DSM III-R Axis I categories of psychopathology in adolescents (Hodges, Kline, Stern, Cytryn, & McKnew, 1982; Kashani, Orvaschel, Rosenberg, & Reid, 1989; Teichner et al., 2000). The CAS has excellent psychometric properties, and includes both a parent and child version (Hodges, McKnew, Burback, & Roebuck, 1987; Hodges & Saunders, 1990). On the CAS, 16 items measure CD, including such items as "lied a lot," "stole when others weren't looking," and "physically cruel to animals." The items are summed and used as a dimensional score for CD, which has been reported as a strength in studying externalizing behaviors (Becker & McCloskey, 2002; Levy, Hay, McStephen, Wood, & Waldman, 1997).

Composite International Diagnostic Interview

The World Health Organization's (WHO) Composite International Diagnostic Interview (CIDI) may also be used for assessment of CD (Kessler & Ustun, 2004). The CIDI is a fully structured diagnostic interview designed for use by laypersons that generates diagnoses according to the definitions and criteria of the DSM-IV and the 10th edition of the ICD (ICD-10) diagnostic systems (Nock et al., 2006). The CIDI has been found to have strong concordance with clinical diagnoses developed through the Structured Clinical Interview for DSM-IV (SCID; Kessler et al., 2005).

Development and Well-Being Assessment

An interview schedule that uses multiple informants to increase the validity of assessment is the Development and Well-Being Assessment (DAWBA), which consists of a parent interview, a child interview, and a teacher questionnaire (Goodman, Ford, Richards, Gatward, & Meltzer, 2000). The DAWBA combines features of structured and semistructured interviews. The parent version of the instrument is administered by a trained interviewer who questions parents regarding their child's psychiatric symptoms, including antisocial behaviors, and their functional impact. Additionally, the interviewer enters parent comments regarding the child's positive symptoms verbatim on the computer, which are then followed by a series of open-ended questions and supplemental prompts.

The teacher form of the DAWBA includes a questionnaire on common symptoms and their impact, while the self-report DAWBA module includes a direct interview for 11- to 16-year-olds. Diagnoses are then generated by computer algorithms based on the DSM-IV (American Psychiatric Association, 1994) and the ICD-10 Diagnostic Criteria for Research (Heyman et al., 2003; World Health Organization, 1993). The psychometrics of this instrument appear to be adequate; the chance-corrected reliability for the presence of any disorder is .86 (standard error [SE] .04; Heyman et al., 2003), .57 for internalizing disorders (SE .11), and .98 for externalizing disorders (SE .02), and there is substantial agreement between clinic diagnoses and DAWBA diagnoses, a testament to the measure's validity (Ford, Goodman, & Meltzer, 2003; Goodman et al., 2000).

Diagnostic Interview of Children and Adolescents

Another interview form is the Diagnostic Interview of Children and Adolescents, 4th edition (DICA-IV), a semistructured diagnostic interview available in parent, child, and adolescent versions. It provides an assessment of symptoms and related consequences associated with DSM-IV criteria, including CD (Latimer, Stone, Voight, Winters, & August, 2002; Reich, 2000; Reich, Shayla, & Taibelson, 1992; Reich & Weiner, 1988). The DICA is organized to explore the presence or absence of each symptom in different pediatric syndromes, and has adequate levels of reliability and validity (Masi et al., 2003). The DICA has also been adapted and validated for the Spanish population, and has been found to have satisfactory psychometric properties in this form (de la Osa, Ezpeleta, Domènech, Navarro, & Losilla, 1996; Ezpeleta et al., 1997; Ezpeleta, Domènech, & Angold, 2006).

Diagnostic Interview Schedule for Children

Another commonly used interview form is the Diagnostic Interview Schedule for Children, 4th edition (DISC-4; Robins, Marcus, Reich, Cunningham, & Gallagher, 1996), which is available in child (C), parent (P), and teacher (T) forms, and in a computerized version (DISC 2.3) that eliminates the requirement for a trained interviewer for administration (Shaffer et al., 1996). The DISC, which is highly structured and available in both English and Spanish, provides a dichotomous classification of disorders based on DSM nosology (Bravo, Woodbury-Farina, Canino, & Rubio-Stipec, 1993), assesses the presence of disorders during the past 6 months, and contains detailed symptom probes (Teplin, Abram, McClelland, Dulcan, & Mericle, 2002). To determine whether a child meets the criteria for a disorder, the DISC taps into DSM symptomatology through a set of questions, some of which are contingent upon a skip pattern. The DISC has been found to have acceptable levels of reliability and validity, and is able to discriminate between CD and ODD, even when the child version is used independently of the other forms (Fisher et al., 1993; Friman et al., 2000; Placentini et al., 1993; Schwab-Stone, 1993). However, the reliability of the DISC is increased when child reports and parent reports are combined (Crowley, Mikulich, Ehlers, Whitmore, & Macdonald, 2001).

In one study, using the questions from the DISC 2.3 that are not contingent upon a skip pattern, four empirically defined scales, relating to depressive, AD/HD, ODD, and CD behaviors, were developed (Rubio-Stipec et al., 1996). These scales may be used in both parent- and self-report formats, and are coded as either 0 (absent) or 1 (present). Rubio-Stipek and colleagues (2002) report that for CD, symptoms that had the highest associated probabilities included "robs" on both the parent and self-report, "belongs to gangs" on the parent report, and "initiates fight" on the self-report, the last of which also has the highest impact. The researchers recommend that use of such dimensional measures to provide additional information about the prevalence of disorders in investigating childhood psychopathology in a population.

Schedule for Affective Disorders and Schizophrenia for School-Age Children

The Schedule for Affective Disorders and Schizophrenia for School-Age Children, abbreviated K-SADS for its colloquial reference to the kiddie version of this instrument (Ambrosini, 2000; Stahl & Clarizio, 1999), is a semistructured interview, subdivided into three indices, and provides both current and lifetime diagnoses. The first part of the interview includes identification, demographics, general health history and present health care, development, past history of abuse, psychiatric history, school background, and social relations. The second component of the instrument consists of an 82-symptom screen that provides a rating of key symptoms for current and past episodes in 20 different diagnostic areas. Finally, the third index offers five supplementary diagnostic score sheets (e.g., affective, psychotic, anxiety, behavioral, and substance abuse/other disorders) that provide confirmatory diagnostic symptom ratings after a positive screening (Andrade, Silva, & Assumpçáo, 2004).

Laboratory and Performance-Based Measures

Laboratory and performance-based measures may be unfamiliar to school-based professionals. Frick and Loney (2000) describe the importance of incorporating results derived from these measures as a part of a comprehensive assessment. Psychometric considerations are included along with the practical implications of these measures.

Provocation Paradigms

Provocation paradigms are standardized stimuli designed to elicit children's and adolescents' antisocial behavior for purposes of observation in laboratory or clinical settings. Each of the following techniques has been found to reveal certain antisocial symptomatology, as well as to distinguish children and adolescents with CD from controls. Aggression in competitive situations, temptation provocation tasks, and situations involving parental demands for compliance each elicit a different type of conduct problem, and will be briefly discussed in this section.

Aggression in Competitive Situations
In this type of provocation paradigm, children are placed in a competitive situation with a confederate peer who engages in hostile, instrumental provocations, while the target child's responses are measured. For example, children are presented with a simulated pinball game in which he or she is in competition with the confederate to earn the most points. The standardized-administered provocation comes in the form of a hostile, loud burst of white noise or interference with the child's ability to successfully complete the task, such as causing the pinball game to tilt and freeze, which is purportedly initiated by the (confederate) peer. Findings from these kinds of tasks have differentiated highly aggressive children, including children with an ODD or CD diagnosis, are significantly correlated with negative peer interactions outside the context of testing, and have resulted in less physiological reactivity in highly aggressive children in comparison to other stimuli (Atkins & Stoff, 1993; Atkins, Stoff, Osborne, & Brown, 1993; Murphy, Pelham, & Lang, 1992; Pelham et al., 1991 as cited in Frick & Loney, 2000).

Temptation Provocation Tasks
Temptation provocation tasks are those designed to assess covert conduct problems in children and adolescents. For example, children are left alone in a room for 6 to 8 minutes, and are asked to work on an assignment involving hidden picture searches (for young children) or word puzzles (for older children). Several objects are partially hidden around the desk where the child is working, including money (less than two dollars), toy cards, baseball cards, other small toys, and the answer key to the child's work assignment, which is partially visible to the child. The level of cheating (0 = no cheating, 1 = occasional cheating, and 2 = clear, repeated cheating) and stealing (0 = none, 1 = one dollar or less, 2 = more than one dollar; number of other objects taken is coded 0 to 3), is measured, and instances of destroyed or defaced property is coded from 0 (no evidence of property destruction) to 3 (writing on furniture or walls, ripping paper, breaking pencils). After these measurements, children are debriefed, informed that stealing and cheating are not permitted, and are encouraged to return any stolen items. While higher rates of stealing and property destruction are evidenced by children who exhibit antisocial behavior, and are correlated with parental ratings of these behaviors, cheating does not differentiate between CD children and controls, nor does it significantly correlate with parent reports of the child's cheating (Hinshaw, Heller, & McHale, 1992; Hinshaw, Simmel, & Heller, 1995; Hinshaw, Zupan, Simmel, Nigg, & Melnick, 1997).

Situations Involving Parental Demands for Compliance
Frick and Loney (2000) indicate that the third provocation paradigm, which is the most widely used laboratory measure of CD, is the assessment of child

noncompliance and oppositional behavior during standardized parent–child interactions. One example of this kind of paradigm is the Dyadic Parent–Child Interaction Coding System (DPICS), initially developed by Eyberg and Robinson, and then revised by Eyberg, Bessmer, Newcomb, Edwards, and Robinson (1994), which was discussed earlier (see Behavioral Observations). In the DPICS, parents and their young children, ages 4 to 8 years, are observed interacting in a clinic playroom during three conditions—a free-play situation (5 minutes), a parent-guided interaction (5 minutes), and a cleanup request (5 minutes)—the latter two of which are designed to elicit children's responses to parental demands for compliance. During all three conditions, children's responses to parental demands are coded, from which a compliance ratio is figured, which is the proportion of parental demands with which the child immediately complies. Conduct-disordered children have been found to have a lower compliance ratio than do control children, and performance on these tasks has been significantly correlated with antisocial behavior observed in naturalistic home environments (Forehand & McMahon, 1981; McMahon & Estes, 1997; Roberts & Powers, 1988). Frick and Loney (2000) also describe laboratory and performance-based techniques that do not directly assess CD, but instead measure underlying processes that contribute to antisocial behavior. For a full description of these measures, readers are suggested to consult Frick and Loney.

Personality Measures

Personality instruments assist examiners in assessing major symptoms of social and personal maladjustment, and may be used in conjunction with behavior rating scales to provide a fuller picture of an individual's functioning.

Minnesota Multiphasic Personality Inventory–Adolescent

The Minnesota Multiphasic Personality Inventory–Adolescent (MMPI-A; Butcher et al., 1992) is a frequently used standardized measure of adolescent psychopathology designed for use with adolescents from 14 to 18 years of age with a 7th grade reading level and normed on a diverse, fairly representative sample of adolescents in the United States. The MMPI-A contains 478 items, with raw responses converted to T scores based on norms by gender. Factor analysis has revealed eight factors of this instrument—general maladjustment, immaturity, disinhibition/excitatory potential, social discomfort, health concerns, naiveté, familial alienation, and psychoticism—two of which, general maladjustment and disinhibition, may provide information about antisocial behavior (Archer, Belevich, & Elkins, 1994). Additionally, validity of the MMPI-A has been established through convergence with other measures of personality and psychopathology, clinical descriptions of adolescents with various behavioral elevations, and clinical utility (Archer, 1997; Weis, Crockett, & Vieth, 2004).

Freiburg Personality Inventory

The Freiburg Personality Inventory–Revised (FPI-R) is a measure often employed in European nations that has been used to distinguish between those with antisocial and normal behavior in 15 studies of a total of 3,450 delinquent participants. In comparison to nondelinquents, antisocial participants showed increased scores in depression, nervousness, aggression, sociability, emotional instability, and extraversion (Steller & Hunze, 1984). In another study of 103 young-adult male imprisoned offenders in Germany, antisocial participants tended to have higher scores in negative attitude to life on the FPI-R (Hinrichs, 2001).

Rorschach Inkblot Method

The Rorschach Inkblot Method (RIM) is composed of 10 cards, each of which contains an ambiguous inkblot with varying achromatic or chromatic coloring. Over the years, there have been several scoring systems used to interpret responses to the inkblots. The most common and well-researched method is Exner's Comprehensive System (CS), now in its third revision (Exner & Erdberg, 2005). The RIM cards are administered in a standardized, sequential format by an examiner to a single subject. Following RIM administration, each response is scored (or coded) on several primary dimensions that address both perceptual aspects of the responses and how the responses are verbalized by the examinee. The scores (or codes) for each response are used to compute various ratios and frequencies which, in turn, provide information about aspects of the individual's cognitive, emotional, and social functioning.

Reliability and validity studies support the use of RIM for both clinical and research settings (Piotrowski, 1996; Piotrowski & Keller, 1989; Piotrowski, Sherry, & Keller, 1985). Kappa (interrater reliability) and interclass correlations (ICC; agreement between repeated measures) studies are in the good (>.60) to excellent (>.75 to .80s) range (Gacono, Evans, & Viglione, 2002; Garb, 1998; Meyer et al., 2002; Shrout & Fliess, 1979). Meta-analyses of interrater reliability studies also report excellent support with a mean estimated kappa of .86 (Meyer, 1997). Hiller, Rosenthal, Bornstein, Berry, and Brunell-Neuleib (1999), having corrected some of the problems in earlier meta-analyses, found that the RIM indices have an unweighted mean effect size of .29, as compared to those of the MMPI, which was found to have a mean effect size of .30; both findings are at the high end of the effect size range for personality tests. Consistent with the uses of both these instruments, the MMPI was found to have larger validity coefficients than the RIM for studies using psychiatric diagnoses and self-report measures as criterion variables, whereas the RIM had larger validity coefficients than the MMPI for studies using objective criterion variables (Exner, 2003). Meyer and Archer (2001) found validity to be similar among the RIM, MMPI, and IQ measures.

The RIM involves little projection. Rather, the RIM is essentially a problem-solving, perceptual-association task that provides information about the person's psychology (personality) underlying his or her behavior (Exner, 2003). The RIM has been used to measure differences in aggressive behaviors in psychopathic and nonpsychopathic CD children (Gacono & Meloy, 1994; Loving & Russel, 2000; Smith, Gacono, & Kaufman, 1997), how childhood delinquency is related to adolescent and adulthood delinquency (Janson & Stattin, 2003), and the role of attachment and anxiety in conduct or dysthymic adolescents (Weber, Meloy, & Gacono, 1992).

Pictorial Assessments

Loeber and colleagues (2000) report that another way in which to assess CD is through self-report pictorial assessments that portray DSM criteria concretely and through multisensory stimuli, thus minimizing potential sources of error. Initial investigations of the psychometric properties of instruments for the assessment of children using pictorial items, such as the Pictorial Instrument for Children and Adolescents-III-R (Ernst, Cookus, & Moravec, 2000) and the Dominic-R (Valla, Bergeron, & Smolla, 2000) appear to be strong according to Loeber and colleagues (2000).

Pictorial Instrument for Children and Adolescents

The Pictorial Instrument for Children and Adolescents, 3rd edition revised (PICA-III-R), developed by Ernst and colleagues (2000), is a semistructured interview that provides an assessment of all DSM-III-R Axis I psychiatric disorders in children aged 6 to 16 years, categorically (diagnosis present or absent) and dimensionally (range of severity). The instrument is composed of 137 pictures organized in modules that cover five diagnostic categories, including disorders of anxiety, mood, psychosis, disruptive behavior, and substance abuse, and 14 subscales, each corresponding to an Axis I psychiatric diagnosis. Additionally, the PICA-III-R can be used for the assessment of non–English-speaking or hearing/speech-impaired children.

The PICA-III-R psychometric properties are sound, with good internal consistency, significant discriminative power for diagnoses, and sensitivity to change. As a measure of discriminant validity, the diagnostic power of the PICA-III-R was assessed through a canonical discriminant function analysis, and the three subscales with the highest internal reliabilities and greatest clinical relevance to the study sample (depression, psychotic disorder, and ODD/CD) were entered in the analysis. The instrument significantly discriminated among these diagnostic groups (Wilkes [lambda] = 0.67, $p < .02$). Validity was further assessed through comparing the scores of the PICA-III-R to clinical diagnosis of improvement, to which the instrument was also sensitive.

The content of each picture is simple, schematic, and neutral, and refers to a single DSM-III-R criterion. The pictures encompass emotions, behaviors, thought content, thought process, or vegetative signs relevant to each criterion. The gender of the child in the pictures is intentionally ambiguous in order to facilitate the identification of the patient with the child and situation depicted in the drawings. Each picture is accompanied by a set of comments and questions provided for the interviewer to help children understand the drawings and rate themselves. Additionally, the examiner can supply additional explanations if the child seems to have difficulty with the content of the pictures. Once the picture is understood, questions are asked to probe the severity of the symptom, frequency of occurrence, and period of time when the symptom was present. The answer to the "How much" question is rated on the 5-point visual analog scale (1 = just a little, to 5 = very much), with a score of 2 or greater considered positive. The authors indicate that answers are noted on the score sheet, which requires both present and past to be recorded and includes extra space for remarks (Ernst et al., 2000).

Dominic-R

The Dominic-R is a structured, pictorial instrument developed by Valla and colleagues (2000), designed to assess mental disorders in 6- to 11-year-olds based on symptoms represented in the disorders of the DSM-III-R, and more recent DSM-IV. The computerized version of this assessment also includes specific (simple) phobias, separation anxiety, generalized anxiety, depression/dysthymia, attention deficit hyperactivity, oppositional defiant, and CD. Symptom descriptions in the Dominic-R complement the visual stimuli, and are included in an effort to provide better information processing than visual or auditory stimuli alone. Test-retest reliability of symptoms and symptom scores and criterion validity against clinical judgment support the visual-auditory combination of stimuli to assess child mental health.

The authors have also developed an adolescent Dominic (AD), appropriate for children ages 12 to 16 years, a pictorial screen for the most frequent Axis I children mental disorders, which include 113 picture items based on DSM-III-R diagnostic criteria. The symptom reliability of the AD compares well with data from other assessment interviews of children's mental disorders. Following these positive results, a computerized DSM-IV version of the AD has focused on the assessment of symptoms and is currently being tested for reliability and criterion validity (Smolla, Valla, Bergeron, Berthiaume, & St.-Georges, 2004).

Assessment and Gender Issues

One of the problems in diagnosis of CD that is frequently recognized is that the diagnostic criteria used for boys may not be as appropriate in identifying antisocial behavior in girls. Delligatti and colleagues (2003) argue for including more nonphysically aggressive behaviors, such as relational aggression, as well as more covert rule violations that may be more common among girls, in the criteria for the diagnosis for CD. These researchers suggest that taking these steps would potentially avoid the gender differences in rates of CD among different age groups. Furthermore, awareness of socialization effects on the development of disruptive behaviors should be considered when diagnosing girls with CD, as should records of police contact, rather than felony records, which may not be the best indicator of girls' rule violations. Additionally, although self-report methods are not often considered to be the most reliable means of diagnosing CD, in girls they may yield valuable information, since others may not be aware of the covert forms of deviance and rule violations engaged in by girls. Thus, combining information from both male and female parents and teachers is important because there may be gender differences in which behaviors evidenced by the girl are viewed as problematic. Other research, however, has suggested that from a family genetic perspective, the diagnostic threshold for CD does not appear to differ by gender, and the authors feel that these results support the possibility that differential rates of CD reflect true differences in rates of antisocial behavior across gender (Doyle et al., 2003).

Finally, it is important to consider the possibility of comorbidity of problem behaviors, especially in adolescents. Comorbidity refers to the presence of one or more disorders in addition to a primary disorder (Table 5.7). It is estimated that of all persons diagnosed with CD, 50% are comorbid with AD/HD, 32% to 37% comorbid with anxiety and affective disorders (e.g. depression), and at least 60% are likely to display one or more mental health or learning disorders (Tynan, 2001). The American Academy of Child and Adolescent Psychiatry (1997) delineates possible alternate primary diagnoses with conduct symptoms, which may require a comprehensive assessment to clarify the manifestation of behaviors that may be concurrent with CD.

Conclusion

A review of the literature shows that there is no one method that can fully capture all the necessary elements for the assessment of conduct disorder. Therefore, the best possible form of assessment would require multiple methods, gathering data from multiple informants, and the use of qualitative as well as quantitative methods for obtaining information about the child's strengths and needs beyond making the diagnosis of CD. Specifically, a comprehensive view of the child or adolescent's level of impairment would likely require examination of data from behavior rating scales (broad- and narrow-band), clinical interviews (developmental, medical, and legal records), behavioral observations, and personality measures (Table 5.8). There are several options of assessment tests and techniques available for each of these areas. The AACAP (1997) provides an extensive and detailed outline of practice parameters for the diagnostic assessment of CD (see Appendix 5.1), incorporating the above-mentioned assessment tools in a step-by-step approach for obtaining patient and family history, school and academic information, and locus points for a physical evaluation. This outline also provides a guide to making a diagnostic formulation based on DSM-IV-TR criteria and offers a list of possible alternate primary diagnoses that are sometimes confused with CD because of their complicated presentation.

TABLE 5.7. Possible alternate or comorbid diagnoses with conduct symptoms.

1. Attention deficit/hyperactivity disorder
2. Oppositional defiant disorder
3. Intermittent explosive disorder
4. Substance use disorders
5. Mood disorders (bipolar and depressive)
6. Posttraumatic stress disorder and dissociative disorders
7. Borderline personality disorder
8. Somatization disorder
9. Adjustment disorder
10. Organic brain disorder and seizure disorder
11. Paraphilias
12. Narcissistic personality disorder
13. Specific developmental disorders (e.g., learning disabilities)
14. Mental retardation
15. Schizophrenia

Adapted from American Academy of Child and Adolescent Psychiatry (1997).

TABLE 5.8. Overview of the assessment process.

1. Documentation of information related to the specific referral (referrals may emerge from teachers, staff, parents or others)
2. Clarification of the purpose of the assessment process (e.g., advance understanding of individual behaviors, diagnosis, inform intervention strategies)
3. Systematically obtain additional information about the behaviors of the individual from multiple sources (i.e., parent, teacher, or self-report available). Methods may include the following:
   a. Standardized instruments
   b. Structured diagnostic interviews
   c. Observations of the children (in multiple contexts)
   d. Discussion with the child and family
   e. A complete medical and family/social history
4. Systematically examine information obtained to discern the age of onset, specific series and scope of behavior problems (and adaptive behaviors), and severity of behavior problems (including an estimate of impairment in functioning in various contexts).
5. Incorporate information yielded through the assessment process to develop a plan for intervention strategies to reduce the behavior problems and promote the social, cognitive, and academic competence of the children.

Appendix 5.1.   American Academy of Child and Adolescent Psychiatry outline of practice parameters for the assessment and treatment of children and adolescents with conduct disorder

I. Diagnostic assessment: every child presenting with significant conduct problems merits a careful diagnostic assessment. Interview patient and parents (separately and together) to obtain history. Interview other family members and medical, school, and probation personnel as indicated. (The order of obtaining data may vary.)

A. Obtain patient's history
   1. Prenatal and birth history, focusing on substance abuse by mother, maternal infections, and medications
   2. Developmental history, focusing on disorders of attachment (e.g., parental depression and substance abuse), temperament, aggression, oppositionality, attention, and impulse control
   3. Physical and sexual abuse history (as victim and perpetrator)
   4. DSM-IV target symptoms
   5. History of symptom development, including impact on family and peer relationships and academic problems (with attention to IQ, language, attention, and learning disabilities)
   6. Medical history, focusing on central nervous system (CNS) pathology (i.e., head trauma, other illnesses involving CNS, chronic illnesses, extensive somatization)

B. Obtain family history
   1. Family coping style, resources (socioeconomic status, social support/ isolation, problem-solving skills, conflict-resolution skills), and stressors; assess parenting skills, including limit setting, structure, harshness, abuse, neglect, permissiveness, inconsistency, and management of child's aggression; explore the parents' and patient's coercive interaction cycles leading to reinforcement of noncompliance
   2. Antisocial behaviors in family members, including incarceration, violence, physical or sexual abuse of patient or family members
   3. Attention deficit/hyperactivity disorder, conduct disorder, substance use disorders, developmental disorders (e.g., learning disabilities), tic disorders, somatization disorder, mood disorders, and personality disorders in family members
   4. Adoptions and placements in foster care and institutions

C. Interviews: interview patient; adolescent interview may precede parental interview; review family history, the patient's personal history, substance use history, and sexual history (including sexual abuse of others); DSM-IV target symptoms may not be apparent or acknowledged during the patient interview, but may be discovered by interviewing parents and other informants; evaluate the following:
   1. Capacity for attachment, trust, and empathy
   2. Tolerance for and discharge of impulses
   3. Capacity for showing restraint, accepting responsibility for actions, experiencing guilt, using anger constructively, and acknowledging negative emotions
   4. Cognitive functioning
   5. Mood, affect, self-esteem, and suicide potential
   6. Peer relationships (loner, popular, drug-, crime-, or gang-oriented friends)
   7. Disturbances of ideation (inappropriate reactions to environment, paranoia, dissociative episodes, and suggestibility)

8. History of early, persistent use of tobacco, alcohol, or other substances
9. Psychometric self-report instruments might provide useful information

D. School information
1. Functioning (IQ, achievement test data, academic performance, and behavior); data may be obtained in person, by phone, or through written reports from appropriate staff, such as school principal, psychologist, teacher, and nurse
2. Standard parent- and teacher-rating scales of the patient's behavior may be useful
3. Referral for IQ, speech and language, and learning disability (high incidence of concurrence) and neuropsychiatric testing if available test data are not sufficient

E. Physical evaluation
1. Physical examination within last 12 months; baseline pulse rate
2. Collaboration with family doctor, pediatrician, or other health care providers
3. Vision and hearing screening as indicated
4. Evaluation of medical and neurological conditions (e.g., head injury, seizure disorder, chronic illnesses) as indicated
5. Urine and blood drug screening as indicated, especially when clinical evidence suggests substance abuse that patient denies

II. Diagnostic formulation

A. Identify DSM-IV target symptoms

B. In the assessment of adolescents and children with symptoms suggestive of CD, consider, the following:
1. Biopsychosocial stressors (especially sexual and physical abuse, separation, divorce, or death of key attachment figures)
2. Educational potential, disabilities, and achievement
3. Peer, sibling, and family problems and strengths
4. Environmental factors including disorganized home, lack of supervision, presence of child abuse or neglect, psychiatric illness (especially substance abuse) in parents, and environmental neurotoxins (e.g., lead intoxication)
5. Adolescent or child ego development, especially ability to form and maintain relationships

C. The subtype of the disorder (childhood onset versus adolescent onset; overt versus covert versus authority; underrestrained versus overrestrained; socialized vs. undersocialized)

D. Possible alternate primary diagnoses with conduct symptoms complicating their presentation, especially in adolescents; these syndromes may be confused or concurrent with CD
1. Attention deficit/hyperactivity disorder
2. Oppositional defiant disorder
3. Intermittent explosive disorder
4. Substance use disorders
5. Mood disorders (bipolar and depressive)

6.   Posttraumatic stress disorder and dissociative disorders
7.   Borderline personality disorder
8.   Somatization disorder
9.   Adjustment disorder
10. Organic brain disorder and seizure disorder
11. Paraphilias
12. Narcissistic personality disorder
13. Specific developmental disorders (e.g., learning disabilities)
14. Mental retardation
15. Schizophrenia

Note: Reprinted with permission from American Academy of Child and Adolescent Psychiatry (AACAP), Work Group on Quality Issues (1997). Practice parameters for the assessment and treatment of children and adolescents with conduct disorder. *Journal of the American Academy of Child and Adolescent Psychiatry, 36* (10, Suppl.), 122S–139S.

6
Psychoeducational Assessment

Determining the presence of conduct disorder (CD) is a relatively straightforward process. As described in Chapters 1, 3, and 5, CD is the diagnostic classification applied to children who display a pervasive and persistent pattern of problem behaviors characterized by aggression, destruction, deceitfulness, and serious violations of rules (American Psychiatric Association, 2000). To meet diagnostic criteria, three or more of the criteria must be present in the past 12 months, with at least one criterion present in the past 6 months. Since CD behaviors are typically externalized behaviors demonstrated by the individual, such actions are often readily measured through observation and broad-band and narrow-band rating scales as described in Chapter 5. However, for school personnel, the diagnosis of CD alone provides limited information for two main reasons. First, the diagnosis of CD may or may not qualify the child for special-education services. Special-education eligibility has implications for the type and location of treatment and also impacts on disciplinary decisions made in response to antisocial behaviors committed on school property (Slenkovich, 1983). Second, diagnosis alone does not provide adequate information regarding treatment for the individual with CD. As discussed in Chapter 5, the goal of assessment in CD is to surpass diagnosis to provide better understanding of the child or adolescent's psychosocial strengths and needs for the purpose of treatment planning (Frick, 1998b). Thus, assessment is a critical step not only for determining diagnosis, but also for informing education decisions and planning for treatment.

Conduct Disorder in the Schools

Conduct disorder is a *Diagnostic and Statistical Manual of Mental Disorders*, text revision, 4th edition (DSM-IV-TR) diagnosis that by itself is not sufficient for a child to be eligible for special-education services. Special-education eligibility decisions are a product of individualized education program (IEP) team meetings, and special-education categories are not necessarily the same as the psychological disorders defined in the DSM-IV-TR. Some children with CD may qualify for special education under the eligibility category of emotional disturbance, while others may not qualify as they may not reach diagnostic threshold (e.g., behaviors do not interfere with their learning or the learning of others) or their behavior difficulties are better described as socially maladjustment (SM). Moreover, whether intervention services for children with CD occur within or outside of special education may be immaterial. Rather, what is important is whether or not the child's difficulties and strengths are described in a manner that will result in the most appropriate treatment (Gacono & Hughes, 2004).

Controversy Regarding Classification

Some argue that there is a continuum of emotional and behavioral disturbances among children and that they cannot be meaningfully differentiated for classification or treatment purposes (Bower, 1982; CCBD Executive Committee, 1987; Merrell & Walker, 2004). Others agree that behaviors do not differentiate groups, but point out that personality traits can meaningfully differentiate emotional and behavior disorders (Gacono & Hughes, 2004). Thus, the issue of how to provide support services for children with CD diagnoses often presents challenges for school systems as they consider (1) an educational category that is not well matched with a recognized psychological disorder in the DSM; (2) poorly defined definitions of the special education terms of emotional disturbance and social maladjustment that are open to interpretation by multidisciplinary teams; (3) legal mandates to exclude those who are socially maladjusted, although this term is undefined; and (4) the reality that CD extends across both emotional disturbance and social maladjustment educational categories.

Definition of Emotional Disturbance

To help clarify how the issue of CD diagnosis impacts on special education, it is useful to consider the definition of emotional disturbance in detail. The key criterion in defining an emotional disturbance is "a condition whereby a child exhibits one or more ... characteristics *over a long period of time* and *to a marked degree* that *adversely affects educational performance...*" (Individuals with Disabilities Education Improvement Act Amendments of 2004 § 300.8[c][4][i]). The phrase, "a long period of time" emphasizes that the condition is not transient, often interpreted as being present for a minimum of 6 months. This is consistent with the diagnostic minimum for CD and other DSM disorders. Further, the phrase, "a marked degree" connotes a severe departure from typical functioning as compared to normative behavior. Finally, the phrase "adversely affects educational performance" refers to the negative impact on children's social, emotional, behavioral, and academic functioning in the school setting. Many states and districts have established guidelines regarding the way in which school functioning is defined. The IDEIA (2004) does not specify any criteria for these conditions. Thus, it is critical for school psychologists to address these presumptions in psychoeducational reports. In addition, it is important to recognize that the multidisciplinary team can accept or reject the conclusions of the school psychologist when determining special-education eligibility. An emotional disturbance (ED) is defined in the following way when the conditions described above are met:

- *An inability to learn that cannot be explained by intellectual, sensory, or health factors.* This criterion is met when there is a decrement in academic achievement, significant emotional problems, and no intellectual, sensory, or health factors to account for the diminishment in academic performance (Kelly, 1990).
- *An inability to build or maintain satisfactory interpersonal relationships with peers and teachers.* When the child demonstrates significant impairment in initiation and satisfactory maintenance of interpersonal relationships due to anxiety, depressed mood, avoidance, withdrawal, isolation, self-abuse, and so on, this criterion has been established (Kelly, 1990).
- *Inappropriate types of behavior or feelings under normal circumstances.* Evidence that this criterion is being met includes the child demonstrating significantly inappropriate behavior or emotions (reflective of depression, anxiety, or distortion of reality), particularly when these behaviors and feelings are not triggered by specific circumstances (Kelly, 1990).
- *A general pervasive mood of unhappiness or depression.* This criterion is most specifically met when the child consistently and significantly engages in impaired affective modulation (e.g., overreacts to perceived transgressions with rage, withdrawal, or crying spells); expressions of sadness, depressed mood, feelings of worthlessness, or irritability; morbid preoccupation; inability to establish or execute simple goals; or absence of interest in previously valued activities (i.e., anhedonia) (Kelly, 1990).
- *A tendency to develop physical symptoms or fears associated with personal or school problems.* When the child demonstrates significant physical symptoms without an organic base, physical symptoms with a known stress-related link (e.g., ulcers, headaches, etc.), persistent irrational fears, and phobias, there is evidence that this criterion has been satisfied (Kelly, 1990).
- *Includes children who are schizophrenic.* This criterion is most specifically met when the child demonstrates symptoms of childhood schizophrenia including inadequate reality testing, distorted thinking (not reality-based), delusions, and hallucinations (Kelly, 1990).
- *But does not include children who are socially maladjusted, unless they are also determined to have an emotional disturbance as determined by evaluation.* This, more so that the other criteria, is the diagnostic issue that has been met with much controversy. Nelson (1992) argues that this exclusionary clause is no different than the criterion that defines ED and is therefore illogical. However, most mental disorders have shared or overlapping symptoms that require decision trees and rule out procedures to sort through similarities and ultimately distinguish between disorders. Skiba and Grizzle (1991) contend that rather

than being illogical, the social maladjustment clause was a legislative "accident of history" (p. 581) that was made in 1975. However, including all children with social maladjustment under the umbrella of special education could significantly increase the costs of providing such services at the federal, state, and local levels. The risk of increased cost ostensibly leads legislators to be reluctant to include those children and adolescents with social maladjustment under federal special education protection.

Definitions of Social Maladjustment

The term *social maladjustment* was introduced to the special-education literature by Samuel Kirk in 1962. In 1975, Congress added social maladjustment to P.L. 94–142 to avoid "opening the floodgates" by providing special education to juvenile delinquents (Skiba & Grizzle, 1991). No substantial changes in the definition of emotional disturbance have been made since 1975. In fact, the most recent reauthorization of IDEIA (2004) again retains social maladjustment as an exclusionary clause when determining if a child is ED. Congress has ruled on this distinction for determining special-education eligibility.

The operational definition of social maladjustment remains elusive. There are several responses to this problem; some ignore the requirement to distinguish ED and SM, others characterize SM as equivalent to meeting the criteria for CD, while others use more arbitrary distinctions in school team decisions. There is general agreement that the context in which the antisocial behavior occurs is also important for the diagnostic distinction between social maladjustment and emotional disturbance. Consider the comparisons reported in the literature (Table 6.1).

Gacono and Hughes (2004) used the personality symptoms associated with psychopathy to define SM, arguing that because both ED and SM children exhibit behavioral problems, the DSM criteria fail to distinguish between them (Bodholdt, Richards, & Gacono, 2000; Loving & Gacono, 2002). On the other hand, personality traits associated with psychopathy have been shown to meaningfully distinguish antisocial groups. Hare's (1993) two-factor model is an empirical model useful for describing traits versus behaviors (Table 6.2). More recent studies have statistically

TABLE 6.1. Comparison of definitions of emotional disturbance and social maladjustment.

Emotional disturbance (Clarizio, 1992b; Costenbader & Buntaine, 1999)	Social maladjustment (Clarizio, 1992a,b; Kelly, 1990)
• Behavior is involuntary or reactive • Disruptive behaviors are emotionally driven • Child feels remorseful • Child is self-critical • Child experiences feelings of inadequacy • Child tends to be anxious and guilt-ridden • Child has few if any friends	• Knows and understands rules and norms, but intentionally breaks and rejects conventions. • Perceives self to be "normal" and able to behave "normally" when needed • Views rule-breaking as acceptable • Misbehavior is motivated by self-gain • Misbehavior does not result in anxiety or remorse unless there is risk of being caught

TABLE 6.2. Hare's (1993) two-factor personality model.

Factor 1 Personality traits	Factor 2 Socially deviant behaviors
• Pathological lying	• Need for stimulation/proneness to boredom
• Grandiose sense of self worth	• Irresponsibility
• Callous/lack of empathy	• Parasitic lifestyle
• Glibness/superficial charm	• Early behavioral problems
• Lack of remorse or guilt shallow affect	• Juvenile delinquency
• Conning/manipulative	• Poor behavioral controls
• Failure to accept responsibility	• Revocation of conditional release
	• Promiscuous sexual behavior
	• Impulsivity
	• Criminal versatility
	• Lack of realistic long-term goals
	• Many short-term relationships

separated the interpersonal and emotional symptoms, but continue to show the basic distinction between traits and behaviors (Neumann, Hare, & Newman, 2007; Neumann, Kosson, Forth, & Hare, 2006).

In forensic or correctional settings, 50% to 80% of individuals may meet the criteria for CD or antisocial personality disorder (ASPD). Of this group of behavior disorders, only 15% to 30% of adult offenders meet the criteria for psychopathy (Hare, 1993; Salekin, Leistico, Neumann, DiCicco, & Duros, 2004). Similarly, the prevalence of psychopathic traits in the young offender population has been estimated at 21% (Salekin et al., 2004). Using both traits and behaviors to define SM enables the school psychologist to identify a much more homogeneous group than would be designated through the DSM diagnosis of CD. Most importantly, these groups show different treatment outcomes that are consistent with the framework of special-education services. For example, researchers report that individuals high on psychopathic traits typically demonstrate a variety of problematic outcomes, including institutional misbehavior, reoffending, violent reoffending, and treatment failure (Gretton, McBride, Hare, O'Shaughnessy, & Kumka, 2001; Hare, 2003) consistent with the SM exclusionary clause. The same prediction should not be assumed for the more heterogeneous CD and ASPD diagnoses (Gacono, 2000). The prognosis for children who meet only the criteria to be diagnosed with CD is likely overly negative (Gacono & Hughes, 2004), and they may benefit from interventions.

For school psychologists working with children with CD, the importance of assessing psychopathy in children and adolescents is twofold. First, elevated psychopathy levels alert professionals to individuals who are at high risk for preying upon others (Rutter et al., 1998), which is a serious concern when children with and without psychopathic features are placed in the same educational category and ultimately the same settings. Mixing these two groups gives access and opportunity for those high on psychopathic traits to exploit children and adolescents with an emotional disturbance. Second, elevated psychopathy levels are associated with disruptive patients for whom more traditional treatment approaches tend to be ineffective (Fisher & Blair, 1998; Samenow, 1998). In fact, traditional treatment approaches may make the socially maladjusted worse (Arnold & Hughes, 1999; Dishion & Andrews, 1995; Dishion, McCord & Poulin, 1999; Hare, 1993; Mager, 2005). Indeed, for children with high psychopathic traits, behavior management strategies within a secure setting, rather than treatment, may be the recommended mode of intervention (Gacono, Nieberding, Owen, Rubel, & Bodholdt, 2001).

Assessment of Conduct Disorder

For school psychologists, training in understanding conduct difficulties is required for adequate assessment and interpretation of the needs for children with CD in the school setting. Without adequate investigation by properly trained professionals, inappropriate treatment for children can result in long-standing negative consequences. For example, for the individual, children receiving inappropriate treatment can have an increase in number, type, and severity of antisocial symptoms (Arnold & Hughes, 1999; Dishion & Andrews, 1995; Dishion et al., 1999; Mager, 2005; Rutter et al., 1998). In addition, some may adopt scripts heard during their treatment to deflect responsibility for their actions. Explaining that neglectful parenting or rowdy peers, for example, are the driving force for their difficulties can keep professionals sufficiently distracted from making true therapeutic gains with such children and adolescents, sometimes for years. At the classroom level, all children with behavior disorders may be placed in the same intervention setting, leaving children with depression and anxiety in close proximity to those with externalizing disorders such as CD, a reality that may be mutually disadvantageous depending on the type of symptoms the child with CD manifests.

Conduct disorders involve a heterogeneous group of behaviors that range in type and severity and ultimately have important implications for treatment. Furthermore, there are a number of causes that lead to the development of CD. Therefore, it is important to keep these factors in mind when selecting the assessment tools and criteria for the individual child. Ultimately, there is a framework that can be followed when assessing CD. However, it is crucial to think of the individual child when assessing and recommending interventions to obtain the most effective therapeutic and educational outcomes.

Assessment Framework

In children, identification of individual and contextual predictors of behavior difficulties is complicated by rapidly changing social, cognitive, and emotional developmental processes. Thus, a coherent classification system for organizing causes of conduct problems for children remains elusive, hindering efforts to prevent and treat antisocial behavior in a prescriptive, research-based manner. However, following a structured protocol for assessment of CD that is flexible enough to allow for individual variations will improve decision making and intervention planning. An adequate assessment battery must be (1) multitheoretical, in which behavior, cognitive, neurobiological, and family systems are evaluated; (2) allow for interpretations of multicausality, so that biological, environmental, psychological, and social influences are maintained by multiple systems (e.g., children, parents, family, school, community) in the environment; and (3) embrace a developmental framework because changes in maturity will influence opportunities for intervention (Conner & Fisher, 1997).

Specific Educational Assessment Practices

Conduct disorder is a severe form of psychopathology that affects multiple domains of the individual's functioning. In 1997, the American Academy of Child and Adolescent Psychiatry (AACAP) provided practice parameters for the assessment and treatment of children and adolescents with CD. This group concluded that mental health interventions for CD must be coordinated, aimed at multiple areas of dysfunction, and delivered over an extended period of time. The first step in accomplishing this goal is an adequate assessment. An extensive list of available assessments are reviewed in Chapter 5, but a recommended assessment battery for a comprehensive intervention strategy is presented in this section.

Special Testing Issues to Obtain Valid Test Scores

It is important to have some understanding of the child being evaluated before any testing and assessment procedures begin. First, begin by conducting a thorough record review, being sure to note patterns in grades, standardized test scores, and discipline referrals. Clarify if the child has had any involvement with the juvenile justice system, including probation and parole documents, lists of charges that are pending or have been dropped, type and number of adjudications, and time served in detention facilities, deterrent programs, drug treatment, and community service. Since deceitfulness (and theft) is one of the four categories of CD symptoms, psychologists need to address this issue during the assessment process. Ultimately, professionals will need to determine if discrepancies documented in the records and those reported by the child (or others) are a result of intentional lying/manipulation and other antisocial processes, drug use, poor cognitive skills (e.g., memory, verbal abilities), poor social relations, or emotional disturbances. Anticipating these discrepancies so that appropriate data can be collected will ultimately improve decision making.

Accessing Juvenile Court Records

In schools, working with parents and legal guardians is the best way to access a child's legal records. Developing a working partnership with caregivers is important for treatment issues; thus, the following is the recommended process for gathering all information regarding legal proceedings. Often, admissions procedures for alternative education programs and other specialty programs (e.g., approved private schools, residential and day treatment) require disclosure of legal records. Schools that have formal relationships with probation departments should establish a written communication procedure so that important information can be legally accessed by qualified school personnel. School psychologists should be aware of their state's regulations regarding public access to juvenile records. Since regulations vary widely, it is important to be well informed regarding the procedures followed by the state; information can be accessed on the web at http://www.rcfp.org/juvcts/index.html.

Behavior Observation

Consistent with all comprehensive evaluation procedures, behavioral observations are essential. Children with CD are a very heterogeneous group, and in addition to the core features of CD, it is not unusual for them to display a range of behavioral symptoms that vary across settings. By using behavioral observations, the evaluator is able to capture the in-situ environmental conditions around the behavior without the explicit request for an informant's perception requested in a rating scale. In children with CD, there are many important behaviors that will not be readily available for observation. However, that which is not observed is also important. That is, observing the context that facilitates the child's behavioral control will also be useful for intervention planning.

Behavior Rating Scales

The behavior rating scale is a time-efficient way of collecting reliable information (Frick, 1998a). This assessment tool allows the psychologist to compare the findings from rating scales obtained from parents, teachers, and children (self-report), allowing the evaluator to achieve an understanding of the severity of CD in relation to the normative group. Rating scales provide an assessment of the child's emotional and behavioral functioning as well as the contextual factor that could be contributing to the CD.

The Behavior Assessment Scale for Children, 2nd edition (BASC-2; Reynolds & Kamphaus, 2004) and the Minnesota Multiphasic Personality Inventory adolescent version (MMPI-A; Butcher et al., 1992) are particularly useful for assessment of CD. First, both tests offer validity scales that provide information about the respondents approach to the test (e.g., overreporting, underreporting, and inconsistent reporting). Often children with externalizing disorders underestimate the severity of the difficulties experienced. Thus, being able to measure and compare symptom reports across informants is important for decision making. Interestingly, it is not only children who tend to embellish descriptions of their behaviors; frustrated adults (e.g., parents and teachers) may also complete protocols in which the validity of the information is compromised. The validity scales also provide context to elevations in the clinical scales. Second, both are broad-band scales that provide a consideration of clinical difficulties alongside of conduct problems. If a child endorses attention difficulties, a symptom that often occurs with CD, these tests aggregate the other relevant data to determine the nature of the attention problem. This helps to clarify not only the presence of CD, but also comorbid disorders and possible alternate primary diagnosis that are sometimes confused with CD because of their complicated presentation (AACAP, 1997).

Although behavior rating scales are an effective measure of CD, they provide only a retrospective assessment of a child's behavior; therefore, it is recommended to complement this tool with direct behavior observation. Further, because it is inappropriate to use only a behavior rating scale to determine diagnosis or make adequate decisions for intervention (Myers & Winters, 2002), these measures must be accompanied by a comprehensive battery.

Structured Interviews

Another useful assessment tool is the structured and semistructured interview. Semistructured interviews allow professionals to gather relevant developmental and family histories. Clinical interviews also may assist professionals in determining the duration and age of onset of behavior problems. These interviews can help shed light on the developmental progression and the degree of impairment with regard to the child's CD (Frick, 1998b). Again, as with the behavioral rating scales, clinical interviews provide a detailed description of the child or adolescent's emotional and behavioral functioning through the interviewing of multiple informants. Due to potential social perception deficits, oppositionality toward the assessment process, and other characteristic behaviors of CD that may lead to suspect responses, it is best practice to also interview the parents and teachers, in addition to the child. Clinical interviews are typically updated to adapt to the changes made in the DSM system (Frick, 1998b). One commonly used interview form is the Diagnostic Interview Schedule for Children (DISC), 4th edition, that also is available in a computerized version that eliminates the need for a trained interviewers to administer it. Another useful tool is the Problem Guidesheet (Forehand & McMahon, 1981), an interview format guide that helps professionals structure the questions to obtain specific information on the duration, frequency, and parent or child responses to the problem behaviors.

Performance-Based Measures

Performance-based measures are problem-solving perceptual-association tasks in which structured responses are not provided. In contrast to self-report, in which responses are based on how respondents see themselves or how they like to be seen by others, performance-based measures can provide the assessment of affect, behavior, or skill in situ, and predict spontaneous choices and responses in the absence of external prompts (McClelland, Koestner, & Weinberger, 1989). The Rorschach Inkblot Method (RIM) has standardized administration and reliable scoring procedures with favorable psychometric properties (Society for Personality Assessment, 2005) that allows the examiner to observe how children conceptualize and approach their environment and provides an opportunity to see where their processing breaks down (Hughes, Gacono, & Owen, 2007). Performance-based measures are typically used to provide a contextualized perspective to observed and reported behaviors.

Specific Domains to Clarify the Nature of Conduct Disorder

While determining if a child or adolescent with CD meets the criteria for special-education eligibility criteria as a child with ED, or is more appropriately classified as SM may be an important first step in decision making. Such eligibility decisions, however, do little to describe a person's strengths and weakness, which is needed for coordinated comprehensive intervention planning. This section highlights the areas that may be relevant for the children with CD.

Biological Risk and Development

As discussed in Chapters 4, biological risk factors are important considerations for violent and aggressive behaviors that are associated with CD (Meloy, 2000). In providing a comprehensive assessment of CD, examiners need to determine the children's in utero exposure to toxins or birth trauma, history of central nervous system (CNS) abnormalities (e.g., head trauma, seizures), and temperament. This can be accomplished by using a semistructured developmental interview.

Trauma

Sexual and physical abuse, neglect, and witnessing of violence needs to be documented as a part of the comprehensive assessment process. Also, determining the presence of acute stress disorders and posttraumatic stress disorder (PTSD) are important. Examiners need to understand the extent to which chaotic or violent family factors (e.g., domestic violence, poverty) and neighborhoods (e.g., drug and gang activity) are contributing to or maintaining the children's behavior (Connor, 2002). This can be accomplished in the developmental and clinical interviews.

Socialization Skills

To assess social functioning, school psychologists need to determine the quality of family and peer relationships, and the individual's capacity for empathy. Schema-related biases in appraising social situations are reported to contribute to the interpersonal difficulties of children (Dodge & Tomlin, 1987; Shirk & Russell, 1996). This can be accomplished by interview, a rating scale, or a performance-based measure.

Cognitive Skills

Cognitive skill assessment includes determining if there are comorbid learning disabilities, attention problems, hyperactivity problems, memory problems, poor academic progress, or the content of biased cognitions such as violent fantasies and disordered thinking. Because children with CD often show a significant difference in their verbal and spatial reasoning skills (Connor, 2002; Meloy, 2000), this portion of the assessment may be helpful in determining the best method for delivering instruction and will have implications for teaching prosocial problem-solving skills in therapeutic interventions. In addition to the cognitive abilities tests (e.g., Wechsler Intelligence Scale for Children, 4th edition [WISC-IV]; Woodcock-Johnson Intelligence Battery, 3rd edition [WJ-III]; Stanford-Binet Intelligence Scale, 5th edition [SB-V]; and Differential Ability Scales-Second Edition [DAS-II]), it is also recommended that memory skills be assessed to help in planning intervention strategies. Neuropsychological tests such as the Connor Continuous Performance Tests (CPT) can clarify the presence of attention problems along with behavior ratings and observations. Performance measures may provide further insights to help understand disordered thinking, including the nature of the cognitive distortion (e.g., input, mediation, ideation). Additionally, interviews can clarify the presence and nature of violent fantasies.

There is emerging evidence in the contemporary neuroscience literature (e.g., Luna, 2005, 2007) that the adolescent brain does not function like an adult brain. Instead, although the brain functioning of adolescents can resemble that of an adult, it is at the cost of inefficient processing that can break down and result in lapses in judgment and behavior control. These preliminary findings may have important implications for understanding antisocial behaviors in children. Already, issues of culpability are being raised in legal settings, and professionals treating children with CD are consequently following this research closely.

Emotional Skills

The nature of the child's or adolescent's emotion regulation skills also needs to be clarified. Children with CD can have difficulties in the identification, expression, and regulation of emotion. Conversely, as discussed earlier, socially maladjusted youngsters may not evidence difficulty in controlling their emotions. In fact, the SM group may appear emotionally cool and unresponsive to emotionally charged situations (Gacono & Hughes, 2004).

Measuring a child's problematic emotional functioning can be accomplished through behavior rating scales such as the BASC-2 and contextualize with performance-based measures. Often, it is important to examine affective expression in the family. One common rating scale is the Global Family Environment Scale (GFES; Moos et al., 1974), in which the adequacy of emotional expression in the family environment can be assessed (Frick, 1998a; Rey et al., 2000).

Aggression

At times, it is useful to determine the type of aggression (overt–covert, predatory–reactive, socialized–solitary, physical–verbal, self–others) in which children are engaging. Typically, this information is available through school and legal records, observation, and teacher-, parent-, or self-report. However, there may be occasion for using a rating scale (e.g., the child is new in the school district and records have not been forthcoming). The New York Teacher Rating Scale for Disruptive and Antisocial Behavior was developed in 1995, has adequate psychometric properties, and has been reported as the best teacher rating scale for measuring hostility and aggression (Connor, 2002). Other such instruments have not yet shown adequate empirical support.

Psychopathy

Children are not labeled as psychopaths. Rather, psychopathic traits that are reported in children are used for description of the level of disturbance (more or less) to inform decision making. As detailed above, the recent focus in schools on the diagnosis of emotional disturbance and its exclusion of social maladjustment (conduct-related behaviors) has prompted the evaluation of psychopathic traits to make meaningful distinctions between these groups, which both exhibit antisocial behaviors.

While the adult literature has extensive empirical support for the construct of psychopathy, similar research with children has been conducted only in the last decade, with limited use in schools (Gacono & Hughes, 2004). The most commonly used instrument is the Psychopathy Checklist–Youth Version (PCL:YV), which has adequate psychometric properties and empirical support for its use, and is matched to the psychopathy construct in adults. However, it is important to note that this 20-item interview requires thorough record review to score the items.

Other assessment instruments include the Antisocial Process Screening Device (APSD; Frick & Hare, 2001), and Childhood Psychopathy Scale (CPS; Lynam, 1997), which use a hallmark of psychopathy (callous and unemotional traits), rather than the total construct of CD, as rated by teachers or parents. Empirical support for these tests is developing. In a recent study, Morris (2007) demonstrated that children in alternative school placements who scored high on the callous/unemotional trait did not expect tangible rewards, punishment, or to alter aversive treatment by their behaviors. Interestingly, they reported that when punishment, reward, or opportunity to decrease aversive treatment was imminent, however, they did care about the consequences. Thus, when teams are designing behavioral programs, the type and timing of reinforcement may be particularly important for children with these traits.

Developmental Level

As detailed in Chapter 4, it is important when assessing children and adolescents with CD to keep in mind their developmental level. This includes both the type of assessments that the examiner utilizes to determine the diagnosis of CD, as well as framing results in the context of age-appropriate tasks for intervention planning. The unique skills that the school psychologist brings to school teams are (1) knowledge of the various theoretical and empirical foundations of human development including pathogenic processes resulting in psychopathology and in this case CD, (2) how to select measures (in a variety of formats) to help clarify the importance of specific issues for the child, and (3) the ability to match theoretical information with the empirical literature to inform intervention strategies in the school setting.

Assessment batteries must be selected to be appropriate for the child's current level of development, including cognitive, social, and emotional domains. Conduct disorder may be difficult to diagnose in very young children who may exhibit antisocial behaviors because of their immature development of cognitive and social understanding. In addition, some behaviors may not be recognized as antisocial until they are seen to be age-inappropriate. For example, the truancy behavior of a child in elementary school may be documented only as "absence" but in middle school may be documented as "truancy." Loeber (1990) notes that manifestations of behavior problems are often dependent on age and a child's behaviors, and are therefore reflective of the developing ability to display different behaviors.

In addition to test selection, typical developmental tasks need to be included in the context of test interpretation. For example, the type and quality of peer relationships should be considered in the assessment process for adolescents exhibiting behaviors of CD. In the recent past, high-profile cases (e.g., Columbine, Colorado; Jonesboro, Arkansas; Pearl, Mississippi) of violence committed on school property showed that these children acted with accomplices or co-conspirators. These behaviors are in sharp contrast to adult crimes of mass homicide in which it is very rare for adults to involve accomplices, co-conspirators, or a second perpetrator (Meloy, Hempel, Mohandie, Shiva & Gray, 2001). Meloy and colleagues (2001) concluded that developmental issues regarding a sense of belonging to a social group may have accounted for these differences. Further, needs for belonging may elevate risk for acting aggressively (Monhandie, 2000).

Because there are an abundance of violent role models in the media (e.g., Internet, television, video games) as well as an availability of weapons (e.g., guns), children who are dealing with the developmental tasks of coping with increased or irregular emotional, social, and cognitive skills may be well equipped to commit violent acts. Thus, the importance of development should not be over looked.

Evaluation Parameters and Organizers

In choosing an optimal assessment tool, it has been concluded in the relevant source literature that there is no one method that can fully capture all the necessary elements for the assessment of CD (McConaughy, 2005). Thus, to gain a comprehensive view of the child's or adolescent's level of impairment, multiple methods that offer multitheoretical contributions to this multidetermined disorder should be taken, including the assessment domains stated above; biological risk and development; trauma; social, cognitive, and emotional skills; as well as type of aggression and psychopathy. Each of these areas can be assessed in various formats, such as behavioral observations, behavior rating scales, clinical interviews, and performance-based measures. These options should be carefully selected by the examiner, keeping the individual's developmental level and cognitive capacity in mind. In the case of ED and SM, treatment tailored to the individual's needs is required for an improved outcome. Thus, organizational strategies to ensure informed decision making regarding placement and intervention strategies are essential.

Multimodal Functional Behavioral Assessment

Multimodal functional behavioral assessment (MFBA), as described by Miller, Tansy, and Hughes (1998), is an assessment procedure that considers the multiple contributions of the causes of children's disruptive behavior. The MFBA process gathers the data outlined in the AACAP parameters and considers the impact of each variable for the purpose of developing a comprehensive behavior intervention plan (BIP). Miller, Williams, and McCoy (2004) used MFBA to differentiate the causal factors that drive behaviors for children with ED and SM. Multimodal functional behavioral assessment is also school-friendly, as it meets the requirements for conducting a functional analysis to determine the cause of behaviors that are not adequately treated by current behavior plans and IEP goals (Miller & Leffard, 2007). Figures 6.1 and 6.2 provide materials to facilitate the MFBA process (additional information and materials can be accessed via the web at http://www.mfba.net).

Considerations for Evaluation Reports

Many school districts have required formats for evaluation reports, while others accept best practice formats that cover the relevant information required for decision making. Certainly, the primary requirement for an evaluation report is to answer the referral question (usually regarding an eligibility decision). In addition, data in the report should allow for generation of hypotheses about the cause and nature of the problem, provide information about baseline and preintervention functioning, recommend a specific course of action, and create a legal document or record of the assessment for future use (Ownby, 1997; Sattler, 2001). In the case of CD,

Child Name: _____   ID: ___   DOB: ___

Case Manager: ___

Data Sources: ❑ Observation | ❑ Child Interview | ❑ Teacher Interview | ❑ Parent Interview | ❑ Rating Scales | ❑ Normative Testing

Description of Behavior (No. ___):

Setting(s) in which behavior occurs:

Frequency:

Intensity (consequences of problem behavior on child, peers, instructional environment):

Duration:

Describe previous interventions:

Educational impact:

Function of behavior (No. ___): Specify hypothesized function for each area checked below.

❑ Affective regulation/emotional reactivity (identify emotional factors; anxiety, depression, anger, poor self-concept; that play a role in organizing or directing problem behavior):

❑ Cognitive distortion (identify distorted thoughts; inaccurate attributions, negative self-statements, erroneous interpretations of events; that play a role in organizing or directing problem behavior):

❑ Reinforcement (identify environmental triggers and payoffs that play a role in organizing and directing problem behavior):

Antecedents:

Consequences:

❑ Modeling (dentify the degree to which the behavior is copied, who the child is copying the behavior from, and why the child is copying the behavior):

❑ Family issues (identify family issues that play a part in organizing and directing problem behavior):

❑ Physiological/constitutional (identify physiological and/or personality characteristics; developmental disabilities, temperament; that play a part in organizing and directing problem behavior):

❑ Communicate need (identify what the child is trying to say through the problem behavior):

❑ Curriculum/instruction (identify how instruction, curriculum, or educational environment play a part in organizing and directing problem behavior):

FIGURE 6.1.   Functional Behavioral Assessment form.

Child Name: _____   ID: _____   DOB: _____   Case Manager: _____

Behavior Number(s)	Expected Outcome(s) Goal(s)	Intervention(s) and Frequency of Intervention	Person Responsible	Goal/Intervention Review Notes

* Review Codes: GA = Goal Achieved | C = Continue | DC = Discontinue   Expected Review Dates: _____|_____

Signatures: _____

FIGURE 6.2.   Behavior intervention planning materials.

school psychologists may consider adding supplemental data to provide information of relative risk assessment.

Examining relative risks as described by Meloy (2000) and Monhandie (2000) can help inform decisions regarding placement and treatment strategies of children with CD. Table 6.3 describes three categories of symptoms: (1) psychological, (2) social-environmental, and (3) biological. It is valuable to consider whether these factors are dynamic or static. Static variables are not available for interventions, while dynamic factors present opportunity for intervention.

School psychologists may also consider describing variables associated with risk for violent and aggressive behavior. Such reporting should not be intended to replace a formal risk assessment or threat evaluation, but rather to serve as

TABLE 6.3. Three categories of conduct disorder symptoms.

1. Psychological
   a. Male (10:1, for every 10 men, one woman is violent); gender is a static variable
   b. Age (15–24 is high-risk period); age is a static variable
   c. Past history of violent behavior (frequency, recency, severity); note presence of hallmark symptoms (cruelty to animals); past history is a static variable
   d. Paranoia (paranoid schizophrenia, paranoid personality disorder, delusional disorder, stimulant induced paranoid states); paranoia can be static or dynamic
   e. Intelligence (below 90 IQ on average, Verbal–Performance split in delinquents, not correlated with psychopathy); intelligence is static
   f. Anger/fear problems (identification and expressing emotions): anger and fear are dynamic
   g. Psychopathy and other attachment problems
      i. Psychopathy (good predictor of violence)
      ii. Attachment (note: the relationship between attachment and violence is theoretical) Psychopathy and other attachment problems is a static variable

2. Social/environmental
   a. Family of origin, violence in the family, harsh discipline; family of origin violence is static in adults (possibly dynamic in children)
   b. Adolescent peer group violence or peer provocations (encouragement); adolescent peer group violence is dynamic
   c. School environment (inconsistent implementation of policies/discipline, passive responses to bullying); school environment can be static or dynamic
   d. Financial instability or poverty; financial instability or poverty can be static or dynamic
   e. Weapons history, skill, interest, and approach

      i. Weapon History Assessment Method (WHAM: Meloy, 1992); weapons history is static; skill, interest, and approach are dynamic

   f. Victim pool; usually dynamic.
   g. Alcohol or psychostimulant use; dynamic
   h. Popular culture (TV, movie/video game or Web site scenes) interests; a static variable
   3. Biological
   a. History of central nervous system (CNS) trauma; static
   b. Current CNS signs and symptoms; can be either static or dynamic, depending on cause
   c. Objective CNS measures; either static or dynamic
   d. Major mental disorder as defined by the DSM (especially depression & bipolar in children); dynamic

Adapted from Meloy (2000) and Mondandie (2000).

an organizing list to consider when planning for intervention. It is important to note that these variables are not associated with cutoff scores for diagnostic purposes. Rather, they describe areas that provide an opportunity for intervention planning.

Conclusion

It is important to recognize that many children with CD do not go on to become antisocial adults. However, almost all antisocial adults have demonstrated CD symptoms as children (Frick, 1998a). It is essential for all professionals to keep in mind that there are many owpportunities for intervention to be implemented targeting CD to promote prosocial and adaptive coping skills. It is essential that school psychologists be knowledgeable about the strategies and techniques helpful in obtaining valid assessment data. A quality psychoeducational assessment process is the foundation for obtaining information about the various strengths and challenges that will inform instructional and behavioral interventions and objectives. The comprehensive assessment reciprocally considers the child's current needs along with tailored recommended intervention strategies. To assist teams in constructing intervention strategies, it is helpful to describe the developmental lag or deficit, along with what the child can do, the next skill in the developmental sequence, and any related requisite skills, in order to achieve the goal. An example of how to write this information in a psychoeducational evaluation is presented in Table 6.4. Further, school teams should routinely anticipate developmental issues

TABLE 6.4.   Example of information for a psychoeducational evaluation useful for intervention

Report information	Emotional disturbance	Social maladjustment
Describe the developmental lag or deficit	Emotional dysregulation	Callous disregard for others
Describe what the child can do	Can identify and differentiate emotions	Can understand there are two points of view in a situation
Describe the next skill in the developmental sequence	Needs to be able to appropriately express verbally his/her emotion/feeling	Needs to articulate the perspective (cognitively and emotionally) of the experience of others where there is more than one valence, positive and negative (cognitively and emotionally), toward the same person
Describe related requisite skills	Needs to practice perspective-taking, does not differentiate emotions in self versus emotions in others	Needs to practice perspective-taking, does not integrate the experience of others in to decision making
Describe goal	Emotion regulation for behavioral control	Respond to the experience of others to inform behavioral choices

(described above and in Chapter 4), provide prevention techniques when possible, and monitor skills that are developing typically so that these strengths can be utilized in interventions. The context of the school environment provides an opportunity to comprehensively meet these treatment requirements regardless of the child's or adolescent's special-education status. Moreover, the school psychologist is in an excellent position to lead a school-based treatment team when an in-depth evaluation has been conducted.

7
Treatment

As previously discussed in Chapters 1 and 2, conduct disorder (CD) is a behaviorally defined disorder that appears to have multiple etiologic pathways (Patterson & Yoerger, 2002; Pettit et al., 1997; Rutter et al., 1975), thus, a variety of treatment strategies have been developed. Treatment refers to systematic efforts to reduce, eliminate, or alleviate a particular problem or set of problems. Treating children and adolescents who suffer from CD is a difficult task due to the complexity of factors associated with this particular disorder (Frick, 1998a, 2001; Kazdin, 1995). A variety of treatments have been applied to children and adolescents with CD. However, only a small number of treatments have been shown to reduce CD behaviors. Treatment procedures tend to be most effective when the child is young (under 8 years of age) and early in the development of problem behaviors (Frick, 1998a; Kazdin 1996; McMahon & Wells, 1998). In addition, intervention strategies need to include multimodal and multicomponent efforts that are tailored to the needs of the individual (Connor & Fisher, 1997; Kazdin, 1996, 1997; Miller et al., 1998; Shirk & Russell, 1996). The evidence-based recommendations emphasizing prevention, early intervention, and multimodal and multicomponent efforts are consistent with the central tenets of the transactional ecological developmental model (cf., Sameroff, 2000) described in Chapter 2. This is particularly important given professional perspectives regarding etiological influences are inevitably intertwined with the selection of intervention strategies; thus, both should be evidence based.

In a review of effective interventions for children and adolescents with CD, Frick (2001) suggests that one reason for the findings of limited effectiveness of most treatments is likely the failure to directly address the causal mechanisms implicated in the development of CD. Moreover, research has consistently pointed to the failure of single-component treatment interventions (Connor, 2002). Indeed, intervention efforts in schools may commit both errors, focusing on single-component interventions (managing behaviors) targeted only in the education setting. It is important for school psychologists and other educational professionals to consider the importance of comprehensive, coordinated, and sustained intervention strategies that have been recommend by the American Academy of Child and Adolescent Psychiatry (AACAP, 1997) for the treatment of CD (see Appendix 7.1). It is the role of the school psychologist to help school teams understand the complex nature of CD through a comprehensive evaluation as discussed in Chapter 6, to acknowledge and communicate that the most effective treatment program gains remain modest, and to build individualized intervention programs for children diagnosed with CD regardless of special-education placement so that all children can have access to a free and appropriate public education.

This chapter reviews the essential components for establishing school programming for children with CD, including structural and pragmatic issues for treating emotional disturbance (ED) and social maladjustment (SM); presents developmental issues pertinent for selecting intervention strategies; and reviews specific independent psychotherapeutic and pharmacological interventions and multidimensional approaches (e.g., multisystemic therapy and the Families and Schools Together [FAST] Track).

School-Based Intervention Strategies

Treating emotional and behavioral disturbances in a school setting involves more than formulating and administering a treatment protocol. School is an integrated educational experience where academic and socialization practices occur in real time for several hours a day and throughout the course of a school year. For these reasons, it is important to consider the structural and pragmatic issues of teaching and treating children who require specialized delivery of their instruction. Prior to selecting treatment programs, it is important for school psychologists and other education professionals to have a fundamental understanding of how to build effective programs that are comprehensive in scope to meet the needs of all children. Once the structure of the program is built, then intervention strategies required for individual children can be adapted and accommodated within the school setting.

Specialized Programming: Classroom Level

Most children with behavioral disturbances benefit from a structured setting where rules and routines are predictable (Connor, 2002). Instruction (educational and social development) should be intensive (i.e., consistent, systematic and cumulative). Specifically, material should be presented in (1) a consistent manner, entailing teacher-directed preparation for assignments, followed by individual or group work; (2) systematic instructional routines (e.g., direct instruction or skills streaming), applying individual, classroom, and schoolwide behavioral feedback; and (3) a cumulative manner, where lessons (educational and social) are explicitly connected to previous learning experiences. Movies, board games, or other such activities can be used only if they are tied directly to the educational topics at hand. There should be a sufficient number of staff that are adequately trained and intellectually and emotionally stable, so that they can provide objective and frequent feedback for students on their target behaviors. Table 7.1 lists

TABLE 7.1. Considerations for school-based interventions for children with conduct disorder (CD), emotional disturbance (ED), and social maladjustment (SM).

- Structured, intensive, richly staffed environment
- Frequent feedback on target behavior
- Goals include return to the regular educational setting
- Systematic plan
  - Individual
  - Classroom (self-contained and general)
  - Schoolwide
  - Family support/interventions

Important details:

- Separate children with ED from children with SM
- SM children have an identified deficit in inhibiting predatory behavior
- ED children have an identified deficit in resisting predatory behavior

Adapted from Tansy (2007).

important considerations in providing school-based support services for children with CD

It is important to separate and closely monitor ED and SM children, since their proximity can interfere with progress. Another goal to consider at the program level is to prepare the child for success in engaging in schoolwide activities, discussed in the next section.

Specialized Programming: Schoolwide Issues

When an individualized education program (IEP) teams decide that the least restrictive environment where a child can benefit from instruction is a pull-out classroom or alternative placement, skill-building that would allow a student to return to general education activities is a critical component of programming. It is also important to prepare the environment for the child's return. This includes consultation with regular education teachers on a child's skill strengths and weakness as well as providing strategies for educators to be successful with this child. In addition to consultation regarding individual children, schoolwide activities that promote education and tolerance of individuals with disabilities are also important (Table 7.2).

For children with SM, schoolwide incentives include much of what would be helpful for students with ED, with some additions. For example, monitoring activities is critical, including staff training on nonverbal gestures used for communication (e.g., gang signs), the use of interpersonal physical contact to transfer drug and weapon paraphernalia (e.g., handshakes, incidental bumping), and the use of coordinated distraction techniques to gather staff in one area (where there is a fight) so that other students can complete transactions (money, drugs, weapons, etc). When staff members have a comprehensive plan for monitoring (e.g., only

TABLE 7.2. Program considerations for students with ED and SM.

Considerations for ED:

- Remove the ED student for part or all of the educational day and provide skill-building activities
- Prepare the regular education teacher and students for the reintroduction of the student into the classroom (acceptance-building activities)
- Conduct schoolwide tolerance-building activities

Considerations for SM:

- Separate the student for all or part of the day and provide skill-building activities
- Provide direct individual and group skill-building activities coupled with monitoring
- Provide significant structure, clear-cut rules, and limits to reduce "deviancy training" by members of the group
- Prepare the regular classroom teacher and students for the reintroduction of the student into the regular classroom setting (assertion training)
- Prepare the entire campus through schoolwide bully programs.

Adapted from Dishion et al. (1999) and Mager (2005).

one teacher will disperse students in a physical altercation unless aid is requested) and clear lines of communication are established for reporting incidents, a safe environment will be provided for both teachers and students.

Once the classroom environment is safe and there is a clear understanding of how the classroom should work, then teachers and relevant school personnel (e.g., school psychologists, counselors, social workers) can sort through intervention strategies designed to fit their individual setting and children.

Specialized Programming: Comprehensive Strategies

Comprehensive intervention strategies for children with CD (ED and SM) should be (1) student-focused, (2) parent-focused, and (3) school-focused (Sanders, Gooley, & Nicholson, 2000). Student-focused approaches address cognitive and social processes that drive behavior. To meet student needs, teachers and mental health personnel will teach problem solving, and provide interventions to target problem behaviors. The structure of delivering student-focused approaches is provided in Table 7.3, along with some suggested examples. Then, in the next section, specific intervention programs are reviewed.

Because negative affect is a common problem for children with CD, there are several styles of interaction that teachers can use in classrooms focusing on emotional support. Negative affective regulation strategies, as described by Larsen and Prizmic (2004), are outlined in Appendix 7.2.

Parent-focused approaches address social influences in the home that may contribute to the child's behaviors. Mental health providers can train parents to increase positive social interactions so that parents can then teach and model prosocial interactions to their children (Brestan & Eyberg, 1998; Taylor & Biglan, 1998). The structure of delivering parent-focused approaches

TABLE 7.3. Considerations for student-focused intervention strategies for students with CD, ED, and SM.

Student-focused approaches
- Focus: cognitive processes and interpersonal problem-solving skills that underlie social behavior
- Key processes: teach problem-solving skills to child via a step-by-step approach to interpersonal situations
- Interventions: modeling, practice, rehearsal, role play, and direct reinforcement of target behaviors
  - Develop an internal dialogue or private speech that utilizes the processes of identifying prosocial solutions to problems
  - Monitor and reward successive approximation of increasingly complex social situations
- Examples:
  - Anger Coping Program (Lochman & Wells, 1996)
  - Brainpower Program (Hudley & Graham, 1995)
  - Dinosaur School (Webster-Stratton & Hammond, 1997)
  - Peer Coping Skills Training (Prinz, Blechman, & Dumas, 1994)
  - Problem-Solving Skills Training (Kazdin, 1996)
  - Social Relations Program (Lochman et al., 1993)

Adapted from Tansy (2007).

TABLE 7.4. Considerations for parent-focused intervention strategies for students with CD, ED, and SM.

- Focus: interactions in the home, especially those involving coercive exchanges; altering the parental behavior to change the child's behavior; trainer of trainers model; teach the parents to teach the child
- Key processes:
  - Direct training of parents (rather than direct work with the child) to develop prosocial behavior in the child
  - Explicit use of social-learning techniques to influence the child
- Interventions:
  - Modeling
  - Rehearsal
  - Coaching
  - Prompting
  - Feedback
  - Graduated homework assignments
- Examples:
  - Helping the Noncompliant Child Parent Training Program (Forehand & McMahon, 1981).
  - Troubled Families–Problem Children (Webster-Stratton & Hammond, 1994).
  - Triple P-Positive Parenting Program (Sanders, 1999).

Adapted from Tansy (2007).

is provided in Table 7.4, along with some suggested examples. In the next section, specific intervention programs aimed at parents are reviewed.

Teacher-focused interventions address both educator behaviors and curricular issues. Teachers should have direct instruction in balancing general classroom management with the management needs of specific children. Teachers require

TABLE 7.5. Considerations for student-focused intervention strategies for students with CD, ED, and SM.

Teacher/school-based interventions
- Teacher behavior
  - General classroom management (Little & Hudson, 1998)
    - Effective monitoring
    - Good time management (increased time on task, smooth transitions)
    - Contingent responding to specific behaviors (praise and redirection)
    - Clear classroom rules, developed early, posted, and referenced
    - Classwide discipline plan
    - Individual behavior plans
    - Home-school contracts/partnership
  - Curriculum-based interventions
    - Bullying intervention programs
    - Social skills curriculum
    - Problem-solving curriculum
    - Schoolwide programs
  - Resources:
    - Adolescent Curriculum for Communication and Effective Social Skills (ACCESS; Walker & Holmes, 1987)
    - Bullying Intervention Program (Olweus, 1994)
    - Contingencies for Learning Academic and Social Skills (CLASS; Hops & Walker, 1995)
    - First Step to Success (Walker et al., 1988)
    - Group Exercises for Enhancing Social Skills and Self-Esteem (Khalsa, 1996)
    - Improving Social Awareness–Social Problem Solving (Hunter, Elias, & Norris, 2001)
    - The Incredible Years Teacher Training (Webster-Stratton & Reid, 1999)
    - The Prepare Curriculum (Goldstein, 1988)
    - Promoting Alternative Thinking Strategies (PATHS) (Greenberg & Kusche, 1996)
    - Ready-to-Use Social Skills Lessons and Activities for Grades 1–3 (Begun, 1995)
    - Second Step (Grossman et al., 1997)
    - Social Skills Intervention Guide (Elliott & Gresham, 1991)
    - Reprogramming Environmental Contingencies for Effective Social Skills (RECESS; Walker, Hops, & Greenwood, 1993)
    - Teaching Social Skills to Youth (Tierney & Dowd, 2000)

Adapted from Tansy (2007).

access to tailored academic curriculum as well as skill building curriculums. A list of teacher and school-based intervention resources is provided in Table 7.5.

Developmental Considerations

It is essential when designing and implementing a treatment program that the pathogenic developmental pathway be considered along with its inherent multiple causal factors that are unique for each child and family (Shirk & Russell, 1996). It is the developmental causal mechanisms that provide the guide and focus for the decisions to be made regarding interventions and treatment. Further, being able to identify the developmental progression and the variety of causal factors enables a greater understanding of the particular nature and character of the disorder and provides earlier and more effective treatment.

For example, a recent study by Wisniewski (2006) examining a longitudinal sample of 503 males over the course of 10 years from the Pittsburgh Youth Study showed that when considering attention deficit/hyperactivity disorder (AD/HD), academic underachievement (AU), and delinquency, the most common developmental path was AD/HD → AU → delinquency. Interestingly, only two children were delinquent without first experiencing AD/HD or AU. In the vast majority of the cases, delinquency followed AD/HD and AU. Wisniewski (2006) also examined these variables as they are related to school bonding, parent involvement, and achievement motivation, with results showing that bonding, motivation, and parent involvement provide an opportunity to influence the development of delinquency through the developmental pathway at various time periods. For example, parent involvement was important in early childhood and showed a negative relationship with delinquency across time. Low achievement motivation was related to delinquency across the developmental period, highlighting motivation as an important target for sustained intervention. Moreover, this study illuminates the opportunity for different interventions based on the child's developmental history and contextual considerations.

The current *Diagnostic and Statistical Manual of Mental Disorders*, text revision, 4th edition (DSM-IV-TR) differentiates only between childhood and adolescent onset CD (as described in Chapter 5). However, there have been numerous efforts to further subtype among children with CD (Frick, Barry, & Bodin, 2000). As described in Chapter 6, children high on psychopathic traits comprise a subset of the CD population (Gacono & Hughes, 2004). Quay and Peterson (1987) described a group of children and adolescents, termed "undersocialized youths"; Lynam (1996, 1997, 1998) described children who display a combination of hyperactive, impulsive, and inattentive symptoms (HIA) and conduct problems (CP), while Frick (2001) delineates impulsive and callous-unemotional types of CD. Diverse pathways reveal different causal characteristics and progression and will therefore require a different approach to treatment.

According to Frick (2001), when conceptualizing CD from a developmental perspective, there are several considerations when designing and implementing a treatment program. First, consider the multiple causal processes that can be involved in its development. Next, based on the extant developmental research and theory, examine the most likely factors that contribute to the development, maintenance, and exacerbation of problems. Third, coordinate the professionals and multiple community agencies to address the child's needs in an effort to continue a typical developmental sequence. Fourth, acknowledge the importance of development as it directly impacts the selection of interventions. That is, interventions need to match the current developmental skills of the child regardless of where age-mates are functioning.

Consider the following example: although one can teach children to memorize the multiplication tables, they cannot understand multiplication before understanding addition, and they cannot add until they understand the number line (a line in which real numbers are placed in order according to their value). Curiously, this straightforward reasoning is often not applied to children with CD, with many behavioral interventions being selected based on the norms of the age group rather than on the skill of the child. In the case of a disorder in which behaviors are substantially deviant from average, interventions cannot just start with age-appropriate behaviors. Instead, children with CD (and other disorders) need interventions that target deficient prerequisite skills in order to reach developmentally appropriate goals.

Developmental Level and School Policies

Developmentally informed practice is implied in various ways in district policies, but may not be explicitly understood by school personnel. For example, schools do not typically move students into alternative education placements until after the age of 12, with the average age being 15 years (Foley & Pang, 2006). Alternative school is typically a regular education initiative (although some children in special education can be accepted) where at-risk children can be placed due to disruptive behaviors. For children with CD, this placement trend is consistent with developmental theorists who identify when children can be considered culpable for their actions. Inherent in school teams selecting alternative education in contrast to special education is the assumption that the children (and not the disorder) are responsible for their actions, and disciplinary actions are appropriate. As discussed in Chapter 1, this warrants careful consideration to be certain the children are receiving appropriate educational resources to facilitate their learning and to promote their social and cognitive competence.

Culpability and discipline are related to cognitive development. Piaget's theory of cognitive development suggests that children act on their environment to learn. After completing the concrete operational stage around the age of 11 to 12 years, the child is able to carry out actions in thoughts and does not require behaviors for reasoning. Further, the child should be able to effectively deal with hypothetical issues, engage in abstract reasoning, recognize reversibility and reciprocity, as well as master the concept of compensation (one action can cause changes in another) and conservation (Woolfolk, 2004). Vygotsky, who offered an alternative to Piaget's stages of cognitive development, stated that students learn through social interactions and their culture. For Vygotsky, self-directed speech was important. He considered private speech as self-directed regulation and communication with the self, which becomes internalized after about 9 years (Woolfolk, 2004). In either case, both agree that cognitive control is typically adequate by age 12 years. Generally by this age underdeveloped cognitive patterns (e.g., not understanding the impact of one's actions) are no longer a viable explanation for disruptive behaviors, and can result in disciplinary sanctions at school.

Culpability and discipline are related to moral development. Piaget's theory of moral development closely parallels his theory of cognitive development. Once children move from the concrete operational to the formal operational stage, their moral actions can be based on cooperation versus constraint. That is, they can see more than one point of view, can judge individuals' actions by their intentions, find that rules can be altered, can demonstrate mutual respect for authority figures and peers, believe that punishment is associated with restitution or getting even, and no longer confuse misfortune with punishment. After the age of 12 years, children increasingly understand reciprocal actions or getting even for good or bad actions (Woolfolk, 2004).

Kolberg's theory of moral development was strongly influenced by Piaget's work, and while he did not assign age-based stages, he describes the conventional level of moral reasoning as it is typical of adolescents and adults. Adolescents and adults reason in a conventional way, judging the morality of actions by comparing these actions to societal views and expectations, trying to be a good person, and living by the Golden Rule: "Do unto others as one would have done unto you" (Kohlberg, 1973). The intentions of actions play a more significant role in reasoning at this stage. Both Piaget and Kohlberg agree that moral control is adequate by around age 12 years.

Culpability and discipline are related to emotional development. Lane and Schwartz (1998) present a model of emotional awareness that includes comparisons to Piaget's stages. Emotions at the formal operational stages allow for experiencing nuances in affect, rich expression of emotional material, and recognition of self and others in affect. Specifically, by the age of 12 years, children demonstrate adequate levels of emotional control, and can experience both positive and negative valance emotions toward the same person, which is similar to the emotional processing of adults. To accomplish this task, a child needs multiple representations of the person (both positive and negative) as well as the cognitive skills to coordinate those ideas in response to the relevant situation at hand. Children who are from primarily negative environments can have difficulty accessing role models in a variety of representations (Shirk & Russell, 1996). Coordinating experience, expression, and differentiation of emotion are the requisite skills needed for emotion regulation.

Culpability and discipline are related to developmental skills. Considering the above discussion, it appears evident why alternative settings are typically only considered after the child reaches the age of 12 years. Alternative regular education initiatives assume culpability and assign discipline sensitive to the child's developmental skill, and are often considered as appropriate placements with children with disruptive behavior disorders, such as CD.

Interventions to Promote Prosocial Skills

Given the heterogeneity of age of onset, symptom variation, and risk factors associated with CD, treatment teams require many options for crafting an effective treatment plan. It is important to understand the underlying theoretical assumptions and treatment techniques so that there is an appropriate match among the child's difficulty, the treatment strategies, and the expected outcome (Reschly & Ysseldyke, 1995). This section reviews the individual therapeutic counseling and pharmacotherapy strategies that may be considered within the school programming for an individual child, along with combined multidimensional strategies.

Contingency Management Programs

Contingency management programs (CMPs) are structured behavior management systems whereby children are assisted to overcome deficiencies in their previous social behaviors resulting from socialization and developmental history. Such programs are based on the assumption that inappropriate feedback from the environment leads to poor psychological and behavioral adjustment. Specifically, families that have not been consistent or contingent in their environment greatly undermine a child's ability to modulate behaviors such as delaying gratification or conforming to parental or societal expectations. Researchers have also determined that children's temperamental vulnerability may render them more susceptible to a noncontingent environment. For example, a child's determination to acquire an iPod may lead to stealing it with little or no regard for the negative consequences of getting arrested or for it being a loss for someone else.

Contingency management systems involve four factors: (1) clearly defining behavioral goals, especially in the areas of concern; (2) developing a monitoring system that determines whether children are reaching their goals; (3) developing a system that reinforces the appropriate steps to reaching goals; and (4) providing consequences for inappropriate behavior.

Although CMP has been effective in altering undesirable behaviors at home, school, and in residential treatment centers, there are some disadvantages. Poor choices in determining goals, reinforcers, and punishments are likely to inhibit a child's motivation. Some goals are difficult to monitor, and thus it is difficult to determine whether the child is achieving them, hence the importance of providing a clear operational definition of behaviors to be monitored. Another concern is when punishment for negative behaviors is utilized (Rutter, Giller, & Hagell, 1998), rather than praise or rewards for positive modifications of behavior.

Parent Management Training

Parent management training (PMT) programs have been the single most effective treatment approach for CD, in which two thirds of young children treated have had clinically significant and sustained improvements (Brestan & Eyberg, 1998; Taylor & Biglan, 1998). Based on social learning theory, these programs assume that coercive parent–child interactions result in conduct problems. The purpose and focus of PMT according to Frick (2001) is to teach parents how to develop and implement structured contingency management plans in the home. There are four main areas of focus: (1) improving parent–child interactions, which includes more parental involvement in child's activities, improving parent–child interactions, and increasing parental warmth and responsiveness; (2) promoting prosocial behaviors by learning how to time and present requests, explicit rules, and expectations; (3) improving parents' ability to monitor and supervise their children; and

(4) teaching various discipline techniques, particularly low power-assertive types, and how to be consistent in enforcing them. Parent management training encourages the participation of both parents in addition to providing long-term follow-up sessions where interventions are reviewed and modified as needed (Frick, 1998a). Further, these programs are among the most researched intervention strategies for CD, where outcomes have been studied with children of varying ages and degrees of severity of dysfunction (Kazdin, 1997). The PMT method appears to be more effective for childhood-onset CD (Tynan, 2001).

Functional Family Therapy

Functional family therapy (FFT) appears to be more successful in treating adolescent–onset CD (Frick, 2001). It identifies how parental issues are influencing the family system and provides guidance as to how to enhance positive parental engagement within the family system. This approach has been effective when parents have had problems with substance abuse, marital conflict, parental depression, or lack of social support. There are a wide variety of FFT treatment manuals that focus on different age groups as well as specific needs (e.g., children with CD and comorbid AD/HD). In this way FFT, may be adapted in method and intensity to the needs of the individual family.

Despite the success of parent training, there are some limitations. Even when parents' efforts result in children changing their behavior at home, there is evidence to suggest that such modifications do not always translate to their behavior at school. Additionally, some parents cannot, or will not, participate in training because of work conflicts, life stress, personal psychopathology, or limited motivation. Lastly, interpersonal and family issues may result in inconsistent implementation or maintenance strategies (Webster-Stratton et al., 2001). Thus, parent involvement in intervention strategies is both important and complex.

Cognitive Problem-Solving Skills Training

Cognitive problem-solving skills training (CPST) is a behavioral approach that addresses deficits in social cognition and social problem solving in children with CD. This approach assumes that children who display problematic social skills do so to secure rewards from the environment. Research has consistently shown that, as a group, aggressive children have deficits in processing social information. Specifically, they demonstrate errors in accurately perceiving social cues and developing social goals, as well as deciding upon and enacting appropriate responses. In CPST, children take a step-by-step approach to solve interpersonal problems. These steps include (1) recognizing problem situations, (2) the use of self-statements to reduce impulsive behaviors, (3) generating multiple solutions to problems, (4) evaluating possible consequences to actions, and (5) taking the perspective of others (Frick, 1998a, 2001). Although the key features of CPST make this type of treatment a promising approach, there are several limitations (Kazdin, 1997). First, the child's cognitive development appears to influence treatment successes. Specifically, the more cognitively sophisticated children are, the better able they are to benefit from CPST (Kazdin, 1997). Also, there are better outcomes for children with fewer and less severe symptoms who remain in treatment over an extended period. Even with some progress, often children do not use the CPST skills outside of the group or fail to sustain treatment gains over an extended period of time (Frick, 1998b, 2001). However, when social skills training, problem solving and anger management strategies for children are combined with PMT, conduct problems have been demonstrated to be effectively reduced, and positive peer relations have been promoted (Webster-Stratton et al., 2001).

Group Therapy

Carlin (1996) advocates group therapy with teenagers who exhibit CD to capitalize on the importance of peer influences, with therapeutic groups being effective in positively influencing behavior and facilitating and altering the perceptions of oneself and others. This type of therapy relies on access to positive peer role models. Tynan (2001) has found that for children under 12 years, group therapy is effective in the development of social skills and problem solving, especially when combined with their parents' attending PMT programs. However, he cautions that evidence shows that group therapy for adolescents can actually worsen their behavior, particularly if they engage in discussions regarding oppositional or illegal behavior.

Psychopharmacologic Interventions

Since the causes of CD are multifaceted and partly determined by biological influences, medications aimed at treating aggression may be considered as adjunctive strategies to psychoeducational interventions. However, medications for children are controversial and require careful evaluation for successful treatments. One approach to treating aggression is to use medications that target a symptom (irritability) that could occur across many disorders. The second approach is to consider medications that target a disorder (psychosis) that is responsive to medication to alleviate the underlying causes of aggression (Connor, 2002). In either method, CD is not a direct target for pharmacological intervention. Determining the type of aggressive symptom an child presents is relevant for determining which medications may be appropriate. For example, predatory aggression (associated with psychopathy) does not appear to be responsive to biological interventions (Eichelman, 1988). Thus, medications are used only with a coordinated multidisciplinary evaluation and as adjunctive to psychoeducational treatment plans (Connor, 2002).

Stimulants (e.g., methylphenidate) have been shown to effectively treat both overt and covert aggression occurring in the context of disruptive behavior disorders (AD/HD, CD, oppositional defiant disorder [ODD]) in children (Hindshaw et al., 1992). Tynan (2001) suggests that methylphenidate should be the choice for the treatment of aggression followed by anticonvulsants (nonspecific aggression), lithium, and clonidine.

Anticonvulsant (valproate) research is still developing. Initial results suggest that anticonvulsants are useful for treating rage and temper outbursts in children (Donovan et al., 2000). These results were found in children with CD or ODD.

Lithium trails have produced mixed results for treating aggression. There is some evidence that reactive explosive aggression is more responsive to lithium (Campbell et al., 1995). However, young children (ages 5 to 12) show more side effects than adolescents, and long-term effects have not yet been documented.

Clonidine is an antihypertensive that has been used to treat overarousal in children. Initial findings suggest that aggression associated with disruptive behavior disorders has been responsive to clonidine (Connor, Barkley, & Davis, 2000; Kemph, DeVane, Levin, Jarecke, & Miller, 1993), although medication trials are still in the early stages.

Neuroleptics (e.g., chlorpromazine, haloperidol) and atypical antipsychotics (e.g., clozapine, risperidone) have been used as an adjunctive treatment for CD in severe chronic and refractory impulsive aggression (Toren, Laor, & Weisman, 1998), overt aggression (Findling et al., 2000), nonspecific severe aggression of the emotionally disturbed (Connor, Ozbayrak, Harrison, & Melloni, 1998), and maladaptive aggression in autism, pervasive developmental disorders, and mental retardation (Buitelaar, 2000). There is evidence in the literature that these medications are effective for treating aggression in children (Connor, 2002). It is unclear, however, if these drugs treat aggression in particular, or if many behaviors are suppressed, including aggression. In addition, these medications have many side effects that may outweigh their usefulness.

Multidimensional Interventions

Multisystemic Therapy

Multisystemic therapy (MST) is geared primarily toward older children and adolescents (Frick, 1998b), where a family-systems–based approach is taken because the child is believed to be embedded problematically in a number of systems, including the family, peers, school, and neighborhood (Frick, 1998b, 2001; Kazdin, 1997), that both interact with one another and affect the child. Multisystemic therapy emphasizes a comprehensive and individualized approach that addresses the many factors that contribute to the development of the child's disorder. For instance, MST considers the individual circumstances and severity of the disorder to indicate the need for individual, family or marital therapy, school interventions (e.g., parent–teacher communication, CBST, classroom behavior management), peer support in the community (Boy Scouts and Girl Scouts or athletic teams) that are developmentally informed (Frick, 2001). Multisystemic therapy assumes several principles: (1) the identified problems are understood within the greater systemic context; (2) therapeutic contacts emphasize positive or strength-oriented levers for change; (3) responsible behavior is promoted among family members; (4) interventions are present-focused and action-oriented, targeting specific and well-defined problems; (5) interventions target sequences of behavior within and among multiple systems; (6) interventions are developmentally appropriate; (7) interventions are designed to require daily or weekly effort by family members; (8) intervention effectiveness must be evaluated continuously from multiple perspectives; and (9) interventions are designed to promote maintenance of the therapeutic change by empowering caregivers. Although MST is a time-limited intervention, there is adequate duration (3 to 5 months) to address chronic issues. Multisystemic therapy also requires a therapist who determines how these principles will be implemented, and to closely monitor the progress throughout the intervention to ensure the principles are being followed. Since MST is designed to be community-based, in which the services are provided in the family's environment and the intervention is under the close direction of a professional, the program is well suited for evaluating treatment-outcome findings. Several outcome studies have shown MST to be effective in reducing delinquency and emotional and behavioral problems, even in severely disturbed children, and also improve family functioning (Henggeler, Schoenwald, Borduin, Rowland, & Cunningham, 1998).

Families and Schools Together (FAST Track)

The FAST Track program is designed for the early intervention of children who demonstrate conduct problems at school entry, providing continuous and intensive interventions to prevent the escalation of behaviors. This is a community-based intervention in which much of the intervention takes place at the school. However, a designated case manager implements an intensive treatment plan that is closely monitored over long periods of time with frequent interactions with the family. Typical interventions include PMT for the parents, CBST, academic tutoring for the child, and developing communication between family and school. The case manager may also help the family with practical problems, such as gaining support from their local community and neighborhood agencies to improve family stability. Although the long-term effectiveness of FAST Track is not yet known, initial results suggest that children show increased social skills, greater social capabilities, and thus better peer relations and academic achievement after participating in the program (Bierman et al., 1999). Additionally, parents were found to be warmer and more positive with their children and demonstrated more consistent and appropriate methods of discipline. Although FAST Track intervenes at the earliest sign of problems, there are concerns that the interventions are not flexible enough to be appropriately individualized. At present, case management and tutoring create the most flexibility (Frick, 2001).

Summary of Evidence-Based Interventions

In selecting adequate treatment in schools for the child or adolescent with CD, there must be sufficient structure and programming that allow for a multimodal intervention addressing child, parent, and teacher needs (Conner & Fisher, 1997; Kazdin, 1996, 1997; Miller et al., 1998; Shirk & Russell, 1996). The individual child's plan should follow a comprehensive assessment that allows for the selection of developmentally informed intervention strategies matched to the pathogenic development of the disorder. Within an appropriate educational environment designed to meet the needs of children with CD who are either ED or SM or both, children can be provided support services through strategically selected interventions that are tailored to individual needs, be able to practice the skills learned, participate in systematic monitoring, and receive constructive feedback. Intervention impact should be measured through the diminishment in the number and severity of CD symptoms, increase in prosocial behaviors, and progression in emotional, social, and cognitive functioning along the developmental path. Although most intervention outcomes for CD are modest (Connor, 2002), detailed progress monitoring will facilitate the modification of interventions in the areas that show limited improvements (Miller et al., 1998). Moreover, the more that schools work along with families, the greater the opportunity to positively affect the functioning of children with CD.

The preponderance of the evidence suggests treatment for CD is complex, requiring long-term coordinated multimodal strategies (AACAP, 1999; Connor, 2002). Multisystemic therapy, FFT, and the FAST Track program have empirical support for their integrated programs. Positive parent participation is a critical component that should be incorporated into the treatment program (Frick, 1998a, 2001). When children with CD are separated into ED and SM categories, the benefits of group therapy may be especially useful with younger children with ED to learn real-life interactions. As detailed in Chapter 6, traditional group therapies should be used with caution for children with SM (Arnold & Hughes, 1999; Dishion & Andrews, 1995; Dishion et al., 1999; Hare, 1993; Mager, 2005).

In terms of pharmacological interventions, research suggests that medication may be appropriate when used in the context of a comprehensive psychoeducational evaluation (Connor, 2002). There are several options for use with children and adolescents with CD; however, results show that medication is most effective when CD is comorbid with AD/HD (Frick, 2001; Tynan, 2001). As with medication for any problem, this option should be considered with caution and effects need to be monitored in both the school and home setting.

Conclusion

Conduct disorder is a complex disorder with various etiologies. There are many risk factors that can lead to CD and high rates of comorbid conditions (e.g., AD/HD), complicating the behavioral presentation. In children, identification of individual and contextual predictors of CD is difficult due to the rapidly changing social, cognitive, and emotional developmental processes. Thus, comprehensive assessment is a demanding and daunting task. However, there are adequate assessment instruments to inform decision making regarding diagnosis, special education eligibility, and treatment planning. Also, there are effective school program structures that allow for implementation of multimodal treatments that may also be tailored to the individual while incorporating interventions to meet parent and teacher needs. Moreover, children with CD are a difficult population to treat, requiring the services of highly trained school personnel rather than paraprofessionals primarily focused on containment and crisis management. These children can learn and for that they need access to trained regular, alternative, special-education teachers, and mental health support services professionals. With the support of school psychologists, counselors, social workers, and administration, educators collectively can effect positive change for many children with CD.

Appendix 7.1. American Academy of Child and Adolescent Psychiatry, Recommendations for the Treatment of Conduct Disorder

Treatment should be provided in a continuum of care that allows flexible application of modalities by a cohesive treatment team. Outpatient treatment of CD includes intervention in the family, school, and peer group. The predominance of externalizing symptoms in multiple domains of functioning call for interpersonal psychoeducational modalities rather than an exclusive emphasis on intrapsychic and psychopharmacological approaches. As a chronic condition, CD requires extensive treatment and long-term follow-up. Mild CD, as seen in private practice, might respond to minor intervention, for example, consultation with parents and schools. Patients with severe CD are likely to have comorbidities (consider entries D.1 to D.15, below) that require treatment.

A. Treat comorbid disorders (e.g., AD/HD, specific developmental disabilities, intermittent explosive disorder, affective or bipolar disorder, anxiety disorder, and substance use disorder).
B. Family interventions include parent guidance, training, and family therapy.
 1. Identify and work with parental strengths.
 2. Train parents to establish consistent positive and negative consequences and well-defined expectations and rules. Work to eliminate harsh, excessively permissive, and inconsistent behavior management practices.
 3. Arrange for treatment of parental psychopathology (i.e., substance abuse).
C. Individual and group psychotherapy with adolescent or child: The technique of intervention (supportive versus explorative; cognitive versus behavioral) depends on patient's age, processing style, and ability to engage in treatment. Usually a combination of behavioral and explorative approaches is indicated, especially when there are internalizing and externalizing comorbidities.

D. Psychosocial skill-building training should supplement therapy.
E. Other psychosocial interventions should be considered as indicated.
  1. Peer intervention to discourage deviant peer association and promote a socially appropriate peer network.
  2. School intervention for appropriate placement, to promote an alliance between parents and school, and to promote prosocial peer group contact. Vocational training may be useful.
  3. Juvenile justice system intervention, including court supervision and limit-setting, as well as special programs when available.
  4. Social services referral, to help the family access benefits and service providers, e.g., case managers.
  5. Other community resources, such as Big Brother and Big Sister programs, Friends Outside, and Planned Parenthood as indicated.
  6. Out-of-home placement (crisis shelters, group homes, residential treatment) when indicated.
  7. Job and independent-living skills training.
F. Psychopharmacology
  1. Medications are recommended only for treatment of target symptoms and comorbid disorders, and are recommended only on the basis of clinical experience, which shows them to be efficacious in some patients. Adequate efficacy studies are lacking in patients with CD and comorbidity (e.g., stimulants for AD/HD, antidepressants for mood and anxiety disorders, low dose major tranquilizers for paranoid ideation with aggression, anticonvulsants for partial complex seizure disorder).
  2. Antidepressants, lithium carbonate, carbamazepine, and propranolol are currently used clinically for CD, but rigorous scientific studies to demonstrate their efficacy have not been performed.
  3. The risks of neuroleptics may outweigh their usefulness in the treatment of aggression in CD and require careful consideration before use.
G. Level-of-care decision making
  1. There is significant agreement on criteria for hospitalization of patients with CD (Lock & Strauss, 1994), but level of care decision making continues to be complex and unsupported by empirical data. The psychiatric professional should choose the least restrictive level of intervention that fulfills both the short- and long-term needs of the patient. Imminent risk to self or others, such as suicidal, self-injurious, homicidal, or aggressive behavior, and imminent deterioration in medical status remain clear indications of the need for hospitalization.
  2. Inpatient, partial-hospitalization, and residential treatment should include the following:
    a. Therapeutic milieu, including community processes and structure (e.g., level system, behavior modification).
    b. Significant family involvement tailored to the needs of the patient (conjoint or without patient present), including parent training and family therapy. If family treatment is not provided, the reasoning for its omission

should be documented. The younger the patient, the more critical the involvement of the family or other caregivers.
  c. Individual and group therapy.
  d. School programming, including special education and vocational training.
  e. Specific therapies for comorbid disorders.
  f. Psychosocial skills training to improve social function (e.g., assertiveness, anger control).
  g. Ongoing coordination with school, social services, and juvenile justice personnel to ensure timely and appropriate discharge to step-down facilities and return to community.

(From American Academy of Child and Adolescent Psychiatry (AACAP). (1997). Practice parameters for the assessment and treatment of children and adolescents with conduct disorder. *Journal of the American Academy of Child and Adolescent Psychiatry, 36* (10, Suppl.), 122S–139S.)

Appendix 7.2. Student-Focused Negative Affective Regulation Strategies (Larsen & Prizmic, 2004)

- Distraction (+): low effort engaging activities
- Downward social comparison (+): feeling better by comparing yourself to someone worse off
- Problem-directed activity/problem solving (+): reflecting on problem events to plan to avoid them in the future
- Self-reward (+): thinking about or doing pleasant activities
- Exercise (+): moderate exercise increases energy levels, distracts, and increases one's sense of well-being
- Socializing (+): interacting with happy people, made worse if interacting with other sad or angry people
- Suppression (+/−): inhibiting/containing negative emotions
- Withdrawal, isolation, spending time alone (+/−): effective in interrupting a cycle of escalation, but results in flooding negative emotions if prolonged
- Venting (−): discharging negative emotions
- Eating (−): eating offers immediate satisfaction but easily develops into a pathological form of self-reward with long-term adverse consequences
- Gratitude (+): counting one's blessings, focusing on what is going well in one's life
- Altruism (+): helping others, committing acts of kindness
- Positive induction (+): humor, laughter, expressing positive emotions

Note: (+) most positive results, (+/−) mixed results, (−) least positive results. Adapted from Tansy (2007).

Appendix
Conduct Disorder Resources

Valuable Information on the Internet

The Internet can be an important tool for parents, teachers, and practitioners seeking information on conduct disorder and related topics. The preponderance of information that can be retrieved in any given search, however, can also make it a time-consuming and unwieldy resource. In order to make the search more manageable, some useful Web sites are listed below. The list is by no means exhaustive, but it contains links to some of the most valuable Web-based materials that are currently available.

Epidemiology and General Information

Report of the Surgeon General on Youth Violence

http://www.surgeongeneral.gov/library/youthviolence/

This report by the Surgeon General of the United States provides a detailed summary of scientific data on youth violence, including discussions pertaining to pervasiveness, developmental dynamics, and potential risk factors. It also offers information and best practices relating to prevention and intervention, as well as an exploration of future trends in empirically based research and methods that may effectively reduce incidence of youth violence. Extensive tables and a glossary are included.

National Center for Education Statistics (NCES)

http://www.nces.ed.gov

This site is sponsored by the NCES, a research arm of the U.S. Department of Education and Institute of Education Sciences that is responsible for compiling data on education in the United States. The Annual Reports section includes the extensive Indicators of School Crime and Safety. This is a compendium that includes data, summaries, and tables covering topics like school environments, threats and attacks on teachers, violent deaths, nonfatal student victimization, fights, weapons, illegal substances, discipline, safety, and security measures. The site's Publications section also contains a lengthy report entitled Violence in U.S. Public Schools; 2000 Survey on Crime and Safety, which is another important resource for data on school violence.

World Health Organization Report on Violence

http://www.who.int/violence_injury_prevention/violence/world_report/en/index.html

Utilizing the expertise of 160 specialists from around the world, the World Health Organization's report represents the first multinational investigation into the problem of violence, its effects, and possible solutions. Included is a lengthy chapter on youth violence that addresses the background and extent of the problem, dynamics, risk factors, and prevention. The report also offers recommendations that have become a serious point of discussion and policy in more than 30 nations.

ConductDisorders.com

http://www.conductdisorders.com

This is a site for parents of children with conduct disorder and its associated conditions. Very detailed information about CD and comorbidity with AD/HD, oppositional defiance, bipolar disorder, and others is provided. Each section typically includes discussions on causes, symptoms, diagnosis, therapies, medications, environmental factors, and treatments. It also offers a message board forum that allows parents to obtain support and receive suggestions from other parents on how to manage children with conduct disorder.

National Youth Violence Prevention Resource Center

http://www.safeyouth.org/scripts/index.asp

This site is operated by a federal entity that is supported by the Centers for Disease Control and Prevention and other agencies, and is devoted to preventing violence against children and adolescents. It offers a wealth of general information, resources, and news dealing with youth violence, including specific pages for professionals, parents, and teens. Its self-proclaimed purpose is to serve as a "one-stop shop" for prevention-related information.

Board on Children, Youth, and Families

http://www7.nationalacademies.org/bocyf/

This is the official Web site of the Board on Children, Youth, and Families, an organization that was created by the National Research Council and Institute of Medicine. The Board elicits expert opinions on policy concerns pertaining to the health of children and families. The site provides key points from summary reports on pregnancy, birth, and infant health, child development, adolescence, and mental health. It also offers publications dealing with children's health, education, and development issues.

Assessment

National Center for Injury Prevention and Control

http://www.cdc.gov/ncipc/pub-res/measure.htm

This site offers over 170 assessment instruments for professionals interested in evaluating violent behaviors, influences, and beliefs. These include aggressive behavior, exposure to violence, attributional biases, neighborhood characteristics, parental supervision, and social and emotional competencies. Each assessment is classified under behavioral, psychosocial/cognitive, attitudinal/belief, and environmental categories. The site also provides appraisals of violence prevention programs.

American Academy of Child and Adolescent Psychiatry (AACAP)

http://www.aacap.org

The AACAP is a national medical association of 7500 psychiatrists whose mission focuses on treating children and families suffering from mental, behavioral, and developmental disorders. It also seeks to promote understanding of mental illness. This site features an article entitled, "Summary of the Practice Parameters for the Assessment and Treatment of Children and Adolescents with Conduct Disorders," which offers a cogent overview of recommendations for diagnostic assessment and formulation, as well as treatment. The site also features a number of informative fact sheets on child and adolescent violence.

United States Secret Service National Threat Assessment Center (NTAC)

http://www.secretservice.gov/ntac_ssi.shtml

This portion of the official U.S. Secret Service Web site is dedicated to the subject of school violence prevention. With the aim of identifying typical behaviors that shooters engage in prior to school shootings, the Secret Service and U.S. Department of Education embarked on a joint series of threat-assessment studies that resulted in two publications: "Final Report and Findings: Implications for Prevention of School Attacks in the United States" and "Threat Assessment in Schools: A Guide to Managing Threatening Situations and to Creating Safe

School Climates." The full text of both studies are available on this Web site and represents a valuable set of data and information. The site also contains information relating to the release of an interactive CD-ROM designed for threat assessment teams entitled "A Safe School and Threat Assessment Experience: Scenarios Exploring the Findings of the Safe School Initiative."

American Academy of Family Physicians (AAFP)

Conduct Disorder: Diagnosis and Treatment in Primary Care: www.aafp.org/afp/20010415/1579.pdf

This site features an article published by the American Academy of Family Physicians, one of the largest medical organizations in the United States. Conduct Disorder: Diagnosis and Treatment in Primary Care was the joint effort of Fred Rottnek, a physician, H. Russell Searight, a professor of community and family medicine and psychology, and Stacey L. Abby, a clinical pharmacist. It provides a valuable overview of information concerning diagnostic criteria, clinical features, etiology, differential diagnosis and comorbidity, interventions, and pharmacotherapy.

Treatment

Prevention of Youth Violence

http://www.cdc.gov/ncipc/dvp/bestpractices/chapter2a.pdf

This site provides an extensive guide that offers home-visiting and parent- and family-based violence intervention and prevention strategies. The strategies are considered best practices, although the authors note that the study of youth violence is a relatively new discipline; therefore, many strategies have not been evaluated after appearing in peer-reviewed literature, and their practical effectiveness has often not been explored. As a result, an important mission of this guide is to describe the experiences of individuals who have used the interventions. Of particular significance are the Web site's Additional Resources sections, which provide important contact information and publications.

Ontario Association of Children's Aid Societies (OACAS): Conduct Problems in Young Children: Effective Early Intervention Strategies

http://www.oacas.org/resources/oacasjournals/1999March/ConductProblems.pdf

This site features an article entitled, "Conduct Problems in Young Children: Effective Early Intervention Strategies," which was based on earlier research utilizing input from parents and clinical experts and a review of literature. It stresses the importance of early intervention and provides information on important programs for preschool and school age children. Cognitive behavioral training, prosocial skill development, child care support, parent training programs, parent support and self-help programs, social skills training, child management coaching, and respite care are some of the interventions that are featured.

Helping America's Youth

http://guide.helpingamericasyouth.gov/programtool-ap.cfm

The primary goal of Helping America's Youth is to focus attention on the contemporary issues children and adolescents face and to encourage adults to form ties with them at the family, school, and community levels. This organization is especially interested in helping at-risk boys. The site offers a large and convenient compendium of 180 intervention programs, each containing a description of the intervention, an empirically based scientific evaluation of the intervention, a rating of outcomes, risk factors, protective factors, references, and contact information.

Center for the Study and Prevention of Violence (CSPV)

Blueprints for Violence Prevention: http://www.colorado.edu/cspv/blueprints

The Center for the Study and Prevention of Violence is a research program of the Institute of Behavioral Science (University of Colorado at Boulder) whose purpose is to disseminate scientific knowledge about violence and how violence can be prevented. The CSPV has scrutinized over 600 intervention programs, and its Blueprints for Violence Prevention features only the small number that have proved efficacious in curtailing aggression, violent crime, substance abuse, and delinquency. Using strict guidelines, the CSPV states that it "sets a gold standard for implementing exemplary, research-based violence and drug programs" and seeks to strictly adhere to program standards during implementation.

Promising Practices Network on Children, Families, and Communities

http://www.promisingpractices.net/programs.asp

The Promising Practices Network was founded by the RAND Corporation, a nonprofit research consortium, to provide unbiased, scientifically based information on effective interventions for children, their families, and their communities. This site is intended for professionals and decision makers and contains relevant data on programs for violent behavior, problem behaviors, and juvenile justice. Each of the program descriptions includes an overview, and information regarding participants, evaluation methods, findings, probable implementers, funding, implementation details, issues, example sites, contact information, and resources. The site also provides important information on research and service delivery.

Legal Issues and Advocacy

Office of Juvenile Justice and Delinquency Prevention (OJJDP)

http://ojjdp.ncjrs.org

The purpose of the Office of Juvenile Justice and Delinquency Prevention is to take a nationwide leadership role in issues of juvenile delinquency and violence. It seeks to promote prevention and intervention, primarily by providing information and resources, supporting states and local communities, and making positive changes in the juvenile justice system. This site offers online publications and an extensive topics section that covers subjects relating to delinquency prevention, courts, corrections and detention, offenses and offenders, and victims. There is also a detailed statistics section with downloadable spreadsheets, and a useful glossary of juvenile justice terms.

Wright's Law

http://www.wrightslaw.com

This site is dedicated to providing comprehensive information about the law as it pertains to education, special education, and children with disabilities so that individuals can be effective advocates for education reform. The site offers a comprehensive section on juvenile justice that addresses delinquency, education, and safe schools, and also offers a number of resources and publications. Each of the topics contains extensive reports and literature. The site also features advocacy and law libraries as well as a voluminous collection of articles.

Access to Juvenile Courts

http://www.rcfp.org/juvcts/index.html

This site provides a succinct summary of legal issues pertaining to juvenile court proceedings, documents, and right to privacy. It includes sections on gaining access to juvenile proceedings and records, the consequences of revealing a juvenile's identity, the issue of transfer proceedings, the use of cameras in juvenile court, and the Juvenile Delinquency Act. The site also offers a state-by-state legal guide.

National Center for Mental Health and Juvenile Justice (NCMHJJ)

http://www.ncmhjj.com

The National Center for Mental Health and Juvenile Justice seeks to improve guidelines and programs for children and adolescents with mental health needs within the juvenile justice system. It also strives to coordinate relevant research and advocacy on a national level. This site offers publications, online training, a resource kit, and links to evidence-based practices. Of special note is "Blueprint for Change: A Comprehensive Model for the Identification and Treatment of Youth with Mental Health Needs in Contact with the Juvenile Justice System," a lengthy report based on research that offers an outline and recommendations for making positive changes in mental health services in the juvenile justice system.

References

Achenbach, T. M. (1991a). *Integrative guide to the 1991 CBCL/4–18, YSR, and TRF profiles.* Burlington, VT: University of Vermont, Department of Psychology.

Achenbach, T. M. (1991b). *Manual of the Teacher's Report Form and 1991 profile.* Burlington, VT: University of Vermont, Department of Psychology.

Achenbach, T. M. (1998). Diagnosis, assessment, taxonomy, and case formulations. In T. Ollendick & M. Hersen (Eds.), *Handbook of child psychopathology* (3rd ed., pp. 63–87). New York: Plenum.

Achenbach, T. M. (1999). The Child Behavior Checklist and related instruments. In M. E. Maruish (Ed.), *The use of psychological testing for treatment planning and outcomes assessment* (2nd ed., pp. 429–466). Mahwah, NJ: Erlbaum.

Achenbach, T. M., & Rescorla, L. A. (2001). *Manual for ASEBA School-Age Forms & Profiles.* Burlington, VT: University of Vermont, Research Center for Children, Youth, & Families.

Achenbach, T. M., Howell, C. T., McConaughy, S. H., & Stanger, C. (1995). Six-year predictors of problems in a national sample: III. Transitions to young adult syndromes. *Journal of the American Academy of Child and Adolescent Psychiatry, 34*, 658–669.

Achenbach, T. M. (2007). *Manual for the Child Behavior Checklist.* Burlington, VT: University of Vermont, Department of Psychiatry.

Ambrosini, P. J. (2000). Historical development and present status of the schedule for affective disorders and schizophrenia for school-age children (K-SADS). *Journal of the American Academy of Child and Adolescent Psychiatry, 39*, 49–58.

American Academy of Child and Adolescent Psychiatry (AACAP), Work Group on Quality Issues (1997). Practice parameters for the assessment and treatment of children and adolescents with conduct disorder. *Journal of the American Academy of Child and Adolescent Psychiatry, 36* (10, Suppl.), 122S–139S.

American Psychiatric Association. (1980). *Diagnostic and statistical manual of mental disorders* (3rd ed.). Washington, DC: American Psychiatric Association.

American Psychiatric Association. (1987). *Diagnostic and statistical manual of mental disorders* (3rd ed., rev.). Washington, DC: American Psychiatric Association.

American Psychiatric Association. (1994). *Diagnostic and statistical manual of mental disorders* (4th ed.). Washington, DC: American Psychiatric Association.

American Psychiatric Association. (2000). *Diagnostic and statistical manual of mental disorders* (4th ed., text rev.). Washington, DC: American Psychiatric Association.

Anderson, S. W., Bechara, A., Damasio, H., Tranel, D., & Damasio, A. R. (1999). Impairment of social and moral behavior related to early damage in human prefrontal cortex. *Nature Neuroscience, 2*, 1032–1037.

Andrade, R. C., Silva, V. A., & Assumpçáo, F. B. (2004). Preliminary data on the prevalence of psychiatric disorders in Brazilian male and female juvenile delinquents. *Brazilian Journal of Medical and Biological Research, 37*, 1155–1160.

Andrews, V. C., Garrison, C. A., Jackson, K. L., Addy, C. L., & McKeown, R. E. (1993). Mother-adolescent agreement on the symptoms and diagnoses of adolescent depression and conduct disorders. *Journal of the American Academy of Child and Adolescent Psychiatry, 23*, 731–738.

Angold, A., & Costello, E. J. (1995). A test-retest reliability study of child-reported psychiatric symptoms and diagnoses using the Child and Adolescent Psychiatric Assessment (CAPA-C). *Psychological Medicine, 25*, 755–762.

Angold, A., Costello, E. J., & Erkanli, A. (1999). Comorbidity. *Journal of Child Psychology and Psychiatry and Allied Disciplines, 40*, 57–87.

Angold, A., Prendergast, M., Cox, A., Harrington, R., Simonoff, E., & Rutter, M. (1995). The Child and Adolescent Psychiatric Assessment (CAPA). *Psychological Medicine, 25*, 739–753.

Angrilli, A., Mauri, A., Palomba, D., Flor, H., Birbaumer, N., Sartori, G., et al. (1996). Startle reflex and emotion modulation impairment after a right amygdala lesion. *Brain, 119*, 1991–2000.

Anonymous. (2000). Clinical practice guideline: Diagnosis and evaluation of the child with Attention-Deficit/Hyperactivity Disorder. *Pediatrics, 105*, 1158–1170.

Archer, R. P. (1997). *MMPI: Assessing adolescent psychopathology.* Mahwah, NJ: Erlbaum.

Archer, R. P., Belevich, J. K. S., & Elkins, D. E. (1994). Item-level and scale-level factor structures of the MMPI-A. *Journal of Personality Assessment, 62*, 332–345.

Arluke, A., Levin, J., Luke, C., & Ascione, F. (1999). The relationship of animal abuse to violence and other forms of antisocial behavior. *Journal of Interpersonal Violence, 14*, 963–975.

Arnold, M. E., & Hughes, J. N. (1999). First do no harm: Adverse effects of grouping deviant youth for social skills training. *Journal of School Psychology, 37*, 99–115.

Atkins, M. S., & Stoff, D. M. (1993). Instrumental and hostile aggression in childhood disruptive behavior disorders. *Journal of Abnormal Child Psychology, 21*, 165–178.

Atkins, M. S., Stoff, D. M., Osborne, M. L., & Brown, K. (1993). Distinguishing instrumental and hostile aggression: Does it make a difference? *Journal of Abnormal Child Psychology, 21*, 165–178.

Augimeri, L., Koegl, C., Webster, C. D., & Levene, K. (2001). *Early Assessment Risk List for Boys (EARL-20B)*, Version 2. Toronto: Earlscourt Child and Family Center.

Bagley, C., & Mallick, K. (2000). Spiralling up and spiralling down: Implications of a long-term study of temperament and conduct disorder for social work with children. *Child and Family Social Work, 5*, 291–301.

Barling, J., O'Leary, K. D., Jouriles, E. N., Vivian, D., & MacEwen, K. E. (1987). Factor similarity of the Conflict Tactics Scale across samples, spouses, and sites: Issues and implications. *Journal of Family Violence, 2*, 37–54.

Barry, C. T., Frick, P. J., DeShazo, T. M., McCoy, M., Ellis, M., & Loney, B. R. (2000). The importance of callous-unemotional traits for extending the concept of psychopathy to children. *Journal of Abnormal Psychology, 109*, 335–340.

Barton, J. (2003). Conduct disorder: Intervention and prevention. *International Journal of Mental Health Promotion, 5*, 32–41.

Bassarath L. (2001). Conduct disorder: A biopsychosocial review. *Canadian Journal of Psychiatry, 46*, 609–616.

Bauer, L. O., & Hesselbrock, V. M. (2001). CSD/BEM localization of P300 sources in adolescents "at-risk": Evidence of frontal cortex dysfunction in conduct disorder. *Biological Psychiatry, 50*, 600–608.

Beauchaine, T. P., Webster-Stratton, C., & Reid, M. J. (2005). Mediators, moderators, and predictors of 1-year outcomes among children treated for early-onset conduct problems. A latent growth curve analysis. *Journal of Consulting and Clinical Psychology, 73*, 371–388.

Bechara, A., Damasio, A. R., Damasio, H., & Anderson, S. W. (1994). Insensitivity to future consequences following damage to human prefrontal cortex. *Cognition, 50*, 7–15.

Becker, K. B., & McCloskey, L. A. (2002). Attention and conduct problems in children exposed to family violence. *American Journal of Orthopsychiatry, 72*, 83–91.

Begun, R. W. (Ed.). (1995). *Ready-to-use social skills lessons & activities for grades 1–3.* West Nyack, NY: Center for Applied Research in Education.

Bergeron, L., Valla, J. P., & Breton, J. J. (1992). Pilot study for the Quebec Child Mental Health survey: Part I. Measurement of the prevalence estimates among 6 to 14 year olds. *Canadian Journal of Psychiatry, 37*, 374–380.

Biederman, J., Faraone, S. V., Milberger, S., Jetton, J. G., Chen, L., Mick, E., et al. (1996). Is childhood oppositional defiant disorder a precursor to adolescent conduct disorder? Findings from a four-year follow-up study of children with ADHD. *Journal of the American Academy of Child and Adolescent Psychiatry, 35*, 1193–1204.

Biederman, J., Mick, E., Wozniak, J., Monuteaux, M. C., Galdo, M., & Faraone, S. V. (2003). Can a subtype of conduct disorder linked to bipolar disorder be identified? Integration of findings from the Massachusetts General Hospital pediatric psychopharmacology research program. *Biological Psychiatry, 53*, 952–960.

Bierman, K. L., Coie, J. D., Dodge, K. A., Greenberg, M. T., Lochman, J. E., McMahon, R. J., & Pinderhughes, E. E. (1999). Initial impact of the fast track prevention trial for conduct problems: I. The high-risk sample. *Journal of Consulting and Clinical Psychology, 67*, 631–347.

Bird, H. R., Canino, G. J., Davies, M., Zhang, H., Ramirez, R., & Lahey, B. B. (2001). Prevalence and correlates of antisocial behaviors among three ethnic groups. *Journal of Abnormal Child Psychology, 29*, 465–478.

Blair, R. J. R. (1999). Responsiveness to distress cues in the child with psychopathic tendencies. *Personality and Individual Differences, 27*, 135–145.

Blair, R. J. R. (2001). Neurocognitive models of aggression, the antisocial personality disorders, and psychopathy. *Journal of Neurology, Neurosurgery, and Psychiatry, 71*, 727–731.

Blair, R. J. R., & Cipolotti, L. (2000). Impaired social response reversal: A case of "acquired sociopathy." *Brain, 123*, 1122–1141.

Bodholdt, R., Richards, H., & Gacono, C. (2000). Assessing psychopathy in adults: The Psychopathy Checklist-Revised and Screening Version. In C. Gacono (Ed.), *The clinical and forensic assessment of psychopathy: A practitioner's guide.* (pp. 55–86). Hillsdale, NJ: Erlbaum.

Bohman, M. (1996). Predisposition to criminality: Swedish adoption studies in retrospect. In G. R. Bock and J. A. Goode (Eds.) *Genetics of criminal and antisocial behaviour* (Ciba Foundation Symposium no. 194) (pp. 99–114). Chichester, England: Wiley.

Borne, R. F. (1998). Serotonin: The neurotransmitter for the 90's. *Drug Topics.*

Bower, E. M. (1982). Defining emotional disturbance: Public policy and research. *Psychology in the Schools, 19*, 55–60.

Bravo, M., Woodbury-Farina, M., Canino, G. J., Rubio-Stipec, M. (1993). The Spanish translation and cultural adaptation of the Diagnostic Interview Schedule for Children (DISC) in Puerto Rico. *Cultural Medical Psychiatry, 17*, 329–344.

Brennan, P. A., Hall, J., & Bor, W. (2003). Integrating biological and social processes in relation to early-onset persistent aggression in boys and girls. *Developmental Psychology, 39*, 309–323.

Brestan, E. V., & Eyberg, S. M. (1998). Effective psychosocial treatments of conduct-disordered children and adolescents: 29 years, 62 studies, and 5272 kids. *Journal of Clinical Child Psychology, 27*, 180–189.

Breton, J. J., Bergeron, L., Valla, J. P., Berthiaume, C., Gaudet, N., Lambert, J., St-Georges, M., Houde, L., & Lépine, S. (1999). Quebec child mental health survey: Prevalence of DSM-III-R mental health disorders. *Journal of Child Psychology and Psychiatry, 40*, 375–384.

Briggs-Gowan, M., Carter, A., Irwin, J. R., Wachtel, K., & Cicchetti, D.V. (2004). The Brief Infant-Toddler Social and Emotional Assessment: Screening for social-emotional problems and delays in competence. *Journal of Pediatric Psychology, 29*, 143–155.

Bronfenbrenner, U. (1986). Ecology of the family as a context for human development: Research perspectives. *Developmental Psychology, 22*, 723–742.

Brotman, L. M., Gouley, K. K., O'Neal, C., & Klein, R. G. (2004). Preschool-aged siblings of adjudicated youths: Multiple risk factors for conduct problems. *Early Education and Development, 15*, 387–406.

Brotman, M. A., Schmajuk, M., Rich, B. A., Dickstein, D. P., Guyer, A. E., Costello, E. J., et al. (2006). Incidence, clinical correlates, and longitudinal course of severe mood dysregulation in children. *Biological Psychiatry, 60*, 991–997.

Büchel, C., Morris, J., Dolan, R. J., & Friston, K. J. (1998). Brain systems mediating aversive conditioning: An event-related fMRI Study. *Neuron, 20*, 947–957.

Bucholz, K. K., Nurnberger, J. I., Kramer, J. R., Hesselbrock, V. M., Schuckit, M. A., & Bierut, L. J. (2006). Comparison of psychiatric diagnoses from interview reports with those from best-estimate procedures. *Journal of Studies on Alcohol, 67*, 157–168.

Buitelaar, J. K. (2000). Open-label treatment with Risperidone of 26 psychiatrically-hospitalized children and adolescents with mixed diagnoses and aggressive behavior. *Journal of Child and Adolescent Psychopharmacology, 10*, 19–26.

Buitelaar, J. K., Montgomery, S. A., van Zwieten-Boot, B. J. (2003). Conduct disorder: Guidelines for investigating efficacy of pharmacological intervention. *European Neuropsychopharmacology, 13*, 305–311.

Burke, J. D., Loeber, R., & Birmaher, B. (2002). Oppositional defiant disorder and conduct disorder: A review of the past 10 years, part II. *Journal of the American Academy of Child and Adolescent Psychiatry, 41*, 1275–1293.

Burke, J. D., Loeber, R., Mutchka, J. S., & Lahey, B. B. (2002). A question for DSM-V: Which better predicts persistent conduct disorder—delinquent acts or conduct symptoms? *Criminal Behaviour and Mental Health, 12*, 37–52.

Burket, R. C., & Myers, W. C. (1995). Axis I and personality comorbidity in adolescents with conduct disorder. *Bulletin of the American Academy of Psychiatry and the Law, 23*, 73–82.

Burt, S. A., Krueger, R. F., & McGue, M. (2001). Sources of covariation among attention-deficit/hyperactivity disorder, oppositional defiant disorder, and conduct disorder: The importance of shared environment. *Journal of Abnormal Psychology, 110*, 516–525.

Bush, G., Luu, P., & Posner, M. I. (2000). Cognitive and emotional influences in anterior cingulate cortex. *Trends in Cognitive Sciences, 4*, 215–222.

Butcher, J. N., Williams, C. L., Graham, J. R., Archer, R. P., Tellegen, A., Ben-Porath, Y. S., & Kaemmer, B. (1992). *MMPI-A (Minnesota Multiphasic Personality Inventory-Adolescent): Manual for administration, scoring, and interpretation.* Minneapolis, MN: University of Minnesota Press.

Button, T. M. M., Scourfield, J., & Martin, N. (2005). Family dysfunction interacts with genes in the causation of antisocial symptoms. *Behavior Genetics, 35,* 115–120.

Cadoret, R., Yates, W., Troughton, E., Woodworth, G., & Stewart, M. A. (1995). Genetic-environmental interaction in the genesis of aggressivity and conduct disorders. *Archives of General Psychiatry, 52,* 916–924.

Cadort, R. J. (1995). Genes, environment and their interaction in the development of psychopathology. In T. Sakai and T. Tsuboi, (Eds.) *Genetic aspects of human behavior* (pp. 165–175). Tokyo: Iagaku-Shoin.

Campbell, M., Adams, P. B., Small, A. M., Kafantaris, V., Silva, R. R., Shell, J., Perry, R., & Overall, J. E. (1995). Lithium in hospitalized aggressive children with conduct disorder: A double-blind placebo-controlled study. *Journal of the American Academy of Child and Adolescent Psychiatry, 34,* 445–453.

Campbell, M., Gonzalez, N. M., & Silva, R. R. (1992). The pharmacologic treatment of conduct disorders and rage outbursts. *Psychiatric Clinics of North America, 15,* 69–85.

Capaldi, D. M., & Patterson, G. R. (1996). Can violent offenders be distinguished from frequent offenders: Prediction from childhood to adolescence. *Journal of Research in Crime and Delinquency, 33,* 206–231.

Carlin, M. E. (1996). Large group treatment of severely disturbed/conduct-disordered adolescents. *International Journal of Group Psychotherapy, 46,* 379–397.

Caron, C., & Rutter, M. (1991). Comorbidity in child psychopathology: Concepts, issues and research strategies. *Journal of Child Psychology and Psychiatry, 32,* 1063–1080.

Center for Child Welfare and Education (2004). *Education status Section 504.* Retrieved January 5, 2007, from http://www.cedu.niu.edu/ccwe/intervention.htm

Center, D., & Kemp, D. (2003). Temperament and personality as potential factors in the development and treatment of conduct disorders. *Education and Treatment of Children, 26,* 75–88.

Chronis, A., M., Lahey, B. B., Pelham, W. E., Kipp, H. L., Baumann, B. L., & Lee, S. (2003). Psychopathology and substance abuse in parents of young children with attention-deficit/hyperactivity disorder. *Journal of the American Academy of Child and Adolescent Psychiatry, 42,* 1424–1432.

Cicchetti, D., & Toth, S. (1995). Developmental psychopathology and disorders of affect. In D. Cicchetti & D. Cohen (Eds.), *Developmental psychopathology and disorders of affect* (pp. 369–420). New York: Wiley.

Clarizio, H. F. (1992a). Social maladjustment and emotional disturbance: Problems and positions: I. *Psychology in the Schools, 29,* 131–140.

Clarizio, H. F. (1992b). Social maladjustment and emotional disturbance: Problems and positions: II. *Psychology in the Schools, 29,* 331–441.

Coccaro, E. F., Kavoussi, R. J., Cooper, T. B., & Hauger, R. L. (1997). Central serotonin activity and aggression: Inverse relationship with prolactin response to d-fenfuramine, but not CSF 5–HIAA concentration, in human subjects. *American Journal of Psychiatry, 154,* 1430–1435.

Cohen, P., Cohen, J., Kasen, S., Velez, C. N., Hartmark, C., Johnson, J., et al. (1993). An epidemiological study of disorders in late childhood and adolescence: I. Age- and gender-specific prevalence. *Journal of Child Psychology and Psychiatry, 34,* 851–867.

Coid, J., Petruckevitch, A., Bebbington, P., Brugha, T., Bhugra, D., Jenkins, R., et al. (2002). Ethnic differences in prisoners I: Criminality and psychiatric comorbidity. *British Journal of Psychiatry, 181*, 473–480.

Collins, W. A., & Sroufe, L. A. (1999). Capacity for intimate relationships: A developmental construction. In W. Furman, B. B. Brown, et al. (Eds.), *The development of romantic relationships in adolescence* (pp. 125–147). New York: Cambridge.

Compton, W. M., Conway, K. P., Stinson, F. S., Colliver, J. D., & Grant, B. F. (2005). Prevalence, correlates, and comorbidity of DSM-IV antisocial personality syndromes and alcohol and specific drug use disorders in the United States: Results from the national epidemiologic survey on alcohol and related conditions. *Journal of Clinical Psychiatry, 66*, 677–685.

Conners, C. K. (1997). *Conners' Rating Scales—Revised Technical Manual.* North Tonawanda, NY: Multi-Health Systems, Inc.

Conners, C. K., Sitarenios, G., Parker, J. D. A., & Epstein, J. N. (1998a). Revision and restandardization of the Conners' Teacher Rating Scale (CTRS-R): Factor structure, reliability, and criterion validity. *Journal of Abnormal Child Psychology, 26*, 279–291.

Conners, C. K., Sitarenios, G., Parker, J. D. A., & Epstein, J. N. (1998b). The revised Conners' Parent Rating Scale (CPRS-R): Factor structure, reliability, and criterion validity. *Journal of Abnormal Child Psychology, 26*, 257–268.

Conners, C. K., Wells, K. C., Parker, J. D. A., Sitarenios, G., Diamond, J. M., & Powell, J. W. (1997). A new self-report scale for assessment of adolescent psychopathology: Factor structure, reliability, validity, and diagnostic sensitivity. *Journal of Abnormal Child Psychology, 25*, 487–497.

Connor, D. F. (2002). *Aggression and antisocial behavior in children and adolescents: Research and treatment.* New York: Guilford Press.

Connor, D. F., & Fisher, S. G. (1997). An international model of child and adolescent mental health clinical case formulation. *Clinical Child Psychology and Psychiatry, 2*, 353–368.

Connor, D. F., Barkley, R. A., & Davis, H. T. (2000). A pilot study of methylphenidate, clonidine, or the combination in ADHD comorbid with aggressive oppositional defiant or conduct disorder. *Clinical Pediatrics, 39*, 15–25.

Connor, D. F., Ozbayrak, K. R., Harrison, R. J., & Melloni, R. H., Jr. (1998). Prevalence and patterns of psychotropic and anticonvulsant medication use in children and adolescents referred to residential treatment. *Journal of Child and Adolescent Psychopharmacology, 8*, 27–38.

Costello, E. J., Mustillo, S., Erkanli, A., Keeler, G., & Angold, A. (2003). Prevalence and development of psychiatric disorders in childhood and adolescence. *Archives of General Psychiatry, 60*, 837–843.

Costenbader, V., & Buntaine, R. (1999). Diagnostic discrimination between social maladjustment and emotional disturbance: An empirical study. *Journal of Emotional and Behavioral Disorders, 7*, 2–7.

Côté, S., Tremblay, R. E., Nagin, D. S., Zoccolillo, M., & Vitaro, F. (2002). Childhood behavioral profiles leading to adolescent conduct disorder: Risk trajectories for boys and girls. *Journal of the American Academy of Child and Adolescent Psychiatry, 41*, 1086–1094.

Council for Children with Behavioral Disorders. (1987). A position paper on definition and identification of students with behavioral disorders. *Behavior Disorders, 15*, 180–189.

Couwenbergh, C., van den Brink, W., Zwart, K., Vreugdenhil, C., van Wijngaarden-Cremers, P., & van der Gaag, R. J. (2006). Comorbid psychopathology in adolescents and young adults treated for substance use disorders: A review. *European Child and Adolescent Psychiatry, 15,* 319–328.

Crowe, R. R. (1974). An adoption study of antisocial personality. *Archives of General Psychiatry, 31,* 785–791.

Crowley, T. J., Mikulich, S. K., Ehlers, K. M., Whitmore, E. A., & Macdonald, M. J. (2001). Validity of structured clinical evaluations in adolescents with conduct and substance problems. *Journal of the American Academy of Child and Adolescent Psychiatry, 40,* 265–273.

Crowley, T. J., Raymond, K. M., Mikulich-Gilbertson, S. K., Thompson, L. L., & Lejuez, C. W. (2006). A risk taking "set" in a novel task among adolescents with serious conduct and substance problems. *Journal of the American Academy of Child and Adolescent Psychiatry, 45,* 175–183.

Crystal, D. S., Ostrander, R., S., Chen, R., & August, G. J. (2001). Multimethod assessment of psychopathology among DSM-IV subtypes of children with Attention Deficit/ Hyperactivity Disorder: Self-, parent, and teacher reports. *Journal of Abnormal Child Psychology, 29,* 189–205.

Dadds, M. R., Fraser, J., & Frost, A. (2005). Disentangling the underlying dimensions of psychopathy and conduct problems in childhood: A community study. *Journal of Consulting and Clinical Psychology, 73,* 400–410.

Damasio, A. R. (1994). *Descartes' error: Emotionality, reason, and the human brain.* New York: Putnam.

Damasio, A. R. (2003). *Looking for Spinoza: Joy, sorrow, and the feeling brain.* Orlando, FL: Harcourt.

Davidson, R. J., Putnam, K. M., & Larson, C. L. (2000). Dysfunction in the neural circuitry of emotion regulation—a possible prelude to violence. *Science, 289,* 591–594.

Davila, R. R., Williams, M. L., & MacDonald, J. T. (1991, September 16). *Memorandum to chief state school officers re: Clarification of policy to address the needs of children with attention deficit disorders with general and/or special education.* Washington, DC: U.S. Department of Education.

de la Osa, N., Ezpeleta, L., Domènech, E., Navarro, J. B., & Losilla, J. M. (1996). Fiabilidad entre entrevista-dores de la Entrevista Diagnóstica Estructurada para Niños y Adolescentes (DICA-R). *Psicohtema, 8,* 359–368.

Deater-Deckard, K., Dodge, K., Bates, J. E., & Petit, G. S. (1996). Physical discipline among African-American and European-American mothers: Links to children's externalizing behaviors. *Developmental Psychology, 32,* 1065–1072.

Delligatti, N., Akin-Little, A., & Little, S. G. (2003). Conduct disorder in girls: Diagnostic and intervention issues. *Psychology in the Schools, 40,* 183–192.

Déry, M., Toupin, J., Pauzé, R., & Verlaan, P. (2004). Frequency of mental health disorders in a sample of elementary school students receiving special education services for behavioural difficulties. *Canadian Journal of Psychiatry, 49,* 769–775.

DeVito, C., & Hopkins, J. (2001). Attachment, parenting, and marital dissatisfaction as predictors of disruptive behavior in preschoolers. *Development and Psychopathology, 13,* 215–231.

Dick, D. M., Li, T-K, Edenberg, H. J., Hesselbrock, V., Kramer, J., Kuperman, S., et al. (2004). A genome-wide screen for genes influencing conduct disorder. *Molecular Psychiatry, 9,* 81–86.

Dishion, T. J., & Andrews, D. W. (1995). Preventing escalation in problem behaviors with high-risk young adolescents: Immediate and 1-year outcomes. *Journal of Consulting and Clinical Psychology, 63,* 538–548.

Dishion, T. J., McCord, J., & Poulin, F. (1999). When interventions harm—Peer groups and problem behavior. *American Psychologist, 54*, 755–764

Dodge, K. A., & Conduct Problems Prevention Research Group. (1996). An initial evaluation of the FAST Track Program. In J.A. Linney (Ed.), Proceedings of the Fifth National Prevention Research Conference (pp. 54–56) Washington, DC: National Institute of Mental Health.

Dodge, K. A., & Tomlin, A. M. (1987). Utilization of self-schemas as a mechanism of interpretational bias in aggressive children. *Social Cognition, 5*, 280–300.

Dodge, K. A., Pettit, G. S., Bates, J. E., & Valente, E. (1995). Social information-processing patterns partially mediate the effect of early physical abuse on later conduct problems. *Journal of Abnormal Psychology, 104*, 632–643.

Doepfner, M., & Lehmkuhl, G. (1998). *Diagnostic system for mental disorders in child and adolescence according to ICD-10 and DSM-IV (DISYP-K)*. Bern, Switzerland: Huber.

Doğan, O., Önder, Z., Doğan, S., & Akyüz, G. (2004). Distribution of symptoms of conduct disorder and antisocial personality disorder in Turkey. *Psychopathology, 37*, 285–289.

Dolan, M., & Rennie, C. (2006). Psychopathy checklist: Youth version and youth psychopathic trait inventory: A comparison study. *Personality and Individual Differences, 41*, 779–789.

Doll, B. (1996). Prevalence of psychiatric disorders in children and youth: An agenda for advocacy by school psychology. *School Psychology Quarterly, 11*, 20–47.

Donovan, J. S., Stewart, J. W., Nunes, E. V., Quitkin, F. M., Parides, M., Daniel, W., Susser, E., & Klien, D. F. (2000). Divalproex treatment of youth with explosive temper and mood lability: A double-blind placebo-controlled crossover design. *American Journal of Psychiatry, 157*, 818–820.

Doyle, A. E., Biederman, J., Monuteaux, M., Cohan, S. L., Schofield, H. T., & Faraone, S. V. (2003). Diagnostic threshold for conduct disorder in girls and boys. *Journal of Nervous and Mental Disease, 191*, 379–386.

Drabick, D. A. G., Gadow, K. D., & Sprafkin, J. (2006). Co-occurrence of conduct disorder and depression in a clinic-based sample of boys with ADHD. *Journal of Child Psychology and Psychiatry, 47*, 766–774.

Dumont, R., & Rauch, M. (2000). Test review: Scale for Assessing Emotional Disturbance (SAED). *Communiqué, 28*, 24–25.

Eaves, L., Rutter, M., Silberg, J. L., Shillady, L., Maes, H., & Pickles, A. (2000). Genetic and environmental causes of covariation in interview assessments of disruptive behavior in child and adolescent twins. *Behavior Genetics, 30*, 321–334.

Edelbrock, C., & Costello, A. J. (1988). Convergence between statistically derived behavior problems syndromes and child psychiatric diagnoses. *Journal of Abnormal Child Psychology, 16*, 219–231.

Eichelman, B. (1988). Toward a rational pharmacotherapy for aggressive and violent behavior. *Hospital and Community Psychiatry, 39*, 31–39.

Elliot, D. S., Huizinga, D., & Ageton, S. S. (1985). *Explaining delinquency and drug use*. Beverly Hills, CA: Sage.

Elliott, S. N., & Gresham, F. M. (1991). *Social skills intervention guide: Practical strategies for social skills training*. Circle Pines, MN: American Guidance Service.

Elliott, C. D. (2006a). *DAS-II Administration and Scoring Manual*. San Antonio, TX: The Psychological Corporation.

Emerson, E. (2003). Prevalence of psychiatric disorders in children and adolescents with and without intellectual disability. *Journal of Intellectual Disability Research, 47*, 51–58.

Emslie, G. J., Portteus, A. M., Kumar, E. C., & Hume, J. H. (2004). Antidepressants: SSRIs and novel atypical antidepressants—an update on psychopharmacology. In H. Steiner (Ed.), *Handbook of mental health interventions in children and adolescents: An integrated developmental approach* (pp. 318–362). San Francisco: Jossey-Bass.

Enebrink, P., Andershed, H., & Långström, N. (2005). Callous-unemotional traits are associated with clinical severity in referred boys with conduct problems. *Nordic Journal of Psychiatry, 59*, 431–440.

Enebrink, P., Långström, N., & Gumpert, C. H. (2006). Predicting aggressive and disruptive behavior in referred 6- to 12-year-old boys: Prospective validation of the EARL-20B risk/needs checklist. *Assessment, 13*, 356–367.

Epstein, M. H., & Cullinan, D. (1998) *Scale for assessing emotional disturbance*. Austin, TX: PRO-ED.

Ernst, M., Cookus, B. A., & Moravec, B. C. (2000). Pictorial Instrument for Children and Adolescents (PICA-III-R). *Journal of the American Academy of Child and Adolescent Psychiatry, 39*, 94–99.

Essau, C. A., Sasagawa, S., & Frick, P. J. (2006). Callous-unemotional traits in a community sample of adolescents. *Assessment, 13*, 454–469.

Exner, J. E. (2003). *The Rorschach: A comprehensive system. Basic foundations and principles of interpretation* (Vol. 1, 4ᵗʰ ed.). New York: Wiley.

Exner, J. E., & Erdberg, P. (2005). *The Rorschach: A comprehensive system. Advanced interpretation* (Vol. 2, 3ʳᵈ ed.). NJ: Wiley.

Eyberg, S. M. (1980). Eyberg Child Behavior Inventory. *Journal of Clinical Child Psychology, 9*, 27.

Eyberg, S. M., & Robinson, E. A. (1983). Conduct problem behavior: Standardization of a behavioral rating scale with adolescents. *Journal of Clinical Child Psychology, 12*, 347–354.

Eyberg, S., Bessmer, J., Newcomb, K., Edwards, D., & Robinson, E. (1994). *Dyadic Parent-Child Interaction Coding System II: A manual*. Social and Behavioral Sciences Documents (Ms. No. 2897). San Rafael, CA: Select Press.

Ezpeleta, L., de la Osa, N., Jude, J., Domènech, J. M., Navarro, J. B., & Losilla, J. M. (1997). Diagnostic agreement between clinician and the Diagnostic Interview for Children and Adolescents—DICA-R in a Spanish outpatient sample. *Journal of Child Psychology and Psychiatry, 38*, 431–440.

Ezpeleta, L., Domènech, J. M., & Angold, A. (2006). A comparison of pure and comorbid CD/ODD and depression. *Journal of Child Psychology and Psychiatry, 47*, 704–712.

Fahrenberg, J., Hampel, R., & Selg, H. (1994). *Freiburg personality inventory (FPI) in the revised form FPI-R*. Göttingen, Germany: Verlag für Psychologie.

Farrington, D. P. (1995). Key issues in the interaction of motivational and opportunity-reducing crime prevention strategies. In P. H. Wikstrom, R.V. Clarke & J. McCord (Eds.), *Integrating crime prevention strategies: Propensity and opportunity* (pp. 333–357). Stockholm: National Counsel for Crime Prevention.

Farrington, D. P. (1997). Early prediction of violent and nonviolent youth offending. *European Journal on Criminal Policy and Research, 5*, 51–66.

Fergusson, D. M., Horwood, L. J., & Lynskey, M. T. (1993). Early dentine lead levels and subsequent cognitive and behavioural development. *Journal of Child Psychology and Psychiatry, 34*, 215–227.

Findling, R. L., McNamara, N. K., Branicky, L. A. Schluchter, M. D., Lemon, E., & Blumer, J. L. (2000). A double-blind pilot study of risperidone in the treatment of conduct disorder. *Journal of the American Academy of Child and Adolescent Psychiatry, 39*, 509–516.

Fisher, L., & Blair, R. J. R. (1998). Cognitive impairment and its relationship to psychopathic tendencies in children with emotional and behavioral difficulties. *Journal of Abnormal Child Psychology, 26*, 511–520.

Fisher, P. W., Shaffer, D., Placentini, J. C., Lapkin, J., Kafantaris, V., Leonard, H., & Herzog, D. B. (1993). Sensitivity of the Diagnostic Interview Schedule for Children (2nd ed.; DISC-2.1) for specific diagnoses of children and adolescents. *Journal of the American Academy of Child and Adolescent Psychiatry, 32*, 666–673.

Foley, D. L., Eaves, L. J., & Wormley, B. (2004). Childhood adversity: Monoamine oxidase A genotype, and risk for conduct disorder. *Archives of General Psychiatry, 61*, 738–744.

Foley, D. L., Pickles, A., Rutter, M., Gardner, C. O., Maes, H. H., Silberg, J. L., & Eaves, L. J. (2004). Risks for conduct disorder symptoms associated with parental alcoholism in stepfather families versus intact families from a community sample. *Journal of Child Psychology and Psychiatry, 45*, 687–696.

Foley, R. M., & Pang, L. (2006). Alternative education programs: programs and student characteristics. *The High School Journal, 89*, 10– 21.

Ford, T., Goodman, R., & Meltzer, H. (2003). The British Child and Adolescent Mental Health Survey 1999: The prevalence of DSM-IV disorders. *Journal of the American Academy of Child and Adolescent Psychiatry, 42*, 1203–1211.

Forehand, R., & McMahon, R. J. (1981). *Helping the noncompliant child: A clinician's guide to parent training*. New York: Guilford Press.

Forth, A. E., Kosson, D. S., & Hare, R. D. (2003). *The Psychopathy Checklist: Youth Version manual*. Toronto: Multi-Health Systems.

Frick, P. J. (1998a). Conduct disorder. In T. Ollendick & M. Hersen (Eds.). *Handbook of child psychopathology* (3rd ed., pp. 213–337). New York: Plenum Press.

Frick, P. J. (1998b). *Conduct disorders and severe antisocial behavior*. New York: Plenum Press.

Frick, P.J. (2001). Effective interventions for children and adolescents with conduct disorder. *Canadian Journal of Psychiatry, 46*, 597–608.

Frick, P. J. (2004). Developmental pathways to conduct disorder: Implications for serving youth who show severe aggressive and antisocial behavior. *Psychology in the Schools, 41*, 823–834.

Frick, P. J. & Hare, R. D. (2001). *The Antisocial Process Screening Device*. Toronto: Multi-Health Systems.

Frick, P. J., & Loney, B. R. (2000). The use of laboratory and performance-based measures in the assessment of children and adolescents with conduct disorders. *Journal of Clinical Child Psychology, 29*, 540–554.

Frick, P. J., Barry, C., & Bodin, S. (2000). Applying the concept of psychopathy to children: Implications for the assessment of antisocial youth. In C. Gacono (Ed.), *The clinical and forensic assessment of psychopathy: A practitioner's guide*. (pp. 3–24). Hillsdale, NJ: Erlbaum.

Frick, P. J., Cornell, A. H., Bodin, S. D., Dane, H. E., Barry, C. T., & Loney, B. R. (2003). Callous-unemotional traits and developmental pathways to severe conduct problems. *Developmental Psychology, 39*, 246–260.

Frick, P. J., Lilienfeld, S. O., Ellis, M., Loney, B., & Silverthorn, P. (1999). The association between anxiety and psychopathy dimensions in children. *Journal of Abnormal Child Psychology, 27*, 383–392.

Frick, P. J., Van Horn, Y., Lahey, B. B., Christ, M. A. G., Loeber, R., Hart, E. A., et al. (1993). Oppositional defiant disorder and conduct disorder: A meta-analytic review of factor analyses and cross-validation in a clinic sample. *Clinical Psychology Review, 13*, 319–340.

Friman, P. C., Handwerk, M. L., Smith, G. L., Larzelere, R. E., Lucas, C. P., & Shaffer, D. M. (2000). External validity of conduct and oppositional defiant disorders determined by the NIMH Diagnostic Interview Schedule for Children. *Journal of Abnormal Child Psychology, 28*, 277–286.

Gabrielli, W. F., & Mednick, S. A. (1983). Genetic correlates of criminal behavior: Implications for research, attribution, and prevention. *American Behavioral Scientist, 27*, 59–74.

Gacono, C. B. (Ed.). (2000). *The clinical and forensic assessment of psychopathy: A practitioner's guide*. Hillsdale, NJ: Erlbaum.

Gacono, C. B., & Hughes, T. L. (2004). Differentiating emotional disturbance from social maladjustment: Assessing psychopathy in aggressive youth. *Psychology in the Schools, 41*, 849–860.

Gacono, C. B., & Meloy, J. R. (1994). *The Rorschach assessment of aggressive and psychopathic personalities*. Hillsdale, NJ: Erlbaum.

Gacono, C. B., Evans, F. B., & Viglione, D. J. (2002). The Rorschach in forensic practice. *Journal of Forensic Psychology Practice, 2*, 33–53.

Gacono, C. B., Nieberding, R., Owen, A., Rubel, J., & Bodholdt, R. (2001). Treating juvenile and adult offenders with conduct disorder, antisocial, and psychopathic personalities. In J. Ashford, B. Sales & W. Reid (Eds.), *Treating clients with special needs* (pp. 99–129). Washington, DC: American Psychological Association.

Garb, H. N. (1998). *Studying the clinician: Judgment research and psychological assessment*. Washington, DC: American Psychological Association.

Garmezy, N., & Rutter, M. (1983) *Stress, coping and development in children*. New York: McGraw-Hill.

Gelhorn, H., Stallings, M., Young, S., Corley, R., Rhee, S. H., Hopfer, C., et al. (2006). Common and specific genetic influences on aggressive and nonaggressive conduct disorder domains. *Journal of the American Academy of Child and Adolescent Psychiatry, 45*, 570–577.

Giancola, P. R., & Mezzich, A. C. (2000). Executive cognitive functioning mediates the relation between language competence and antisocial behavior in conduct-disordered adolescent females. *Aggressive Behavior, 26*, 359–375.

Glascoe, F. P. (2006). *Parents' Evaluation of Developmental Status*. Nashville, TN: Ellsworth & Vandermeer Press LLC, available at www.pedstest.com.

Goldberg, L. R. (1993). The structure of phenotypic personality traits. *American Psychologist, 48*, 26–34.

Goldstein, A. P. (1988). *The prepare curriculum: Teaching prosocial competencies*. Champaign, IL: Research Press.

Goldstein, R. B., Grant, B. F., Ruan, W. J., Smith, S. M., & Saha, T. D. (2006). Antisocial personality disorder with childhood- vs. adolescence-onset conduct disorder: Results from the national epidemiologic survey on alcohol and related conditions. *Journal of Nervous and Mental Disease, 194*, 667–675.

Goldstein, R. B., Prescott, C. A., & Kendler, K. S. (2001). Genetic and environmental factors in conduct problems and adult antisocial behavior among adult female twins. *Journal of Nervous and Mental Disease, 189*, 201–209.

Goodman, R., Ford, T., Richards, H., Gatward, R., & Meltzer, H. (2000). The Development and Well-Being Assessment: Description and initial validation of an integrated assessment of child and adolescent psychopathology. *Journal of Child Psychology and Psychiatry, 41*, 645–655.

Gray, J. A. (1987). *The psychology of fear and stress* (2nd ed.). New York: Cambridge University Press.

Greenberg, M. T., & Kusche, C. A. (1996). *The PATHS project: Preventive intervention for children: Final report to the National Institute of Mental Health.* Grant number R01MH42131. http://www.colorado.edu/cspv/blueprints/model/programs/PATHS.html

Greene, R. W., Biederman, J., Zerwas, S., Monuteaux, M., Goring, J. C., & Faraone, S. V. (2002). Psychiatric comorbidity, family dysfunction, and social impairment in referred youth with oppositional defiant disorder. *American Journal of Psychiatry, 159,* 1214–1224.

Gretton, H., McBride, M., Hare, R., O'Shaughnessy, R., & Kumka, G. (2001). Psychopathy and recidivism in adolescent sex offenders. *Criminal Justice and Behavior, 28,* 427–449.

Grossman, D. C., Necherman, H. J., Koepsell, T. D., Liu, K. N., Beland, K., Frey, K., & Rivera, F. P. (1997). Effectiveness of a violence prevention curriculum among children in elementary school. *Journal of the American Academy of Child and Adolescent Psychiatry, 30,* 208–217.

Guerra, N. G., Huesmann, L. R., Tolan, P. H., Van Acker, R., & Eron, L. D. (1995). Stressful events and individual beliefs as correlates of economic disadvantage and aggression among urban children. *Journal of Consulting and Clinical Psychology, 63,* 518–528.

Hampel, R., & Selg, H. (1975). FAF. *Fragebogen zur Erfassung von Aggressivitatsfaktoren.* Gottingen: Hogrefe.

Hampson, S. E., Goldberg, L. R., Vogt, T. M., & Dubanoski, J. P. (2006). Forty years on: Teachers' assessments of personality traits predict self-reported health behaviors and outcomes at midlife. *Health Psychology, 25,* 57–64.

Harada, Y., Satoh, Y., Sakuma, A., Imai, J., Tamaru, T., Takahashi, T., et al. (2002). Behavioral and developmental disorders among conduct disorder. *Psychiatry and Clinical Neurosciences, 56,* 621–625.

Hare, R. (1993). *Without conscience: The disturbing world of the psychopaths among us.* New York: Guilford Press.

Hare, R. (2003). *The Hare Psychopathy Checklist-Revised* (2nd edition). Toronto: Multi-Health Systems.

Hawkins, J. D., Herrenkohl, T., Farrington, D. P., Brewer, D., Catalano, R. F., & Harachi, T. W. (1998). A review of predictors of youth violence. In R. Loeber & D. P. Farrington (Eds.), *Serious and violent juvenile offenders: Risk factors and successful interventions* (pp. 106–146). Thousand Oaks, CA: Sage.

Henggeler, S. W., Schoenwald, S. K., Borduin, C. M., Rowland, M. D., & Cunningham, P. B. (1998). *Multisystemic treatment of antisocial behavior in children and adolescents.* New York: Guilford Press.

Herkov, M. J., & Myers, W. C. (1996). MMPI profiles of depressed adolescents with and without conduct disorder. *Journal of Clinical Psychology, 52,* 705–710.

Herpertz, S. C., Mueller, B., Qunaibi, M., Lichterfeld, C., Konrad, K., & Herpertz-Dahlmann, B. (2005). Response to emotional stimuli in boys with conduct disorder. *American Journal of Psychiatry, 162,* 1100–1107.

Herrenkohl, T. I., Maguin, E. Hill, K. G., Hawkins, J. D., Abbott, R. D., & Catalano, R. F. (2000). Developmental risk factors for youth violence. *Journal of Adolescent Health, 26,* 176–186.

Heyman, I., Fombonne, E., Simmons, H., Ford, T., Meltzer, H., & Goodman, R. (2003). Prevalence of obsessive-compulsive disorder in the British nationwide survey of child mental health. *International Review of Psychiatry, 15,* 178–184.

Heyman, R. E., & Schlee, K. A. (1997). Toward a better estimate of the prevalence of partner abuse: Adjusting rates based on the sensitivity of the Conflict Tactics Scale. *Journal of Family Psychology, 11,* 332–338.

Hilarski, C. (2004). Victimization history as a risk factor for conduct disorder behaviors: Exploring connections in a national sample of youth. *Stress, Trauma, and Crisis: An International Journal, 7*, 47–59.

Hiller, J. B., Rosenthal, R., Bornstein, R. F., Berry, D. T., & Brunell-Neuleib, S. (1999). A comparative meta-analysis of Rorschach and MMPI validity. *Psychological Assessment, 11*, 278–296.

Hinrichs, G. (2001). Multidimensional assessment of young male offenders in penal institutions. *International Journal of Offender Therapy and Comparative Criminology, 45*, 478–488.

Hinshaw, S. P., Heller, T., & McHale, J. P. (1992). Covert antisocial behavior in boys with attention-deficit hyperactivity disorder: External validation and effects of methylphenidate, *Journal of Consulting and Clinical Psychology, 60*, 274–281.

Hinshaw, S. P., Simmel, C., & Heller, T. L. (1995). Multimethod assessment of covert antisocial behavior in children: Laboratory observations, adult ratings, and child self-report. *Psychological Assessment, 7*, 209–219.

Hinshaw, S. P., Zupan, B. A., Simmel, C., Nigg, J. T., & Melnick, S. (1997). Peer status in boys with and without attention-deficit hyperactivity disorder: Predictions from overt and covert antisocial behavior, social isolation, and authoritative parenting beliefs. *Child Development, 68*, 880–896.

Hodges, K., & Saunders, W. (1990). Internal consistency of a diagnostic interview for children: The Child Assessment Schedule. *Journal of Abnormal Child Psychology, 17*, 691–701.

Hodges, K., Cool, J., & McKnew, D. (1989). Test-retest reliability of a clinical research interview for children: The Child Assessment Schedule. *Psychological Assessment, 1*, 317–322.

Hodges, K., Kline, J., Stern, L., Cytryn, L., & McKnew, D. (1982). The development of a child assessment schedule for research and clinical use. *Journal of Abnormal Child Psychiatry, 10*, 173–189.

Hodges, K., McKnew, D., Burbach, D. J., & Roebuck, L. (1987). Diagnostic concordance between the Child Assessment Schedule (CAS) and the Schedule for Affective Disorders and Schizophrenia in school-age children (K-SADS) in an outpatient sample using lay interviewers. *Journal of the American Academy of Child and Adolescent Psychiatry, 26*, 654–661.

Hogan, A. E., Quay, H. C., Vaughn, S., & Shapiro, S. K. (1989). Revised Behavior Problem Checklist: Stability, prevalence, and incidence of behavior problems in kindergarten and first-grade children. *Psychological Assessment, 1*, 103–111.

Holmes, S. E., Slaughter, J. R., & Kashani, J. (2001). Risk factors in childhood that lead to the development of conduct disorder and antisocial personality disorder. *Child Psychiatry and Human Development, 31*, 183–193.

Hops, H., & Walker, H. M. (1988). *CLASS: Contingencies for Learning Academic and Social Skills*. Seattle, WA: Educational Achievement Systems.

Hornak, J., Bramham, J., Rolls, E. T., Morris, R. G., O'Doherty, J., Bullock, P. R., et al. (2003). Changes in emotion after circumscribed surgical lesions of the orbitofrontal and cingulate cortices. *Brain, 126*, 1691–1712.

Hudley, C., & Graham, S. (1995). School-based interventions for aggressive African-American boys. *Applied & Preventive Psychology, 4*, 185–195.

Hudziak, J. J., Copeland, W., Stanger, C., & Wadsworth, M. (2004). Screening for DSM-IV externalizing disorders with the Child Behavior Checklist: A receiver-operating characteristic analysis. *Journal of Child Psychology and Psychiatry, 45*, 1299–1307.

Hughes, T. L. (2001). Complexity in the causal pathways of aggression in children: A rationale for treatment. In M. Martinez (Ed.) *Prevention and control of aggression and the impacts on its victims*. (1st ed., pp.113–120) New York: Plenum.

Hughes, T. L., Gacono, C. G., & Owen, P. F. (2007). Current status of Rorschach assessment: Implications for the school psychologist. *Psychology in the Schools, 44*, 281–291.

Hunter, L., Elias, M. J., & Norris, J. (2001). School based violence prevention: Challenges and lessons learned from an action research project. *Journal of School Psychology, 39*, 161–175.

IDEIA. (2004). Individuals with Disabilities Education Improvement Act of 2004. 20 USC 1400.

Jaffee, S. R., Belsky, J., Harrington, H., Caspi, A., & Moffitt, T. E. (2006). When parents have a history of conduct disorder: How is the caregiving environment affected? *Journal of Abnormal Psychology, 115*, 309–319.

Jaideep, T., Reddy, Y. C. J., & Srinath, S. (2006). Comorbidity of attention deficit hyperactivity disorder in juvenile bipolar disorder. *Bipolar Disorders, 8*, 182–187.

Janson, H., & Stattin, H. (2003). Prediction of adolescent and adult delinquency from childhood Rorschach ratings. *Journal of Personality Assessment, 8*, 51–63.

Jellinek, M., & Murphy, J. M. (n.d.) *Pediatric Symptom Checklist*. Retrieved February 2007 from http://www.massgeneral.org/allpsych/PediatricSymptomChecklist/psc_english.PDF.

Jimerson, S. R., Morrison, G. M., Pletcher, S. W., & Furlong, M. J. (2006). Youth engaged in antisocial and aggressive behaviors: Who are they? In S. Jimerson & M. Furlong, (Eds.), *Handbook of school violence and school safety: From research to practice*, (pp. 3–19). Mahwah, NJ: Erlbaum.

Johnson, H. R., Thompson, M. J. J., Wilkinson, S., Walsh, L., Balding, J., & Wright, V. (2002). Vulnerability to bullying: Teacher-reported conduct and emotional problems, hyperactivity, peer relationship difficulties, and prosocial behaviour in primary school children. *Educational Psychology, 22*, 553–556.

Kann, R. T., & Hanna, F. J. (2000). Disruptive behavior disorders in children and adolescents: How do girls differ from boys? *Journal of Counseling and Development, 78*, 267–274.

Kashani, J. H., Jones, M. R., Bumby, K. M., & Thomas, L. A. (1999). Youth violence: Psychosocial risk factors, treatment, prevention, and recommendations. *Journal of Emotional & Behavioral Disorders, 7*, 200–210.

Kashani, J. H, Orvaschel, H., Rosenberg, T., & Reid, J. (1989). Psychopathology in a community sample of children and adolescents: A developmental perspective. *Journal of the American Academy of Child and Adolescent Psychiatry, 28*, 701–706.

Kawa, I., Carter, J. D., Joyce, P. R., Doughty, C. J., Frampton, C. M., Wells, J. E., et al. (2005). Gender differences in bipolar disorder: Age of onset, course, comorbidity, and symptom presentation. *Bipolar Disorders, 7*, 119–125.

Kazdin, A. E. (1995). Risk factors, onset, and course of dysfunction. In A.E. Kazdin (Ed.), *Conduct disorders in childhood and adolescence* (2nd ed., pp. 50–74). Thousand Oaks, CA: Sage.

Kazdin, A. E. (1996). *Conduct disorders in childhood and adolescence* (2nd ed.). Thousand Oaks, CA: Sage.

Kazdin, A. E. (1997). Practitioner review: Psychosocial treatments for conduct disorder in children. *Journal of Child Psychology and Psychiatry, 38*, 161–178.

Kazdin, A. E., & Kolko, D. J. (1986). Parent psychopathology and family functioning among childhood firesetters. *Journal of Abnormal Child Psychology, 14*, 315–329.

Keenen, K., Shaw, D. S., Walsh, B., Delliquadri, E., & Giovannelli, J. (1997). DSM-III-R disorders in preschool children from low-income families. *Journal of the American Academy of Child and Adolescent Psychiatry, 36*, 620–627.

Kelly, B. T., Loeber, R., Keenan, K., & DeLamarte, M. (1997). *Developmental pathways in boys' disruptive and delinquent behavior.* Washington, DC: U.S. Department of Justice, Office of Justice Programs, Office of Juvenile Justice and Delinquency Prevention.

Kelly, E. J. (1990). *The Differential Test of Conduct and Emotional Problems.* East Aurora, NY: Slosson.

Kelly, E. J., & Vitali, G. J. (1990). *Differential test of conduct and emotional problems: Manual.* East Aurora, NY: Slosson Educational Publications.

Kelly, T. M., Cornelius, J. R., & Lynch, K. G. (2002). Psychiatric and substance use disorders as risk factors for attempted suicide among adolescents: A case control study. *Suicide and Life-Threatening Behavior, 32*, 301–312.

Kemph, J. P., DeVane, C. L., Levin, G.M., Jarecke, R., & Miller, R. L. (1993). Treatment of aggressive children with clonidine: Results of an open pilot study. *Journal of the American Academy of Child Adolescent Psychiatry, 32*, 577–581.

Kessler, R. C., & Ustun, T. B. (2004). The World Mental Health (WMH) Survey Initiative Version of the World Health Organization (WHO) Composite International Diagnostic Interview (CIDI). *International Journal of Methods in Psychiatric Research, 13*, 93, 121.

Kessler, R. C., Berglund, P., Demler, O., Jin, R., Merikangas, K. R., & Walters, E. E. (2005). Lifetime prevalence and age-of-onset distributions of DSM-IV disorders in National Comorbidity Survey Replication. *Archives of General Psychiatry, 62*, 593–602.

Khalsa, S. S. (1996). *Group exercises for enhancing social skills and self-esteem.* Sarasota, FL: Professional Resource Press/Professional Resource Exchange.

Khan, A. A., Jacobson, K. C., Gardner, C. O., Prescott, C. A., & Kendler, K. S. (2005). Personality and comorbidity of common psychiatric disorders. *British Journal of Psychiatry, 186*, 190–196.

Kim, E. Y., & Miklowitz, D. J. (2002). Childhood mania, attention deficit hyperactivity disorder and conduct disorder: A critical review of diagnostic dilemmas. *Bipolar Disorders, 4*, 215–225.

Kim-Cohen, J., Arseneault, L., Caspi, A., Tomás, M. P., Taylor, A., & Moffitt, T. E. (2005). Validity of DSM-IV conduct disorder in 4½–5-year-old children: A longitudinal epidemiological study. *American Journal of Psychiatry, 162*, 1108–1117.

Kim-Cohen, J., Moffitt, T. E., Taylor, A., Pawlby, S. J., & Caspi, A. (2005). Maternal depression and children's antisocial behavior: Nature and nurture effects. *Archives of General Psychiatry, 62*, 173–181.

Kirk, S. (1962). *Educating exceptional children.* Boston: Houghton Mifflin.

Kirk, S. A., & Hsieh, D. K. (2004). Diagnostic consistency in assessing conduct disorder: An experiment on the effect of social context. *American Journal of Orthopsychiatry, 74*, 43–55.

Kohlberg, L. (1973). The claim to moral adequacy of a highest stage of moral judgment. *Journal of Philosophy, 70*, 630–646.

Kolko, D. J., Bukstein, O. G., & Barron, J. (1999). Methylphenidate and behavior modification in children with ADHD and comorbid ODD or CD: Main and incremental effects across settings. *Journal of the American Academy of Child and Adolescent Psychiatry, 38*, 578–586.

Kovacs, M., & Pollock, M. (1995). Bipolar disorder and comorbid conduct disorder in childhood and adolescence. *Journal of the American Academy of Child and Adolescent Psychiatry, 34*, 715–723.

Kuhne, M., Schachar, R., & Tannock, R. (1997). Impact of comorbid oppositional or conduct problems on attention-deficit hyperactivity disorder. *Journal of the American Academy of Child and Adolescent Psychiatry, 36*, 1715–1725.

LaBar, K. S., Gatenby, J. C., Gore, J. C., LeDoux, J. E., & Phelps, E. A. (1998). Human amygdala activation during conditioned fear acquisition and extinction: A mixed trial fMRI study. *Neuron, 20*, 937–945.

Lahey, B. B., & Waldman, I. D. (2003). A developmental propensity model of the origins of conduct problems during childhood and adolescence. In B. B. Lahey, T. E. Moffitt, & A. Caspi (Eds.), *Causes of conduct disorder and juvenile delinquency* (pp. 76–117). New York: Guilford Press.

Lahey, B. B., Goodman, S. H., Canino, G., Bird, H., Schwab-Stone, M., Waldman, I. D., Rathouz, P. J., Miller, T. L., Dennis, K. D., & Jensen, P. S. (2000). Age and gender differences in oppositional behavior and conduct problems: A cross-sectional house-hold study of middle childhood and adolescence. *Journal of Abnormal Psychology, 109*, 488–503.

Lahey, B. B., Loeber, R., Quay, H. C., Applegate, B., Shaffer, D., Waldman, I., et al. (1998). Validity of DSM-IV subtypes of conduct disorder based on age of onset. *Journal of the American Academy of Child & Adolescent Psychiatry, 37*, 435–442.

Lahey, B. B., Miller, T. L., Gordon, R. A., & Riley, A. W. (1999). Developmental epidemiology of the disruptive behavior disorders. In H. C. Quay & A. E. Hogan (Eds.), *Handbook of disruptive behavior disorders* (pp. 23–48). New York: Plenum.

Lahey, B. B., Schwab-Stone, M. Goodman, S. H., Waldman, I. D., Canino, G., & Rathouz, P. J., et al. (2000). Age and gender differences in oppositional behavior and conduct problems: A cross-sectional household study of middle childhood and adolescence. *Journal of Abnormal Psychology, 109*, 488–503.

Lambert, E. W., Wahler, R. G., Andrade, A. R., & Bickman, L. (2001). Looking for the disorder in conduct disorder. *Journal of Abnormal Psychology, 110*, 110–123.

Lane, R. D., Reiman, E. M., Bradley, M. M., Lang, P. J., Ahern, G. L., Davidson, R. J., et al. (1997). Neuroanatomical correlates of pleasant and unpleasant emotion. *Neuropsychologia, 35*, 1437–1444.

Lane, R. D., & Schwartz, G. E. (1998). Levels of emotional awareness: A cognitive-developmental theory and its application to psychopathology. *American Journal of Psychiatry, 144*, 133–143.

Larsen, R. J. & Prizmic, Z. (2004). Affect regulation. In Baumeister, R. F. & Vohs, K. D. (Eds.). *Handbook of self-regulation: Research, theory, and applications* (pp. 40–61). New York: Guilford Press.

Latimer, W. W., Stone, A. L., Voight, A., Winters, K. C., & August, G. J. (2002). Gender differences in psychiatric comorbidity among adolescents with substance use disorders. *Experimental and Clinical Psychopharmacology, 10*, 310–315.

Lengua, L. J., Sadowski, C. A., Friedrich, W. N., & Fisher, J. (2001). Rationally and empirically derived dissensions of children's symptomatology: Expert ratings and confirmatory factor analyses of the CBCL. *Journal of Consulting and Clinical Psychology, 69*, 683–698.

Levy, F., Hay, D. A., McStephen, M., Wood, C., & Waldman, I. (1997). Attention-deficit hyperactivity disorder: A category or a continuum? Genetic analysis of a large-scale twin study. *Journal of the American Academy of Child and Adolescent Psychiatry, 36,* 737–744.

Lewinsohn, P. M., Hops, H., Roberts, R. E., Seeley, J. R., & Andrews, J. R. (1993). Adolescent psychopathology: I. Prevalence and incidence of depression and other DSM-III-R disorders in high school students. *Journal of Abnormal Psychology, 102,* 133–144.

Lewis, C. E., & Bucholz, K. K. (1991). Alcoholism, antisocial behavior and family history. *British Journal of Addiction, 86,* 177–194.

Lewis, D. O. (2002). Development of the symptoms of violence. In M. Lewis (Ed.) *Child and adolescent psychiatry: A comprehensive textbook* (3rd ed., pp. 387–399). Philadelphia: Lippincott Williams & Wilkins.

Little, E., & Hudson, A. (1998). Conduct problems and treatment across home and school: A review of the literature. *Behavior Change, 15,* 213–227.

Lochman, J. E., Coie, J. D., & Underwood, M. K. (1993). Effectiveness of a social relations intervention program for aggressive and nonaggressive, rejected children. *Journal of Consulting and Clinical Psychology, 61,* 1053–1058.

Lochman, J. E., & Wells, K. C. (1996). A social-cognitive intervention with aggressive children: Prevention effects and contextual implementation issues. In R. Peters & R. J. McMahon (Eds.), *Preventing childhood disorders, substance abuse, and delinquency* (pp. 111–143). Thousand Oaks, CA: Sage Publications.

Lock, J., & Strauss, G. D. (1994). Psychiatric hospitalization of adolescents for conduct disorder. *Hospital & Community Psychiatry, 45,* 925–928.

Loeber, R. (1982). The stability of antisocial and delinquent child behavior: A review. *Child Development, 53,* 1431–1446.

Loeber, R. (1990). Development and risk factors of juvenile antisocial behavior and delinquency. *Clinical Psychology Review, 10,* 1–41.

Loeber, R., Burke, J. D., Lahey, B.B., Winters, A., & Zera, M. (2000). Oppositional defiant and conduct disorder: A review of the past 10 years, Part I. *Journal of the American Academy of Child and Adolescent Psychiatry, 39,* 1468–1484.

Loeber, R., Keenan, K., & Zhang, Q. (1997). Boys' experimentation and persistence in developmental pathways toward serious delinquency. *Journal of Child and Family Studies, 6,* 321–357.

Loeber, R., Farrington, D., Stouthamer-Loeber, M., & Van Kammen, W. B. (1998). *Antisocial behaviors and mental health problems: Explanatory factors in childhood and adolescence.* Mahway, NJ: Lawrence Erlhaum.

Loeber, R., Wung, P., Keenan, K., Giroux, B., Stouthamer-Loeber, M., & Van Kammen, W. B. (1993). Developmental pathways in disruptive child behavior. *Developmental Psychopathology, 5,* 101–132.

Loney, B. R., Frick, P. J., Ellis, M., & McCoy, M. G. (1998). Intelligence, callous-unemotional traits, and antisocial behavior. *Journal of Psychopathology and Behavioral Assessment, 20,* 231–247.

Loving, J., & Gacono, C. (2002). Assessing psychopathy in juveniles: clinical and forensic applications. In N. Ribner (Ed.). *Handbook of juvenile forensic psychology* (pp. 292–317). New York: Wiley.

Loving, J., & Russell, W. F. (2000). Selected Rorschach variables of psychopathic juvenile offenders. *Journal of Personality Assessment, 75,* 126–142.

Luczak, S. E., Wall, T. L., Cook, T. A. R., Shea, S. H., & Carr, L. G. (2004). ALDH2 status and conduct disorder mediate the relationship between ethnicity and alcohol dependence in Chinese, Korean, and White American college students. *Journal of Abnormal Psychology, 113,* 271–278.

Lumley, V. A., McNeil, C. B., Herschell, A. D., & Bahl, A. B. (2002). An examination of gender differences among young children and disruptive behavior disorders. *Child Study Journal, 32*, 89–100.

Luna, B. (2005, October). *Brain and cognitive processes underlying cognitive control of behavior in adolescence.* Paper presented at the University of Pittsburgh, Pittsburgh, PA.

Luna, B. (2007, February). *Adolescent brain development and cognitive control of behavior.* Workshop presented at the School Psychology Speaker Series, Duquesne University, Pittsburgh, PA.

Lynam, D. R. (1996). Early identification of chronic offenders: Who is the fledgling psychopath? *Psychological Bulletin, 120*, 209–234.

Lynam, D. (1997). Pursuing the psychopath: Capturing the fledgling psychopath in a nomological net. *Journal of Abnormal Psychology, 106*, 425–438.

Lynam, D. (1998). Early identification of the fledgling psychopath: Locating the psychopathic child in the current nomenclature. *Journal of Abnormal Psychology, 107*, 566–575.

Lyons-Ruth, K., Alpern, L., & Repacholi, B. (1993). Disorganized infant attachment classification and maternal psychosocial problems as predictors of hostile-aggressive behavior in the preschool classroom. *Child Development, 64*, 572–585.

Mager, W. (2005). Intervention groups for adolescents with conduct problems: Is aggregation harmful or helpful? *Journal of Abnormal Child Psychology, 33*, 349–362.

Maguin, E., & Loeber, R. (1996). Academic performance and delinquency. In M. Tonry & N. Morris (Eds.), *Crime and justice: A review of research* (Vol. 20). Chicago: University of Chicago Press.

Mannuzza, S., Klein, R. G., Abikoff, H., & Moulton, J. L. (2004). Significance of childhood conduct problems to later development of conduct disorder among children with ADHD: A prospective follow-up study. *Journal of Abnormal Child Psychology, 32*, 565–573.

Mantzicopoulos, P. Y., & Morrison, D. (1994). Early prediction of reading achievement: Exploring the relationship of cognitive and noncognitive measures to inaccurate classifications of at-risk status. *Remedial and Special Education, 15*, 244–251.

Marshall, G. N., Wortman, C. B., Vickers, R. R., Kusulas, J. W., & Hervig, L. K. (1994). The five-factor model of personality as a framework for personality-health research. *Journal of Personality and Social Psychology, 67*, 278–286.

Marshal, M. P., & Molina, B. S. G. (2006). Antisocial behaviors moderate the deviant peer pathway to substance use in children with ADHD. *Journal of Clinical Child and Adolescent Psychology, 35*, 216–226.

Masi, G., Millepiedi, S., Mucci, M., Bertini, N., Pfanner, C., & Arcangeli, F. (2006). Comorbidity of obsessive-compulsive disorder and attention-deficit/hyperactivity disorder in referred children and adolescents. *Comprehensive Psychiatry, 47*, 42–47.

Masi, G., Toni, C., Perugi, G., Travierso, M. C., Millepiedi, S., Mucci, M., & Akiskal, H. S. (2003). Externalizing disorders in consecutively referred children and adolescents with bipolar disorder. *Comprehensive Psychiatry, 44*, 184–189.

Mason, D. A., & Frick, P. J. (1994). The heritability of antisocial behavior: A meta-analysis of twin and adoption studies. *Journal of Psychopathology and Behavioral Assessment, 16*, 301–323.

Maughan, B., Rowe, R., Messer, J., Goodman, R., & Meltzer, H. (2004). Conduct Disorder and Oppositional Defiant Disorder in a national sample: Developmental epidemiology. *Journal of Child Psychology and Psychiatry, 45*, 609–621.

McBurnett, K., Lahey, B. B., Rathouz, P. J., & Loeber, R. (2000). Low salivary cortisol and persistent aggression in boys referred for disruptive behavior. *Archives of General Psychiatry, 57*, 38–43.

McCabe, K. M., Hough, R., Wood, P. A., & Yeh, M. (2001). Childhood and adolescent onset conduct disorder: A test of the developmental taxonomy. *Journal of Abnormal Child Psychology, 29*, 305–316.

McClelland, D. C., Koestner, R., & Weinberger, J. (1989). How do self-attributed and implicit motives differ? *Psychological Review, 96*, 690–702.

McConaughy, S. H. (2005). *Clinical interviews for children and adolescents: Assessment to intervention.* New York: Guilford Press.

McCord, J. (1979). Some child-rearing antecedents of criminal behavior in adult men. *Journal of Personality and Social Psychology, 9*, 1477–1486.

McGee, R., Freehan, M., Williams, S., Partridge, F., Silva, P. A., & Kelly, J. (1990). DSM-III disorders in a large sample of adolescents. *Journal of the American Academy of Child and Adolescent Psychiatry, 29*, 611–619.

McMahon, R. J., & Estes, A. M. (1997). Conduct problems. In E. J. Mash & L. G. Terdal (Eds.), *Assessment of childhood disorders* (3rd ed., pp. 130–193). New York: Guilford Press.

McMahon, R. J., & Forehand, R. (1988). Conduct problems. In E. J. Mash & L. G. Terdal (Eds.), *Behavioral Assessment of Childhood Disorders* (2nd ed.). New York: Guilford Press.

McMahon, R. J., & Wells, K. C. (1998). Conduct problems. In E. J. Mash & R. A. Barkley (Eds.), *Treatment of childhood disorders* (2nd ed., pp. 111–207). New York: Guilford Press.

Meller, W. H., & Borchardt, C. M. (1996). Comorbidity of major depression and conduct disorder. *Journal of Affective Disorders, 39*, 123–126.

Meloy, J. R. (1992). *Violence attachments.* San Diego, CA: Specialized Training Services.

Meloy, J. R. (2000). *Violence risk and threat assessment.* San Diego, CA: Specialized Training Services.

Meloy, J. R., Hempel, A. G., Mohandie, K., Shiva, A., & Gray, T. B. (2001). Offender and offense characteristics of a nonrandom sample of adolescent mass murders. *Journal of the American Academy of Child Adolescent Psychiatry, 40*, 719–28.

Merrell, K. W. (1999). *Behavioral, social, and emotional assessment of children and adolescents.* Mahwah, NJ: Erlbaum.

Merrell, K. W. (2003). *Preschool and Kindergarten Behavior Scales* (2nd ed.). Austin, TX: PRO-ED.

Merrell, K.W., & Walker, H.M. (2004). Deconstructing a definition: Social maladjustment versus emotional disturbance and moving the EBD field forward. *Psychology in the Schools, 41*, 899–909.

Meyer, G. J. (1997). Assessing reliability: Critical correlations for a critical examination of the Rorschach Comprehensive System. *Psychological Assessment, 9*, 480–489.

Meyer, G. J., & Archer, R. P. (2001). The hard science of Rorschach research: What do we know and where do we go? *Psychological Assessment, 13*, 486–502.

Meyer, G. J., Hilsenroth, M. J., Baxter, D., Exner, J. E., Fowler, C. J., Piers, C. C., & Resnick, J. (2002). An examination of inter-rater reliability for scoring the Rorschach Comprehensive System in eight data sets. *Journal of Personality Assessment, 78*, 219–274.

Miller, J.A., & Leffard, S. A. (2007). Behavioral assessment. In S. R. Smith & L. Handler (Eds.) *The clinical assessment of children adolescents: A practitioners guide* (pp. 115–137). Hillsdale, NJ: Erlbaum.

Miller, J. A., Tansy, M., & Hughes, T. L. (1998). Functional behavioral assessment: The link between problem behavior and effective intervention in schools. *Current Issues in Education, 1*, 1–18.

Miller, J. A., Williams, S. J., & McCoy, E. L. B. (2004). Using multimodal functional behavioral assessment to inform treatment selection for children with either emotional disturbance or social maladjustment. *Psychology in the Schools, 41*, 867–877.

Moffitt, T. E. (1993). Adolescent-limited and life-course persistent antisocial behavior: A developmental taxonomy. *Psychological Review, 100*, 674–701.

Moffitt, T. E., & Silva, P. A. (1988). Self-reported delinquency: Results from an instrument for New Zealand. *Australian and New Zealand Journal of Criminology, 21*, 227–240.

Moffitt, T. E., Caspi, A., Rutter, M., & Silva, P. A. (2001). *Sex differences in antisocial behavior: Conduct disorder, delinquency, and violence in the Dunedin Longitudinal Study.* Cambridge, UK: Cambridge University Press.

Molina, B. S. G., Bukstein, O. G., & Lynch, K. G. (2002). Attention-deficit/hyperactivity disorder and conduct disorder symptomatology in adolescents with alcohol use disorder. *Psychology of Addictive Behaviors, 16*, 161–164.

Monhandie, K. (2000). *School violence threat management.* San Diego, CA: Specialized Training Services.

Moos, R. H., & Moos, B. S. (1987). *The Family Environment Scale manual.* Palo Alto, CA: Consulting Psychologists Press.

Moos, R. H., Insel, P. M., & Humphrey, B. (1974). *Family, work and group environment scales.* Palo Alto, CA: Consulting Psychologists Press.

Morris, C. (2007). *Psychopathic traits and social cognitive processes in aggressive youth.* Unpublished dissertation, Duquesne University.

Morris, J. S., Frith, C. D., Perrett, D. I., Rowland, D., & Young, A. W. (1996). A differential neural response in the human amygdala to fearful and happy facial expressions. *Nature, 383*, 812–815.

Mpofu, E. (2002). Psychopharmacology in the treatment of conduct disorder children and adolescents: Rationale, prospects, and ethics. *South African Journal of Psychology, 32*, 9–21.

Mpofu, E., & Conyers, L. M. (2003). Neurochemistry in the comorbidity of conduct disorder with other disorders of childhood and adolescence: Implications for counseling. *Counseling Psychology Quarterly, 16*, 37–41.

Mueser, K. T., Rosenberg, S. D., Drake, R. E., Miles, K. M., Wolford, G., Vidaver, R., et al. (1999). Conduct disorder, antisocial personality disorder and substance use disorders in schizophrenia and major affective disorders. *Journal of Studies on Alcohol, 60*, 278–284.

Muntz, R., Hutchings, J., & Edwards, R. T. (2004). Economic evaluation of treatments for children with severe behavioural problems. *Journal of Mental Health Policy and Economics, 7*, 177–189.

Murphy, D. A., Pelham, W. E., & Lang, A. R. (1992). Aggression in boys with attention deficit-hyperactivity disorder: Methylphenidate effects on naturalistically observed aggression, response to provocation, and social information processing. *Journal of Abnormal Child Psychology, 20*, 451–466.

Myers, K., & Winters, N. C. (2002). Ten-year review of rating scales I: Overview of scale functioning, psychometric properties and selection. *Journal of the American Academy of Child Adolescent Psychiatry, 41*, 114–122.

Myers, M. G., Stewart, D. G., & Brown, S. A. (1998). Progression from conduct disorder to antisocial personality disorder following treatment for adolescent substance abuse. *American Journal of Psychiatry, 155*, 479–485.

Myers, W. C., & Scott, K. (1998). Psychotic and conduct disorder symptoms in juvenile murderers. *Homicide Studies, 2*, 160–175.

Nelson, C. M. (1992). Searching for meaning in the behavior of antisocial pupils, public school educators, and lawmakers. *School Psychology Review, 1*, 35–39.

Neumann, C. S., Hare, R. D., & Newman, J. P. (2007). The super-ordinate nature of the Psychopathy Checklist-Revised. Special Section on Psychopathy: *Journal of Personality Disorders, 21*, 102–117.

Neumann, C. S., Kosson, D. S., Forth, A. E., & Hare, R. D. (2006). Factor structure of the Hare Psychopathy Checklist: Youth Version (PCL:YV) in incarcerated adolescents. *Psychological Assessment, 18*, 142–154.

Newcorn, J. H., Miller, S. R., Ivanova, I., Schulz, K. P., Kalmar, J., Marks, D. J., et al. (2004). Adolescent outcome of ADHD: Impact of childhood conduct and anxiety disorders. *CNS Spectrums, 9*, 668–678.

Nock, M. K., Kazdin, A. E., Hiripi, E., & Kessler, R. C. (2006). Prevalence, subtypes, and correlates of DSM-IV conduct disorder in the National Comorbidity Survey Replication. *Psychological Medicine, 36*, 699–710.

Nolan, E. E., Gadow, K. D., & Sprafkin, J. (2001). Teacher reports of DSM-IV ADHD, ODD, and CD symptoms in schoolchildren. *Journal of the American Academy of Child and Adolescent Psychiatry, 40*, 241–249.

O'Brien, B. S., & Frick, P. J. (1996). Reward dominance: Associations with anxiety, conduct problems, and psychopathy in children. *Journal of Abnormal Child Psychology, 24*, 223–240.

Offord, D. R., Boyle, M. H., Fleming, J. E., Munroe-Blum, H., & Rae-Grant, N. I. (1989). Ontario Child Health Study: Summary of selected results. *Canadian Journal of Psychiatry, 34*, 483–491.

Olweus, D. (1994). Annotation: Bullying at school: Basic facts and effects of a school based intervention program. *Journal of Child Psychology and Psychiatry, 35*, 1171–1190.

Olympia, D., Farley, M., Christiansen, E., Petterson, H., Jenson, W., & Clark, E. (2004). Social maladjustment and students with behavioral and emotional disorders: Revisiting basic assumptions and assessment issues. *Psychology in the Schools, 4*, 835–847.

O'Neill, K. B., & Liljequist, L. (2002). Strategies used by teachers to rate student behavior. *Psychology in the Schools, 39*, 77–85.

Oosterlaan, J., Geurts, H. M., Knol, D. L., & Sergeant, J. A. (2005). Low basal salivary cortisol is associated with teacher-reported symptoms of conduct disorder. *Psychiatry Research, 134*, 1–10.

Ownby, R. I. (1997). *Psychological reports: A guide to report writing in professional psychology* (3rd ed.). New York: Wiley.

Pajer, K., Gardner, W., Rubin, R. T., Perel, J., & Neal, S. (2001). Decreased cortisol levels in adolescent girls with conduct disorder. *Archives of General Psychiatry, 58*, 297–302.

Palacio, J. D., Castellanos, F. X., Pineda, D. A., Lopera, F., Arcos-Burgos, M., Quiroz, Y. T., et al. (2004). Attention-deficit/hyperactivity disorder and comorbidities in 18 Paisa Colombian multigenerational families. *Journal of the American Academy of Child and Adolescent Psychiatry, 43*, 1506–1515.

Pardini, D., Obradovic, J., & Loeber, R. (2006). Interpersonal callousness, hyperactivity/impulsivity, inattention, and conduct problems as precursors to delinquency persistence in boys: A comparison of three grade-based cohorts. *Journal of Clinical Child and Adolescent Psychology, 35*, 46–59.

Patrick, C. J., Bradley, M. M., & Lang, P. J. (1993). Emotion in the criminal psychopath: Startle reflex modulation. *Journal of Abnormal Psychology, 102*, 82–92.

Patterson, G. R., & Yoerger, K. (2002). A developmental model for early- and late-onset delinquency. In J. B. Reid, G. R. Patterson, & J. Snyder (Eds.), *Antisocial behavior in children and adolescents: A developmental analysis and model for intervention* (pp. 147–172). Washington, DC: American Psychological Association.

Patterson, G. R., DeGarmo, D. S., & Knutson, N. (2000). Hyperactive and antisocial behaviors: Comorbid or two points in the same process? *Development and Psychopathology, 12*, 91–106.

Pavuluri, M. N., Birmaher, B., & Naylor, M. W. (2005). Pediatric bipolar disorder: A review of the past 10 years. *Journal of the American Academy of Child and Adolescent Psychiatry, 44*, 846–871.

Pelham, W. E., Atkins, M. S., Murphy, H. A., & White, K. (1981, November). *Operationalization and validation of ADD.* Paper presented at the meeting of the Association for the Advancement of Behavior Therapy, Toronto.

Pelham, W. E., Evans, S. W., Gnagy, E. M., & Greenslade, K. E. (1992). Teacher ratings of DSM-III-R symptoms for the disruptive behavior disorders: Prevalence, factor analyses, and conditional probabilities in a special education sample. *School Psychology Review, 21*, 285–299.

Pelham, W. E., Milich, R., Cummings, E. M., Murphy, D. A., Schaughency, E. A., & Greiner, A. R. (1991). Effects of background anger, provocation, and methylphenidate on emotional arousal and aggressive responding in attention-deficit hyperactivity disordered boys with and without concurrent aggressiveness. *Journal of Abnormal Child Psychology, 19*, 407–426.

Pettit, G. S., Laird, R. D., Bates, J. E., & Dodge, K. A. (1997). Patterns of after-school care in middle childhood: Risk factors and developmental outcomes. *Merrill-Palmer Quarterly, 43*, 515–538.

Pierrehumbert, B., Miljkovitch, R., Plancherel., B., Halfon, O., & Ansermet, F. (2000). Attachment and temperament in early childhood: Implications for later behavior problems. *Infant and Child Development, 9*, 17–32.

Pike, A., McGuire, S., Hetherington, E. M., Reiss, D., & Plomin, R. (1996). Family environment and adolescent depressive symptoms and antisocial behavior. A multivariate genetic analysis. *Developmental Psychology, 32*, 590–603.

Piotroski, C. (1996). The status of Exner's Comprehensive System in contemporary research. *Perceptual and Motor Skills, 82*, 1341–1342.

Piotroski, C., & Keller, J. W. (1989). Use of assessment in mental health clinics and services. *Psychological Reports, 64*, 1298.

Piotroski, C., Sherry, D., & Keller, J. W. (1985). Psychodiagnostic test usage: A survey of the Society for Personality Assessment. *Journal of Personality Assessment, 49*, 115–119.

Placentini, J., Shaffer, D., Fisher, P. W., Schwab-Stone, M. E., Davies, M., & Giola, P. (1993). The Diagnostic Interview Schedule for Children—revised version (DISC-R), III: concurrent criterion validity. *Journal of the American Academy of Child and Adolescent Psychiatry, 32*, 651–657.

Prinz, R. J., Blechman, E. A., & Dumas, J. E. (1994). An evaluation of peer coping-skills training for childhood aggression. *Journal of Clinical Child Psychology, 23*, 193–203.

Puig-Antich, J. (1982). Major depression and conduct disorder in prepuberty. *Journal of the American Academy of Child Psychiatry, 21*, 118–128.

Quay, H. C. (1993). The psychobiology of undersocialized aggressive conduct disorder: A theoretical perspective. *Development and Psychopathology, 5*, 165–180.

Quay, H. C., & Peterson, D. R. (1987). *Manual for the Revised Behavior Problem Checklist*. Miami, FL: University of Miami.

Raine, A., & Venables, P. H. (1987). Contingent negative variation, P3 evoked potentials, and antisocial behavior. *Psychophysiology, 24*, 191–199.

Raine, A., Venables, P. H., & Williams, M. (1990). Relationships between central and autonomic measures of arousal at age 15 years and criminality at age 24 years. *Archives of General Psychiatry, 47*, 1003–1007.

Rapp, L. A., & Wodarski, J. S. (1997). The comorbidity of conduct disorder and depression in adolescents: A comprehensive interpersonal treatment technology. *Family Therapy, 24*, 81–100.

Reich, W. (2000). Diagnostic Interview for Children and Adolescents (DICA). *Journal of the American Academy of Child and Adolescent Psychiatry, 39*, 59–66.

Reich, W., & Weiner, Z. (1988). *The Diagnostic Interview for Children and Adolescents (DICA)*. St. Louis: Washington University, Division of Psychiatry.

Reich, W., Shayla, J. J., & Taibelson, C. (1992). *The Diagnostic Interview for Children and Adolescents—Revised (DICA-R)*. St. Louis Washington University, Division of Psychiatry.

Reid, J. B., Baldwin, D. V., Patterson, G. R., & Dishion, T. J. (1988). Observations in the assessment of childhood disorder. In M. Rutter, A. H. Tuma, & I. S. Lann (Eds.), *Assessment and diagnosis in child psychopathology*. New York: Guilford Press.

Renouf, A. G., Kovacs, M., & Mukerji, P. (1997). Relationship of depressive, conduct, and comorbid disorders and social functioning in childhood. *Journal of the American Academy of Child and Adolescent Psychiatry, 36*, 998–1004.

Reschly, D. J., & Ysseldyke, J. E. (1995). School psychology paradigm shift. In A. Thomas & J. Grimes (Eds.), *Best practices in school psychology* (3rd ed., pp. 17–31). Washington, DC: National Association of School Psychologists.

Rey, J. M., Singh, M. M., Hung, S., Dossetor, D. R., Newman, L., Plapp, J. M., & Bird, K. D. (1997). A global scale to measure the quality of the family environment. *Archives of General Psychiatry, 54*, 817–822.

Rey, J. M., Walter, G., Plapp, J. M., & Denshire, E. (2000). Family environment in attention deficit hyperactivity, oppositional defiant and conduct disorders. *Australian and New Zealand Journal of Psychiatry, 34*, 453–457.

Reynolds, C. R., & Kamphaus, R. W. (2004). *Behavioral Assessment for Children manual*. Circle Pines, MN: AGS.

Rhule, D. M., McMahon, R. J., & Spieker, S. J. (2004). Relation of adolescent mothers' history of antisocial behavior to child conduct problems and social competence. *Journal of Clinical Child and Adolescent Psychology, 33*, 524–535.

Riggs, P. D., Mikulich, S. K., Coffman, L. M., & Crowley, T. J. (1997). Fluoxetine in drug-dependent delinquents with major depression: An open trial. *Journal of Child and Adolescent Psychopharmacology, 7*, 87–95.

Roberts, M. W., & Powers, S. W. (1988). The compliance test. *Behavioral Assessment, 10*, 375–389.

Robins, L., Marcus, L., Reich, W., Cunningham, R., & Gallagher, T. (1996). *The Diagnostic Interview Schedule IV*. St. Louis: Washington University.

Robinson, E. A., & Eyberg, S. M. (1981). The Dyadic Parent-Child Interaction Coding System: Standardization and validation. *Journal of Consulting and Clinical Psychology, 49*, 245–250.

Robinson, E. A., Eyberg, S. M., & Ross, A. W. (1980). The standardization of an inventory of child conduct problem behaviors. *Journal of Clinical Child Psychology, 9,* 22–28.

Roethlisberger, F. J. & Dickson, W. J. (1939) *Management and the worker.* Cambridge, MA: Harvard University Press.

Romano, E., Baillargeon, R. H., Wu, H. X., Zoccolillo, M., Vitaro, F. & Tremblay, R. E. (2004). A new look at inter-informant agreement on conduct disorder using a latent class approach. *Psychiatry Research, 129,* 75–89.

Rösler, M., Retz, W., Retz-Junginger, P., Hengesch, G., Schneider, M., Supprian, T., et al. (2004). Prevalence of attention deficit/hyperactivity disorder (ADHD) and comorbid disorders in young male prison inmates. *European Archives of Psychiatry and Clinical Neuroscience, 254,* 365–371.

Rothbart, M. K., & Bates, J. E. (1998). Temperament. In W. Damon & N. Eisenberg (Eds.), *Handbook of child psychology* (5th ed.)*: Vol. 3. Social, emotional, and personality development* (pp. 105–176). Hoboken, NJ: Wiley.

Rowland, A. S., Lesesne, C. A., & Abramowitz, A. J. (2002). The epidemiology of attention-deficit/hyperactivity disorder (ADHD): A public health view. *Mental Retardation and Developmental Disabilities Research Reviews, 8,* 162–170.

Rubio-Stipec, M., Shrout, P. E., Canino, G., Bird, H. R., Jensen, P., Dulcan, M., & Schwab-Stone, M. (1996). Empirically defined symptom scales using the DISC 2.3—Diagnostic Interview Schedule for Children. Journal of Abnormal Child Psychology, 24, 67–83.

Rubio-Stipec, M., Walker, A., Murphy, J., & Fitzmaurice, G. (2002). Dimensional measures of psychopathology: The probability of being classified with a psychiatric disorder using empirically derived symptom scales. *Social Psychiatry and Psychiatric Epidemiology, 37,* 553–560.

Rutter, M., Cox, A., Tupling, C., Berger, M., & Yule, W. (1975). Attainment and adjustment in two geographical areas. *British Journal of Psychiatry, 126,* 493–509.

Rutter, M., Giller, H., & Hagell, A. (1998). *Antisocial behavior by young people.* New York: Cambridge Press.

Rutter, M., Silberg, J., O'Connor, T., & Simonoff, E. (1999). Genetics and child psychiatry: II. Empirical research findings. *Journal of Child Psychology and Psychiatry and Allied Disciplines 40,* 19–55.

Sailor, W., Gerry, M., & Wilson, W. C. (1990). Policy implications of emergent full inclusion models for the education of students with severe disabilities (Report No. EC 302 673). San Francisco State University, CA. California Research Institute. (ERIC Document Reproduction Service No. ED 365 048).

Salekin, R. T., Leistico, A. R., Neumann, C. S., DiCicco, T. M., & Duros, R. L. (2004). Psychopathy and comorbidity in a young offender sample: taking a closer look at psychopathy's potential importance over disruptive behavior disorders. *Journal of Abnormal Psychology, 113,* 416–427.

Samenow, S. E. (1998). *Before it's too late.* New York: Times Books.

Sameroff, A. J. (1995). General systems theories and developmental psychopathology. In D. Cicchetti & D. Cohen (Eds.), *Developmental psychopathology* (pp. 659–689). New York: Wiley.

Sameroff, A. J. (2000). Dialectical processes in developmental psychopathology. In A. J. Sameroff, M. Lewis, & S. M. Miller (Eds.), *Handbook of developmental psychopathology* (2nd ed., pp. 23–40). New York: Kluwer Academic/Plenum.

Sameroff, A. J. & Chandler, M. J. (1975). Reproductive risk and the continuum of caretaker casualty. In F. D. Horowitz (Ed.), Review of child development research (Vol. 4). Chicago: University of Chicago Press.

Sameroff, A. J., Seifer, R., & Bartko, W. T. (1997). Environmental perspectives on adaptation during childhood and adolescence. In S. S. Luthar, J. Burack, D. Cicchelti, & J. Weisz (Eds.), *Developmental psychopathology: Perspectives on adjustment, risk, and disorder* (pp. 507–526). Cambridge: Cambridge University Press.

Sanders, M. R. (1999). Triple P—Positive Parenting Program: Towards an empirically validated multilevel parenting and family support strategy for the prevention of behavior and emotional problems in children. *Clinical Child and Family Psychology Review, 2,* 71–90.

Sanders, M., Arduca, Y., Karamitsios, M., Boots, M., & Vance, A. (2005). Characteristics of internalizing and externalizing disorders in medication-naïve, clinically referred children with attention deficit hyperactivity disorder, combined type and dysthymic disorder. *Australian and New Zealand Journal of Psychiatry, 39,* 359–365.

Sanders, M. R., Gooley, S., & Nicholson, J. (2000). Early intervention in conduct problems in children (Vol. 3). In R. Rosky, A. O'Hanlon, G. Martin, & C. Davis (Series Eds.). *Clinical approaches to early intervention in child and adolescent mental health.* Adelaide, Australia: The Australian Early Intervention Network for Mental Health in Young People.

Sattler, J. M. (2001). *Assessment of children: Cognitive applications* (4th ed.). San Diego, CA: Author.

Schneider, S., Atkinson, D. R., & El-Mallakh, R. S. (1996). CD and ADHD in bipolar disorder. *Journal of the American Academy of Child and Adolescent Psychiatry, 35,* 1422–1423.

Schubiner, H., Tzelepis, A., Milberger, S., Lockhart, N., Kruger, M., Kelley, B. J., et al. (2000). Prevalence of attention-deficit/hyperactivity disorder and conduct disorder among substance abusers. *Journal of Clinical Psychiatry, 61,* 244–251.

Schwab-Stone, M., Fisher, P. W., Placentini, J., Shaffer, D., Davies, M., & Briggs, M. (1993). The Diagnostic Interview Schedule for Children—Revised Version (DISC-R), II: Test-retest reliability. *Journal of the American Academy of Child and Adolescent Psychiatry, 32,* 651–657.

Section 504 of the Rehabilitation Act of 1973, as amended 29 U.S.C. § 794

Shaffer, D., Fisher, P., Dulcan, M., Davies, M., Piacentini, J., Schwab-Stone, M., Lahey, B., Bourdon, K., Jensen, P., Bird, H., & Canino, G. R. D. (1996). The second version of the NIMH Diagnostic Interview Schedule for Children (DISC–2). *Journal of the American Academy of Child and Adolescent Psychiatry, 35,* 865–877.

Shaw, D. S., Dishion, T. J., Supplee, L, Gardner, F., & Arnds, K. (2006). Randomized trial of a family-centered approach to the prevention of early conduct problems: 2-year effects of the family check-up in early childhood. *Journal of Consulting and Clinical Psychology, 74,* 1–9.

Shirk, S. R., & Russell R. L. (1996). *Change processes in child psychotherapy.* New York: Guilford Press.

Shrout, P. E. & Fliess, J. L. (1979). Intraclass correlations: Uses in assessing rater reliability. *Psychological Bulletin, 86,* 420–428.

Silva, R. R., Alpert, M., Pouget, E., Silva, V., Trosper, S., Reyes, K., & Dummit, S. (2005). A rating scale for disruptive behavior disorders based on the DSM-IV pool. *Psychiatric Quarterly, 76,* 327–339.

Silverthorn, P., Frick, P. J., & Reynolds, R. (2001). Timing of onset and correlates of severe conduct problems in adjudicated girls and boys. *Journal of Psychopathology and Behavioral Assessment, 23,* 171–181.

Simonoff, E., Pickles, A., Meyer, J. M., Silberg, J. L., Maes, H. H., Loeber, R., Rutter, M., Hewitt, J. K., & Eaves, L. J. (1997). The Virginia twin study of adolescent behavioral development: Influence of age, sex, and impairment on rates of disorder. *Archives of General Psychiatry, 54*, 801–808.

Skiba, R., & Grizzle, K. (1991). The social maladjustment exclusion: Issues of definition and assessment. *School Psychology Review, 20*, 580–594.

Slenkovich, J. E. (1983). PL 94–142 as applied to the DSM III diagnosis: An analysis of DSM III diagnosis vis-à-vis special education law. Cupertino, CA: Kinghorn.

Slutske, W. S., Heath, A. C., Dinwiddie, S. H., Madden, P. A. F., Bucholz, K. K., Dunne, M. P., Statham, D. J., & Martin, N. G. (1997). Modeling genetic and environmental influences in the etiology of conduct disorder: A study of 2,682 adult twin pairs. *Journal of Abnormal Psychology, 106*, 266–279.

Smith, T. W., & Williams, P. G. (1992). Personality and health: Advantages and limitations of the five factor model. *Journal of Personality, 60*, 395–423.

Smith, A. M., Gacono, C. B., & Kaufman, L. (1997). A Rorschach comparison of psychopathic and non-psychopathic conduct disordered adolescents. *Journal of Clinical Psychology, 53*, 239–300.

Smolla, N., Valla, P., Bergeron, L., Berthiaume, C., & St.-Georges, M. (2004). Development and reliability of a pictorial mental disorders screen for young adolescents. *Canadian Journal of Psychiatry, 49*, 828–837.

Society for Personality Assessment. (2005). The status of the Rorschach in clinical and forensic practice: An official statement by the Board of Trustees of the Society for Personality Assessment. *Journal of Personality Assessment, 85*, 219–237.

Soleil, G. (2000). *AD/HD and school law*. Washington, DC: Office of Educational Research and Improvement. Retrieved November 5, 2006 from www.eric.ed.gov/sitemap/html_0900000b8013425b.html

Sondeijker, F. E. P. L., Ferdinand, R. F., Oldehinkel, A. J., Veenstra, R., De Winter, A. F., Ormel, J., et al. (2005). Classes of adolescents with disruptive behaviors in a general population sample. *Social Psychiatry and Psychiatric Epidemiology, 40*, 931–938.

Speltz, M. L., DeKlyen, M., Calderon, R., Greenberg, M. T., & Fisher, P. A. (1999). Neuropsychological characteristics and test behaviors of boys with early onset conduct problems. *Journal of Abnormal Psychology, 108*, 315–325.

Spitzer, R. L., Davies, M., & Barkley, R. A. (1990). The DSM–III–R field trial of disruptive behavior disorders. *Journal of the American Academy of Child and Adolescent Psychiatry 2*, 690–697.

Sroufe, L. A., & Rutter, M. (1984). The domain of developmental psychopathology. *Child Development, 55*, 17–29.

Stahl, N. D., & Clarizio, H. F. (1999). Conduct disorder and comorbidity. *Psychology in the Schools, 36*, 41–50.

Steller, M., & Hunze, D. (1984). Self-descriptions of delinquents in the Freiburg-Personality-Inventory (FPI)—A secondary analysis of empirical studies. *Periodical for Differential and Diagnostic Psychology, 5*, 87–109.

Sterzer, P., Stadler, C., Krebs, A., Kleinschmidt, A., & Poustka, F. (2005). Abnormal neural responses to emotional visual stimuli in adolescents with conduct disorder. *Biological Psychiatry, 57*, 7–15.

Straus, M. A. (1979). Measuring intrafamily conflict and violence. *Journal of Marriage and the Family, 41*, 75–88.

Straus, M. A., & Gelles, R. J. (1990). *Physical violence in American families*. New Brunswick, NJ: Transaction.

Street, A. E., King, L. A., King, D. W., & Riggs, D. S. (2003). The association among male-perpetrated partner violence, wives' psychological distress and children's behavior problems: A structural equation modeling analysis. *Journal of Comparative Family Studies, 34*, 23–40.

Swanson, J. M., Nolan, W., & Pelham, W. E. (1982). The Snap rating scales. http://www.centerforpediatrics.com

Swartz, M. S., Wagner, H. R., Swanson, J. W., Stroup, T. S., McEvoy, J. P., Canive, J. M., et al. (2006). Substance use in persons with schizophrenia: Baseline prevalence and correlates from the NIMH CATIE study. *Journal of Nervous and Mental Disease, 194*, 164–172.

Tackett, J. L., Krueger, R. F., Sawyer, M. G., & Graetz, B. W. (2003). Subfactors of DSM-IV conduct disorder: Evidence and connections with syndromes from the Child Behavior Checklist. *Journal of Abnormal Child Psychology, 31*, 647–654.

Tansy, M. (2007). *Emotional Disability or Social Maladjustment? Best Practices in Assessing and Treating ED and SM in Children & Adolescents*. Workshop presented at MEDS-PDN in Pittsburgh, PA.

Taylor, T. K., & Biglan, A. (1998). Behavioral family interventions for improving child-rearing: A review of the literature for clinicians and policy makers. *Clinical Child and Family Psychology Review, 1*, 41–60.

Teichner, G., Golden, C. J., Crum, T. A., Azrin, N. H., Donohue, B., & Van Hasselt, V. B. (2000). Identifying patterns of neuropsychological functioning within an adolescent delinquent sample. *Journal of Psychiatric Research, 34*, 29–32.

Teplin, L. A., Abram, K. M., McClelland, G. M., Dulcan, M. K., & Mericle, A. A. (2002). Psychiatric disorders in youth in juvenile detention. *Archives of General Psychiatry, 59*, 1133–1142.

Thompson, A., Hollis, C., & Richards, D. (2003). Authoritarian parenting attitudes as a risk for conduct problems: Results from a British national cohort study. *European Child and Adolescent Psychiatry, 12*, 84–91.

Thompson, L. L., Riggs, P. D., Mikulich, S. K., & Crowley, T. J. (1996). Contribution of ADHD symptoms to substance problems and delinquency in conduct-disordered adolescents. *Journal of Abnormal Child Psychology, 24*, 325–347.

Tierney, T., & Dowd, R. (2000). The use of social skills groups to support girls with emotional difficulties in secondary schools. *Support for Learning, 15*, 82–85.

Tillman, R., Geller, B., Bolhofner, K., Craney, J. L., Williams, M., & Zimerman, B. (2003). Ages of onset and rates of syndromal and subsyndromal comorbid DSM-IV diagnoses in a prepubertal and early adolescent bipolar disorder phenotype. *Journal of the American Academy of Child and Adolescent Psychiatry, 42*, 1486–1493.

Tolan, P. (2001). Youth violence and its prevention in the United States: An overview of current knowledge. *Injury Control and Safety Promotion, 8*, 1–12.

Tolan, P.H., & Gorman-Smith, D. (1998). Development of serious and violent offending careers. In R. Loeber & D.P. Farrington (Eds.), *Serious and violent juvenile offenders: Risk factors and successful interventions* (pp. 68–85). Thousand Oaks, CA: Sage.

Toren, P., Laor, N., & Weisman, A. (1998). Use of atypical neuroleptics in child and adolescent psychiatry. *Journal of Clinical Psychiatry, 59*, 644–656.

Trickett, P. K., & Putnam, F. W. (1998). Developmental consequences of child sexual abuse. In P. K. Trickett & C. J. Schellenbach (Eds.), *Violence against children in the family and the community* (pp. 39–56). Washington, DC: American Psychological Association.

Tynan, D. (2001). Conduct Disorder. EMedicine. Retrieved June 30, 2007, from http://www.emedicine.com/ped/topic2793.htm

Ullmann, R. K., Sleator, E. K., & Sprague, R. L. (2000). *ACTeRS Teacher and Parent Forms Manual*. Champaign, IL: Metritech.

U.S. Department of Health and Human Services. (1999). *Mental health: A report of the Surgeon General.* Rockville, MD: Author.

Valla, J., Bergeron, L., & Smolla, N. (2000). The Dominic-R: A pictorial interview for 6- to 11-year-old children. *Journal of the American Academy of Child and Adolescent Psychiatry, 39*, 85–93.

Van Goozen, S. H. M., Matthys, W., Cohen-Kettenis, P. T., Buitelaar, J. K., & van Engeland, H. (2000). Hypothalamic-pituitary-adrenal axis and autonomic nervous system activity in disruptive children and matched controls. *Journal of the American Academy of Child and Adolescent Psychiatry, 39*, 1438–1445.

Van Goozen, S. H. M., Matthys, W., Cohen-Kettenis, P. T., Gispen-de Wied, C., Wiegant, V. M., & van Engeland, H. (1998). Salivary cortisol and cardiovascular activity during stress in oppositional-defiant disorder boys and normal controls. *Biological Psychiatry, 43*, 531–539.

Vitaro, F., Tremblay, R. E., & Bukowski, W. M. (2001). Friends, friendships and conduct disorders. In J. Hill & B. Maughan (Eds.), *Conduct disorders in childhood and adolescence* (pp. 346–378). New York: Cambridge University Press.

Volavka, J. (1990). Aggression, electroencephalography, and evoked potentials: A critical review. *Neuropsychiatry, Neuropsychology, and Behavioral Neurology, 3*, 249–259.

Vostanis, P., Meltzer, H., Goodman, R., & Ford, T. (2003). Service utilisation by children with conduct disorders: Findings from the GB national study. *European Child and Adolescent Psychiatry, 12*, 231–238.

Wakschlag, L. S., Gordon, R. A., Lahey, B. B., Loeber, R., Green, S. M., & Leventhal, B. L. (2000). Maternal age at first birth and boys' risk for conduct disorder. *Journal of Research on Adolescence, 10*, 417–441.

Walker, H. M., & Holmes, D. (1987). *The ACCESS Program; Adolescent Curriculum for Communication and Effective Social Skills.* Austin, TX: Pro-Ed.

Walker, H., & Severson, H. (1992). *Systematic Screening of Behavior Disorders (SSBD): A multiple gating procedure.* Longmont, CO: Sopris West.

Walker, H. M., Hops, H., & Greenwood, C. (1993). *RECESS: A program for reducing negative-aggressive behavior.* Seattle, WA: Educational Achievement Systems.

Walker, H. M., Kavanagh, K., Stiller, B., Golly, A., Steverson, H. H., & Fell, E. G. (1988). First Step to Success: An early intervention approach for preventing school antisocial behavior. *Journal of Emotional and Behavioral Disorders, 6*, 66–80.

Walker, H. M., Ramsey, E., & Gresham, F. M. (2004). *Antisocial behavior in school: Strategies and best practices* (2nd ed.). Pacific Grove, CA: Brooks/Cole.

Waller, R. J., Waller, K. S., Schramm, M. M., Bresson, D. J. (2006). Conduct Disorder. In R. J. Waller (Ed) *Fostering child & adolescent mental health in the classroom.* (pp. 163–181). Thousand Oaks, CA: Sage.

Weber, C. A., Meloy, J. R., Gacono, C. B. (1992). A Rorschach study of attachment and anxiety in inpatient conduct disordered and dysthymic adolescents. *Journal of Personality Assessment, 58*, 16–26.

Webster-Stratton, C., & Hammond, M. (1997). Treating children with early-onset conduct problems: A comparison of child and parent training interventions. *Journal of Consulting and Clinical Psychology, 65*, 93–109.

Webster-Stratton, C., & Reid, J. (November, 1999). *Treating children with early-onset conduct problems: The importance of teacher training.* Paper presented at the American Association of Behavior Therapy, Toronto.

Webster-Stratton, C., Hollinsworth, T., & Kolpacoff, M. (1989). The long-term effectiveness and clinical significance of three cost-effective training programs for families with conduct-problem children. *Journal of Consulting and Clinical Psychology, 57*, 550–553.

Webster-Stratton, C., Reid, M. J., & Hammond, M. (2001). Social skills and problem solving training for children with early-onset conduct problems: Who benefits? *Journal of Child Psychology and Psychiatry, 42*, 943–952.

Webster-Stratton, C., Reid, M. J., & Hammond, M. (2004). Treating children with early onset conduct problems: Intervention outcomes for parent, child, and teacher training. *Journal of Clinical Child and Adolescent Psychology, 33*, 105–124.

Weis, R., Crockett, T. E., & Vieth, S. (2004). Using MMPI-A profiles to predict success in a military-style residential treatment program for adolescents with academic and conduct problems. *Psychology in the Schools, 41*, 563–574.

West, H. A., & Verhaagen, D. A. (1999). The Differential Test of Conduct and Emotional Problems as an evaluative tool for the Willie M. program. *Adolescence, 34*, 437–441.

West, P., Sweeting, H., Der, G., Barton, J., & Lucas, C. (2003). Voice-DISC identified DSM-IV disorders among 15-year-olds in the West of Scotland. *Journal of the American Academy of Child and Adolescent Psychiatry, 42*, 941–949.

Whalen, P. J., Rauch, S. L., Etcoff, N. L., McInerney, S. C., Lee, M. B., & Jenike, M. A. (1998). Masked presentations of emotional facial expressions modulate amygdala activity without explicit knowledge. *Journal of Neuroscience, 18*, 411–418.

Whitmore, E. A., Mikulich, S. K., Thompson, L. L., Riggs, P. D., Aarons, G. A., & Crowley, T. J. (1997). Influences on adolescent substance dependence: Conduct disorder, depression, attention deficit hyperactivity disorder, and gender. *Drug and Alcohol Dependence, 47*, 87–97.

Wikström, P. H., & Loeber, R. (2000). Do disadvantaged neighborhoods cause well-adjusted children to become adolescent delinquents? A study of male juvenile serious offending, individual risk and protective factors, and neighborhood context. *Criminology, 38*, 1109–1142.

Wisniewski, K. G. (2006). Delinquency, academic underachievement, and attention deficit hyperactivity disorder: A longitudinal investigation of developmental sequencing and interrelated risk factors. Unpublished dissertation, Duquesne University.

Woolfolk, A. (2004). *Educational psychology* (9th ed.). Boston: Allyn and Bacon.

World Health Organization. (1993). *The ICD-10 classification of mental and behavioural disorders: Diagnostic criteria for research.* Geneva: Author.

Yang, J., Zhang, S., & She, Y. (2005). A preliminary study of comorbidities associated with Tourette Syndrome. *Chinese Mental Health, 19*, 413–415.

Yen, C., & Chong, M. (2006). Comorbid psychiatric disorders, sex, and methamphetamine use in adolescents: A case-control study. *Comprehensive Psychiatry, 47*, 215–220.

Yen, C., Yang, Y., & Chong, M. (2006). Correlates of methamphetamine use for Taiwanese adolescents. *Psychiatry and Clinical Neurosciences, 60*, 160–167.

Index

D

DBDs. *See* Disruptive behavior disorders
Degree of heritability, for CD, 15, 22
Delinquency, in males, 43–44
Depression, in children with CD, 3
Development and Well-Being Assessment
  (DAWBA), 64–65
Diagnostic and statistical manual of mental
  disorders, 4–5, 24, 32
  conduct disorder, diagnostic criteria
    for, 50
  oppositional defiant disorder, diagnostic
    criteria for, 51
  severity specifiers, 51–52
  somatoform disorder, 33
Diagnostic Interview Schedule for
  Children (DISC), 29, 63, 65–66
Diagnostic System for Psychiatric
  Disorders in Childhood and
  Adolescence (DISYP), 57, 58
Differential Test of Conduct and
  Emotional Problems (DT/CEP),
  58–59
Disruptive behavior disorders, 15, 34
Disruptive Behavior Disorders Rating
  Scale (DBDRS), 59
Dominic-R, for mental disorder
  assessment, 71
Dyadic Parent-Child Interaction Coding
  System (DPICS-R), 62

E

Early Assessment Risk List for Boys
  (EARL-20B), 59
Emotional disturbance (ED)
  definition, 78–80
  group therapy, 111
  and multimodal functional behavioral
    assessment (MFBA), 90
  psychoeducational evaluation, for
    intervention, 95
  and school-based interventions, 99
  schoolwide incentives, 99
  and social maladjustment, 80
  students with, 58, 100, 102
Eyberg Child Behavior Inventory (ECBI),
  59–60
Eysenck's theory, on personality,
  16–18

F

Family Interaction Coding System (FICS), 62
FAPE. *See* Free and appropriate public
  education
Free and appropriate public education, 2
  children with CD, 6
  and individualized education program
    (IEP), 6
Freiburg Personality Inventory (FPI), 69
Frontal lobe, role in CD, 12
Functional family therapy (FFT), for CD, 107

G

Global Family Environment Scale (GFES),
  for CD assessment, 54–56, 88
Group therapy, for CD, 108

H

Hawthorne effect, 47
Helping America's Youth, 118
Hispanic people, with CD, 31
Hypothalamic-pituitary-adrenal (HPA), 14

I

Individualized education program (IEP)
  and FAPE, 6
  IDEIA direction, 2
  least restrictive environment, 99
Individuals with Disabilities Education
  Improvement Act (IDEIA), 2
  services to infants and toddlers, 46
Intelligence quotient (IQ), of children with
  CD, 41
International Classification of Diseases
  (ICD), for CD identification, 58
Interview, with CD patients
  Child and Adolescent Psychiatric
    Assessment (CAPA), 63–64
  Child Assessment Schedule (CAS), 64
  Composite International Diagnostic
    Interview (CIDI), 64
  Development and Well-Being
    Assessment (DAWBA), 64–65
  Diagnostic Interview of Children and
    Adolescents (DICA), 65
  Diagnostic Interview Schedule for
    Children (DISC), 65–66
  Schedule for Affective Disorders and
    Schizophrenia (K-SADS), 66

Printed in the United States
114401LV00003BA/58-60/A